# SINGIN' IN THE REIGN

*A collection of original musical plays created for the purpose of teaching Biblical lessons to children and also to serve as an "outreach ministry" to nursing and retirement homes and to the community.*

CLARK TYLER

authorHOUSE®

*AuthorHouse™*
*1663 Liberty Drive*
*Bloomington, IN 47403*
*www.authorhouse.com*
*Phone: 1-800-839-8640*



*First published by AuthorHouse 03/24/2011*

*ISBN: 978-1-4567-3917-1 (sc)*
*ISBN: 978-1-4567-3916-4 (e)*

*Printed in the United States of America*



*This book is printed on acid-free paper.*

## About the Author

After graduating from Harvard and serving a stint in the US Army, Clark Tyler began his professional career as a publicist for the American Broadcasting Company, promoting Woody Woodpecker, Superman, Pat Boone and Carol Burnett among others. His first writing contract was as a lyric and comedy writer for the network radio show "Flair" starring Dick Van Dyke.

He joined the Johnson administration in 1963 as a press aide and speechwriter and later received a presidential appointment requiring Senate confirmation. He composed speeches, delivered Congressional testimony and authored a number of dry, but illuminating, works having to do with the GI Bill for Vietnam veterans, Federal contracts for small and minority businesses; public/private partnerships, and growth management around military bases.

The rest of his career was as a senior executive at Amtrak, a regional advertising agency and two minority businesses in the mass transit industry. However, his most fulfilling role was as a Sunday school teacher for the past 21 years – working with and training children age 6 to teens. It was in this role that he began writing musical presentations for his classes to sing before adult audiences at retirement and nursing homes.

His book, "Singin' in the Reign," is not only a collection of seven complete musical Bible-based plays, but a chronicle of how his students' input and ideas helped to construct these presentations for mature audiences. This was done in such a way that takes advantage of that very special chemistry between kids age 6 to12 and older citizens. The photos of this process clearly show the success of this targeted emphasis.

A self-described crowning achievement was accomplished on two recent trips to Romania. A non-profit group engaged in the rescue, rehabilitation and local adoption of abused/abandoned children, asked him to work with groups of these kids at a local summer camp in the foothills of Transylvania. Taking scenes from several of his plays, he taught these special children pantomime presentations of many of the parables of Jesus. In spite of the fact that these kids spoke only Romanian (Tyler, only English), their presentations were the hit of the camp.

Clark currently teaches Sunday school at McLean Presbyterian Church in McLean, Virginia.

* * *

All of the pictures in this book are the work of the well-known Washington photographer, Eric Long - who just happens to be the father of three of these plays' most consistent stars. Eric is a senior photographer and has served the Smithsonian Institution in Washington since 1983. Currently assigned to the National Air and Space Museum, he documents collections, exhibitions and events to support museum research and publications. Eric has participated in the historical documentation of three Presidential Inaugurations, an Oral History of Southern Agriculture and his work has been published in Smithsonian Magazine, Air and Space Magazine, Time Magazine and in a number of books. He has also been an instructor for the National Park Service, teaching documentary photography in Native American Communities.

* * *

The piano arrangements in these musical plays are the work of Andrew Bell. Andrew is a composer/producer/performing musician from Fulton, Maryland and has been an arranger4 for a number of singers with nationally available CDs. He graduated from the University of Maryland with a degree in audio engineering and classical guitar performance. Currently he owns and operates CenterEarth Studios, a full-service recording/production/design studio in the Baltimore-Washington area. Outside of the studio, Andrew performs regularly as a classical guitarist and a singer/songwriter in the Band Bravenoise.

* * *

This book is dedicated to Ethel Telchin, the late wife of my first pastor, Stan Telchin. An indomitable and solid believer, Ethel was a mentor, critic, encourager and admonisher extraordinaire. She was always an enthusiastic audience for many of these plays. Once when I had introduced a new song for our church's Christian Passover Seder, she paid me the ultimate compliment: "Are you sure you're not Jewish?" Ethel was a very great lady.

# Table of Contents

## FOREWORD

As a child I never attended Sunday school. Sure, it was during World War II, there was gas rationing etc. but my family was not "churchgoing." My first exposure to the Bible came in a little one-room school in North Rupert Vermont in 1943. Each Wednesday a lady came to the school with a flannel board and a bunch of Biblical character figures that would be stuck on the board as she taught us the Bible lesson. I was 9 years old… and I remember those lessons very clearly – and the songs we sang ("I'm in the Lord's ar-mee," "the B-I-B-L-E, yes that's the book for me").

Now fast forward to 2009. I am now 75 years old and have taught Sunday school for the last 20 years. I even made a flannel board for one of my classes and replicated those Wednesday lessons with some cutout Bible figures. But I also, in 1989, began writing Bible-based musical plays for my classes to reach out to seniors in nursing and retirement homes. I did this because the programs sent around to churches were not really applicable for children to witness to adults. I learned that the children I taught were fully capable of doing just that… and were very good and effective at it.

Now I am not talking about "evangelizing." Garnering adherents to a given set of beliefs is for those who pursue seminary or theological goals. What I am talking about is reaching out to a hungry adult audience, who may be non-churched, non-believers, or just non-involved in scriptural lessons. Such people are not any less hungry for the simple truths that the Bible contains. That is why I remember fondly and completely the Wednesday lady with the flannel board in 1943. She taught the Bible as a collection of lessons – things that God wants us to know and learn from, so we can be the person he wants us to be.

From what I have seen of curricula that routinely gets sent around to many churches for Sunday school, there is an undue emphasis on verse memorization and presentation of the Bible as just a collection of stories, characters, or prophesies or a chronicle of events, complete with games, crafts etc. Sometimes the Bible is presented as a justification for certain denominational emphasis or a specific doctrine. This type of emphasis misses a great opportunity – the opportunity to present the Bible truths as lessons, a kind of living flannel board. But this approach for children requires simplicity, plain English, a non-theological agenda and, yes, even a little humor.

All this is why children ages 5 through 12 (or so) are ideal faith witnesses for adult audiences, and especially people who reside in retirement and nursing homes. There is that special chemistry between such residents and such children that builds on this natural receptivity. However, this is not just about Sunday school – it's about references to Biblical lessons at home, in the neighborhood or at various non-religious groups.

The status of the usual musical Bible presentation is for the class to practice the pageant, or the toy store coming to life, or some such, and then present it to an audience of adoring parents in a church setting.

Now, don't misunderstand me; there is nothing cuter than your six-year old child dressed up in a costume singing a nice little song. Parents love it; friends and neighbors (kind of) love it; others are "polite." There is no question but that such "performances" build confidence in a child and unquestionably are better than having them watch TV, play endless video games, or listen to rock music.

However in the context of Sunday school, a broader perspective, I believe, is called for... and much more is possible. Over the course of these 20 years, I have watched such children grow spiritually and, with some very different material, become very effective witnesses - to adult audiences. The main requirement to achieve such a wonderful result is that the child understand what he/she is saying or singing; that they have fun doing it; and that the total package be purposeful (beyond "aren't they cute!"). It ***is*** possible to be both entertaining and edifying.

If these conditions are met, I can absolutely guarantee that the children will more than just remember what they did, the scriptural truths will indeed be "engrafted", and, best of all, adults being thus witnessed to will be blessed. Many seeds will be planted and fruit will be produced. I know this because I have seen it happen - often beyond my most optimistic expectations.

One of the major roadblocks to achieving such results is the physical and procedural constraints facing smaller churches. Things such as sophisticated sound systems, rehearsal requirements, the lack of a full stage to handle settings etc., the undue stress on memorization and the lack of a creative vehicle that adults can relate to, plus the time requirements so that already-busy schedules can be accommodated. All of these things can be overcome and an entertaining (and edifying) result can be delivered.

What is contained in this volume are the examples and case studies of seven musical presentations where exactly this was done. Many of my young charges who participated in these productions are now in college, some are in the armed forces, a few have become youth pastors - but all remember the experience (I think fondly), and grew as a result. Best of all, I know that there have been many residents of the nursing and retirement homes we visited who have responded to this rather singular ministry. I like to think that heaven has a few more occupants because of what the children did. Yes, they were cute, but, my, were they effective!

And you'll meet many of them: Gina, Kirstie, Jason, Megan, Kristen, Erin, Jennifer, Marlayna. But you'll also meet the characters they played: Nehemiah, Joshua, Ruth, Gideon, Rahab, Esther, Noah, Moses and Habakkuk, plus a collection of serpents, donkeys, locusts, bees and a whale or a mouse or two. But then there's a roster of other characters...such as:

Rose Bloom and Ivy LaVine - garden consultants extraordinaire
Purlie Gates - concierge at Paradise Inn
Sarah Phim - curator of the Faith Hall of Fame
Joy S. Tydings and Eve VanGelist - Christmas reporters
Woof-Woof Blitzer - dogged newshound
Colonel O'Wheat – commandant of ancient crops
Drs. Angie O'Plasty & Ray D. Ayshun - heart specialists
Manny Arcald - theatrical agent "where the few are chosen"
Gloria Livingstone - angelic guide to an archeological dig
The Grateful Living - a true "rock" group
and, of course, several devilish characters from the other side:
James Bondage - secret agent licensed to kill & destroy
Lucy Fur - night manager of Motel 666
The Power of Darkness - almost champion wrestler (he loses)

These musical plays have been performed in a number of churches and an even greater number of nursing and retirement homes. They have been performed during church services, on special occasions, at seasonal celebrations and before audiences of Christians (Baptists, Pentecostals, Congregationalists, Messianics) Orthodox Jews, families, neighbors, curious onlookers and a large collection of "I'm-not-sure-what-I-believe's." I believe that all have been entertained; many have been edified; I think a great many have been blessed; a lot have been taught; and no one I know of has been offended. Not much material available for consumption these days can make that collection of claims.

I offer these to any church or group that would like to perform them. They are simple, fun, uplifting for the cast, and can be performed with just a piano (or maybe a guitar or two). They are written in a "revue" format, which means they can be telescoped - or cut to fit any time limitation. Musical numbers or scenes can be left in or out without diminishing the point or storyline. There are no "creative rules." The only requirement is that before they are performed, it is important to teach the youngsters (usually age 6 to 12) the basics of the scriptural lessons involved. For this reason, a lesson plan is attached to each script.

The talent level of the performers is not important; heart understanding of what they are performing is very important. To make this point, I have included an introductory section on the background of each play, followed by an outline of a lesson plan (and list of references), and concluding with the script and sheet music of each play. A list of required props is also included.

There are four very significant people involved with these plays: my two Pastors who encouraged me to write and have these performed - Pastor Stan Telchin of the former Living Word Fellowship and Pastor John Bayles of Halpine Church. The other two important people are Rose and Ian - when you read the stories of "Song of Purim" and "Paradise Inn" you will see why.

Clark Tyler
McLean, VA

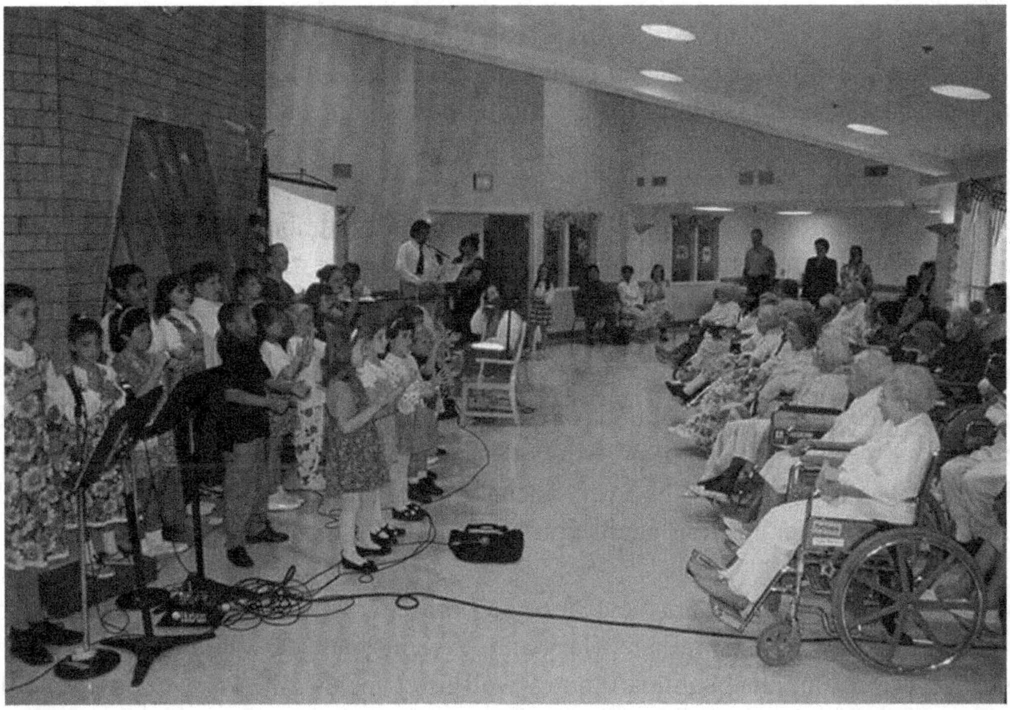

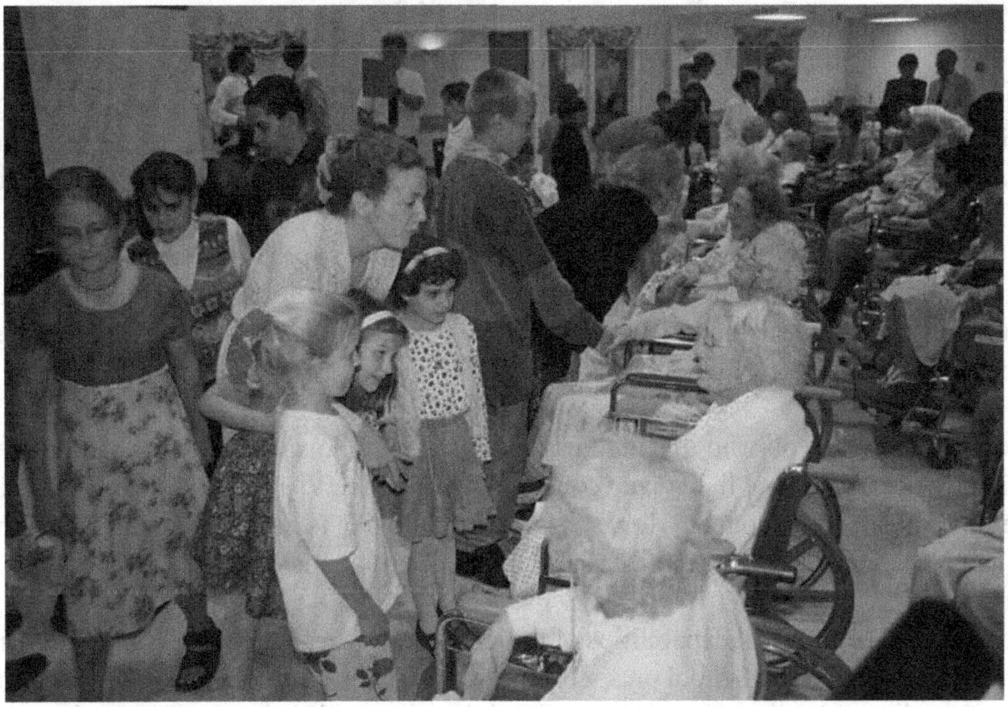

The Sunday School class performs at a nursing home.

## Chapter I - THE MUSTARD SEED

Appropriately enough, it all began with a mustard seed... and a little 5 year-old girl who was upset because she couldn't draw. More about the mustard seed later. First, a little background.

Our pastor was fond of quoting the Apostle Paul's admonition in Romans that the mission of the church is to equip the saints to do the work of ministry. Beginning with the aforementioned mustard seed, what follows is an approach to that "equipping," and a few specific examples of the resulting ministry.

As anyone who has ever taught Sunday School will tell you, the growth process exhibited by children is exceeded only by the growth of the teacher as he or she teaches. I love the line in "The King and I," that says: "It's a very ancient saying, but a true and honest thought; that if you become a teacher, by your pupils you'll be taught." Amen.

We were a small church - maybe 125 or so born-again Christians who met in a rented school gymnasium in suburban Maryland. As our pastor's wife used to say: "our 'incense'was the unmistakable aroma of well used sneakers!" The Sunday School was about a dozen children of various ages between 5 and 11. This was too small to break up into standard class groupings, and thus not a really good fit for most of the curricula sent around by the various Christian publishing houses.

I had tried to adapt these canned lessons to hold the interest of the group, but struggled with the fact that when the older kids were taught at an appropriate level, the younger kids couldn't really relate, and fidgeted. And vice versa... things that appealed to the younger ones tended to bore the older ones.

Something different was needed. I soon found that songs were *the* ingredient that reached and motivated both segments. When a sense of fun was injected into the musical lesson, fidgeting and boredom vanished.

Now for those of you who are anticipating that what follows is a step by step guide that will produce a scriptural light opera company (rivaling the Vienna Boys Choir or the Trapp Family Singers), I apologize. However, if you would like to see how an outreach ministry of young "equipped saints" can bless a whole bunch of adults, read on.

I discovered the musical capabilities of these children when an elder of our church asked me to have the Sunday School present some sort of Christmas program. Well, "program" may be a little grandiose for what happened, but the result is instructive - at least it was for me. Another shepherd-king-angel-creche type pageant seemed a little beyond our talents; what was needed was something simpler, and perhaps a little more interesting for the audience. A simple song seemed to be the answer.

Now my bias was towards songs that used actual words of scripture, but when I looked for such a Christmas song, I was amazed to find that there was no such thing. Except, of course, for Handel's "Messiah," and somehow I just couldn't visualize our being even remotely credible with that!

The answer was in the second chapter of Luke's gospel, the most familiar reading in the celebration of the Christmas season. There, in six short verses was the complete telling of the Christmas story, followed by a natural chorus: "Glory to God in the highest, and on earth, peace, good will to men." No problem for anyone of any age to memorize that.

But setting the six applicable verses to music didn't seem quite right, and I didn't really want to change any of those wonderful words to make them fit tempo or to add any rhymes, just to construct a song. What I decided to do was to write a simple musical theme that would be played underneath, while a child recited each of those six verses. Then all would sing the chorus, "Glory to God etc" after each verse. In order to use all 12 children, I added a short tag line for emphasis after each verse, which would in turn be a cue for all to sing the chorus. This also enabled the director to play the piano without having to wave his hands wildly to cue the children. And the soloists didn't have to sing - only recite a well-known verse that they had all heard many times over.

The words for each verse and tag line were put on numbered 3 by 5 cards and the kids arranged in order of presentation, passing the hand held microphone down the line during the chorus. We practiced both the song and the logistics for six Sundays and our little mini choir was ready. No one got a cold, sore throat or confused, and the pieces all fell into place. When, on the Sunday before Christmas, this "gloratorio" was presented, the kids were blessed to receive a standing ovation. No one tripped over a styrofoam manger, dropped "gold" pieces, lost an ill-fitting crown, had to wear a shepherd bathrobe, or snagged a wing on a mike stand. It was indeed a different Christmas program!

"Glory to God" became a Christmas standard in our church. I later included it in a special Christmas play, "Reports of Christmas"... giving Luke full credit for the lyrics.

And now...about that mustard seed.

With our seasonal triumph behind us, I decided to start teaching the class about the parables of Jesus. I knew from the Christmas experience that some sort of song that incorporated the kids' own efforts would not only work best, but would give them a real performance to work towards. After all, I now had a dozen-plus cast of troupers to work with. The "gee, I could do that" syndrome had resulted in our little class becoming larger - almost 16 or 18 now.

So off I went to the local Christian bookstore. The children's section had a number of books about the parables, but not ALL the parables; only the most familiar ones. I wanted to teach the class about <u>all</u> of them. I found a wonderful book, in the adult section, by William Barclay. It was, "And Jesus Said" (Westminster Press, 1970). It had all the parables. In his introduction, the author referred to a parable as "an *illustration* of an aspect of truth." He stressed that Jesus used parables because, "most of us tend to think in pictures." And again, "He gave us these *cameo-like pictures* we call parables so that the great ideas He wished to teach might become comprehensible." The use of the word "illustration" and "picture" stuck in my mind as I tried to come up with a theme or a song for the kids to learn. Since the theme of most of the parables was, The Kingdom of God, I knew I had a theme.

"Picture the Kingdom" would be our song, and to pick up on Mr. Barclay's words of introduction, it would be "illustrated" by the children's own drawings of each parable. Knowing that kids' drawings are indeed treasures of heart expression, if not great art, we could take a drawing from each child and transfer it to an overhead which would then be projected on a screen as the song was presented.

I just needed the song. Well... I also needed the enthusiastic participation of each child.

That Sunday, we started with the Parable of the Sower and the Seed. Everyone knew that one. I told them the plan. We would learn what the parables were all about, then read and discuss each one. Finally, each child would try and capture the essence of the story in one simple drawing. Since Jesus took the trouble to explain this parable to His disciples, this was a good place to start.

After the reading and the teaching, we had enough time left for the drawings.

When young Chris brought me his drawing, I knew we were on the right track. There on his one page was a simple drawing of a man with a Scott's Turf Builder-type spreader and all kinds of seeds trailing out behind. Others were equally imaginative with hungry birds, scorching sunbursts, evil grappling thorns and hazardous forbidding rocks. There was even a Bible with what looked like a beanstalk sprouting through its cover. I was delighted!

Then I noticed little Kirstie. The more the other kids got into the task and feverishly produced drawing after drawing, the more poor little Kirstie just stared down at her blank sheet of paper. She was the youngest in the class, about five or a little younger. She felt left out. When I went to her and asked what was the matter, she told me she couldn't draw. By now, all the others had composed a veritable gallery of artwork and were ready to start on the next parable.

I told Kirstie to come up to the blackboard with me. I gave her a nice new piece of chalk and took her little hand in mine. As I guided her hand, we made a simple, but distinct dot in the middle of the blackboard. I whispered into Kirstie's ear that the dot was the mustard seed... and it was all *hers*. When one child asked what it was, Kirstie proudly announced that it was the mustard seed...**her** mustard seed. I now had her enthusiastic participation. And she became Miss Mustard Seed. Today she is in high school, but when I call and talk to her, I always ask, "and how is Miss Mustard Seed?" I never fail to get a giggle in reply.

"Picture the Kingdom" became a 12-15 minute production that opened with an introductory song about the Kingdom Of God and then devolved into a musical patter citing something about each of the parables with a chorus after every two or three verses. But the centerpiece was the kids' drawings that illustrated the lyrical treatment of the parables. The drawings were simple, if rudimentary, but they exhibited a very precious understanding of Jesus' lessons. The most important thing was that the drawings gave the children ownership of the production... it was, truly, theirs.

I learned a very valuable lesson. You can't just impose a song or a play or skit on these children and expect it to be perfected with a heavy schedule of rehearsals. If they have heart understanding of the words and the lesson, then what you hear as an end result will be fine. It does not depend on their degree of musical talent, or how well they have memorized their part. If the song or the play is "theirs" in a very real sense, then their confidence and ability to witness will be more than evident.

I found a very unique way of testing this proposition. There were about a dozen nursing homes in the immediate area of where our church was. Since I had recently put my own mother in a nursing home, I was acutely aware of the very special chemistry that exists between people in their 70's and 80's and kids in this particular age group (age 5 to 12). I was also very aware of how hungry nursing home residents were for things spiritual... or just a simple Bible verse or two. It occurred to me that people like this might be a most receptive audience to what the children could offer. After all, it was in my heart to train and equip witnesses, reaching out to others.

A fellow member of our congregation visited most of these homes to see if they might like to have our class come and perform for them. Almost all of them responded most favorably, not really sure of what we were all about. For reasons of logistical simplicity, I chose the nearest one. It was a good choice, since many of the residents there were retired schoolteachers.

So after the class had performed this work for our church, we packed up a mini sound system and shepherded the kids to the nearby nursing home. While the mandatory bathroom break was being orchestrated and the sound system and overhead projector being set up, I explained to the crowd of residents the background of the song. They seemed fascinated that the song had been written especially for the children and that their own drawings would illustrate the presentation. Luckily I had made copies of all the drawings, so I told the audience that the kids would have a present for each of them when we finished.

I had explained to the class beforehand that the nursing home was a very special audience that would undoubtedly love to visit with the kids individually, and even hold their hand and pray with them after the performance. After some initial hesitation on the kids' part, the ice was broken and almost all of the residents were charmed to have them briefly pray with them. Each child had a copy of their own drawing and gave it to the resident they prayed with.

I will never forget the sight of those thirty or so elderly residents (most in wheelchairs), rolling back to their rooms clutching their little parable drawings. And it was a most fortunate resident who proudly accepted Kirstie's "mustard seed." A new ministry was born that day. And a happily equipped bunch of saints was eager to get to work on the next production.

## Chapter 2 - A CHRISTMAS UN-PAGEANT

When you work with small children in plays or musical productions, the last thing you want to do is make the kids anxious. I had seen shy and nervous kids get so uptight about concentrating on parroting lines from memory that the performance became flat, dull and totally without meaning. If the point was to develop heart understanding and the ability to witness to others (especially adults), then the goal should be building confidence and achieving credibility. But how?

As every parent knows, if a child hears a commercial on TV more than once (especially if it strikes them as even remotely amusing), it somehow gets downloaded forever in their cranial hard drive. They can perform it with all the inflections, movements and characterizations of the original. But tell the same child to memorize Psalm 23, and the drudgery of repeating by rote will flatline the faith message. It will come out as one dimensional and devoid of spirituality.

As I began to design and craft these little musical productions, I found that by removing the need to memorize, the anxiety level dropped appreciably. As a result, we became experts in ways to disguise and screen cue cards, lyrics and script pages. In one of my earlier lives I was a poll watcher in New York City elections. Early on, I was instructed in the fine art of "palm cards."

There is a strict law against any candidate material or electioneering within so many feet of the polling place. To get around this, the political types devised the "palm card." This was a small card placed in the voters hand that merely listed the names of those he or she was urged to vote for. In Tyler productions, the palm card was extended to new heights.

Lyrics were affixed to the back of props, pinned to curtains, glued to packages, written on sleeves and hidden in plants. In one play, one singer who was playing Gideon was supposed to be talking to God. Her lines were pinned on the back edge of an upper masking curtain, so when she looked up to heaven, there was her script!

To overcome stage fright and similar public performance anxiety, some of my shyer charges were cast as the voices of puppets. While the puppets performed, their "voice" was positioned behind the curtain with a stationary mike, script in hand. Much confidence was built in this way and many of these "voices" emerged later as full fledged performers... shy no more! Another technique involved judicious blocking which simplified stage movement and kept the helter-skelter appearance to a minimum. This style also was consistent with the physical constraints of not only our rented church space, but the small areas where we often performed in nursing homes.

So, what's an "un-pageant?"

It is a staple of most churches to have a Christmas program, usually included within the service on the Sunday before Christmas. Since our church had a number of families where one parent was a churchgoer and the other not; or where there were many friends, neighbors or family members who preferred the non-threatening format of a separate program as opposed to a church service, we decided to have a longer production at a special evening time followed by carol singing and a fellowship time with juice and cookies. This meant that we needed something a little more imaginative than a toy store coming to life or the standard shepherds-kings-angels type pageant. This format also worked better for the nursing homes, where they really wanted something more than an 8 or 10 minute presentation. A 40 minute production seemed to be about right.

Now you just can't have a Christmas program without Kings, angels, shepherds, Mary, the star, the manger, Herod and all the rest; but what about the most impressive characters of all - the Messianic prophets? Collectively, all these represented an overview of the importance of Christmas, while individually, each was a report of the event's significance from varying perspectives. Hence, "Reports of Christmas."

Now, making all this entertaining as well as edifying meant the inclusion of several characters not automatically associated with the Christmas story. Picking up on the idea of using narrators, I started with two special Christmas reporters, Joy S. Tidings and Gloria N. Excelsis. Representing the commercialization of the season was a bit with a couple of shoppers (one of whom was the epitome of humbug); then to set the stage of the star in the east segment, I added King Herod's Astronomer Royal who gets it all wrong. A special report from Bethlehem was given by a dog puppet newshound named Woof-Woof Blitzer, who reports that the main story was taxes; and finally a manger scene described by one small mouse hidden in the straw, "who saw it all." Of course, my class loved all of this, and the biggest problem was making the choice of which little girl would be the Mouse Who Saw it All.

By adding the narrators, and the shopping couple, it was possible to include 2 older teens and a couple of "non kids" which enhanced the casting opportunities. But the centerpiece was the five Messianic prophets - Jeremiah, Isaiah, Zechariah, Micah and Daniel. I say, "centerpiece" because this is what our class-time focused on. I wanted the children to really understand the importance of prophesies given 500 years before that first Christmas.

One of the more compelling tenets of Christianity is the fulfillment of prophecy. When I became a born again Christian, my pastor was a remarkable man named Stan Telchin. He was a very successful insurance man who happened to be Jewish, and he became a believer at age 50. His remarkable testimony is detailed in his book, "Betrayed," which has been translated into 24 languages and sold probably millions of copies. The telling point for his belief was the fulfillment of Old testament prophecies by Jesus. An astounding chapter in another book, Josh McDowell's "Evidence That Demands a Verdict," details 61 of these prophecies and shows exactly how they were fulfilled by Jesus. He quotes a scientist who figured the odds of probabilities on the fulfillment of these prophecies by any one man. Taking just the key 48 prophecies, he determined these odds as one chance in 10 to the 157$^{th}$ power. Nobody can even imagine the size of that kind of number. Just considering the 8 most prominent prophecies, the chances of fulfillment were one in 10 to the $17^{th}$ power - that is one in seventeen quadrillion. Now that was a number that I knew my class could begin to grapple with. So I conceived of a scene in which the five major messianic prophets would state their prophecies as the first "Report of Christmas."

This scene was called "Thus Saith the Lord," and was introduced by one of the teens dressed as a grandmother reading a poem titled "The Coming King" to a bunch of kids seated on the floor around her. As she finishes, five of the kids stand up and turn around revealing the fact that they have on gold T-shirts emblazoned with letters spelling out the name of each prophet. They can either recite or sing these shortened prophetic statements (we have done it both ways).

When I went to the sporting goods store to order these gold T-shirts, the clerk looked at the five names (Jeremiah, Isaiah, Zechariah, Micah and Daniel) and assumed that I was putting together a Jewish basketball team. Several years later, I incorporated this scene into a Christmas musical I had written for a prison ministry. These five "prophets" averaged about 6 feet 3 inches and each weighed from 200 to 250 pounds. The same clerk was there, so when he saw the same five names and the extra-extra large sizes needed, I told him that the kids had really grown in their faith. It would have taken too long to explain what it was all about, and I knew he would be telling the story anyway for years to come. I only wish I could have heard his version!

Reports of Christmas had one scene in which Mary is told by the angel Gabriel that she would give birth to the Messiah. There was one little girl in the class (Sarah) who was a very polished performer and loved the Lord. The problem was she had a very faint little voice. However, she had been taking ballet lessons and was quite good. So the scene was staged with a narrator reciting a short series of poetic verses, taken from Luke, while Sarah danced a charming little balletic dance choreographed to the words of the narration. It was a very special moment, and when we rehearsed it, the other kids never failed to applaud Sarah's dance.

With this production I found that if certain portions of the script were written in verse, it was easier for the cast to recite. In some cases, I put in some background music which served to slow down their delivery - a very important feature as children tend to speed up when they know something really well. At the nursing homes, where many residents are hard of hearing, this could be disastrous. The poems work well since the hearer anticipates the rhyme. Once the kids are taught not to recite in sing-song fashion, thc mnemonics take over and it makes the performance flow a little better.

As their teacher (me) learned all these things, it became clear that the best ideas came from the kids themselves. An excellent example of this is the "Gifts of God" number from Reports of Christmas. As our little class studied and talked about the various reports that would go into this production, I asked the class one day what was the most important thing about Christmas? Of course, the really spiritual kids said, "the coming of Jesus." Most of the others said, "presents." Anticipating this latter answer, I told them that, yes presents were important, but it was the gifts that we get from God that are the most important...and that Jesus was certainly one of these. Then I asked them to name any of the special gifts that we get from God. It took a little while, but soon the blackboard was filled with things like: joy, love, faith, forgiveness, hope, mercy and salvation. We discussed each of these things and as we did so, the kids began to understand how God was working in their lives. As our list grew, we played a game. I put each of these words (to which I added grace, His Word and the promise of Jesus) on a sheet of paper and then placed them in a box. Each child then came up and pulled a word out of the box and was urged to give a little explanation of what that word meant to them - a mini testimony.

We talked about these "gifts" for a while and fined-tuned their explanation, finding where in scripture each was mentioned or illustrated. Pretty soon, each child had a favorite word. It worked nicely that our 12 member core group each had a word. During the intervening week, as I thought about this game and the class's words, I visualized a stage with two rows of kids singing about the gifts of God. Then, at the end, they would each hold up their "word" to illustrate the gifts. This song wrote itself:

We've received our presents from God
And we're here to say:
That His gifts, His precious gifts
Are all wrapped up in Christmas Day

Gifts of God, gifts of God
Are all wrapped up in Christmas Day:

Joy, peace, mercy and love;
Faith, hope, forgiveness, salvation;
His Word, His grace, His promise in Jesus;
These are the gifts of God.

The next Sunday, I had 12 pieces of foamcore board, cut to various sizes to fit the length of each word. On one side was each word in 3 inch letters; on the other was Christmas wrapping paper with a bow so each looked like a present. Hearing the song just once, the kids held their "present", wrapping paper side out; then when they sang their own word, they flipped the board over, holding it up to reveal the "gift." It didn't take much rehearsing to get this down pat. The only tricky part was for each to hold their word facing them so it was upside down. Then when they turned it over in raising it over their heads, it was right side up facing the audience.

The only change in this number came when a little five year old girl who was, I believe, autistic, joined our class just the week or so before the performance. Although she was too young and unaware to really understand what the song was all about (and she was unable to articulate), she sure knew that she didn't have a word/present like all the other kids. Time for a hasty amendment. The night of the performance, there in the first row of children was little Johanna; And when the gifts were named, she happily held hers up – and the word was: "healing."

# REPORTS OF CHRISTMAS

## Lesson Plan

The key to teaching your class about this Christmas play is to make sure they understand the significance of the Messianic prophets - Jeremiah, Isaiah, Micah, Daniel and Zechariah. Hundreds of years before the birth of Jesus, these prophets articulated not only God's promise of a savior/deliverer, but provided the most minute details of his life, ministry and death/resurrection.

Since most children performing Christmas presentations are familiar only with the shepherd, Wise Men, angels & creche scene, it is important to give them a little broader perspective. My favorite source for understanding the Messianic prophesies is Josh McDowell's book, "Evidence that Demands a Verdict" (Thomas Nelson Publishers, 1972). Chapter 9 of Volume I of this work compresses into 36 pages some truly amazing facts about the prophecies and their fulfillment.

- Find out what your class members know about Christmas - how it is celebrated; what it signifies; what the Bible says about it; what do they hear about it on television. Make a blackboard list of what the kids say in each category.

- In the New Testament, Matthew and Luke are the two gospels that tell parts of the Christmas story. Each contain a genealogy of Jesus; one through his father, Joseph and one through his mother, Mary. Explain why this was important - the inheritance of the throne of David. After the temple was destroyed in 70 AD, all genealogical records were lost. Therefore, no Messianic claims could be verified after that date. That is why Daniel's prophecy about the "70 weeks" is so important.

- So, Matthew and Luke each give a "Christmas report." What is a report? What do they teach reporters in journalism school? They teach that a reporter has to reveal five things: the WHO, the WHAT, the WHERE, the WHEN and the WHY. Illustrate this: stage a simple scene (for instance, a person comes on, looks around, then hides something under a box...then leaves. Another person comes on and just happens to knock the box over...discovers something and picks it up (it's money)...jumps for joy, and then happily rushes off. Ask the kids to "report" what happened. Then critique the reports. Did they put in the who, what, where, when and why? Did Matthew and Luke do this? Read those scriptural verses and see if the children recognize the Who, the what, the where, the when and the why. The birth of Jesus was a defining event - it separated the B.C. from the A.D. It affected the history of the world more than any other event. Spiritually, it was a matter of life and death for all of us. Why?

- The Who, the what and the where of the Christmas story. Classify all the elements of the Christmas story into one of three "buckets" so it comes out like this:

| WHO | WHAT | WHERE |
|---|---|---|
| Jesus | A star | Judea |
| Mary | A manger | Bethlehem |
| Joseph | gold | Israel |
| shepherds | frankincense | the earth |
| wise men | myrrh | Syria |
| King Herod | a covenant | Roman Empire |
| angels | A savior | an inn |
| Gabriel | good news | a stable |
| Luke | Gospel | the East |
| Matthew | hope | The sky |
| Caesar Augustus | peace | Heaven |
| Quirinnius | joy | The hills |
| Immanuel | glory | Nazareth |
| the prophets | salvation | Egypt |
| the animals | a tax | A dream |

- Now have the class make up some headlines that different papers might have run 2,000 years ago. Who and what were the most important things - to believers, to sinners, to the citizens of Bethlehem, to the world, to Satan, to God.... What happened BEFORE that first Christmas that might have had something to do with events? Talk about Mary & Gabriel, Herod, Caesar and the prophets.

- What did the prophets say? When? What is God's purpose in prophecy? Look at the specific prophesies of Jeremiah (23: 5-6), Isaiah (7:14, 9:6, 60:1), Micah (5:2-5), Daniel (9: 23-24) and Zechariah (9: 9-10) (see pages 25, 26 and 27). Explain "fulfillment." (See, "The Coming King" on page 24).

- Why is the gospel good news? Use the lyrics of "And the Good News Is..." and the chorus of "The Gifts of God." Explain redemption, salvation, restoration, reconciliation, forgiveness, righteousness, new creation, hope, new spirit, new song and "new destination." How many of these types of words occur in the standard Christmas carols we know so well. Since most children think that Christmas is all about presents/gifts, have them talk about God's gifts to us: joy, peace, mercy, love, salvation, forgiveness, faith, hope, His word, His grace, His promise in Jesus. Assign each word/gift to a child and get them to try and say what that word means to them. Change these around so they get to try different "gifts." What does God expect us to do with these gifts? (besides giving thanks).

- Why was the star important? The Bible refers to Jesus as "the bright and morning star" (Peter & John) and the Old Testament speaks of a "star out of Jacob" (Deuteronomy) and "the star of your God (Amos). Why did Herod fear the star? What did the Wise Men do because of the star?

## Format

This presentation is configured as what is known as a "revue" style format - that is, it is a series of separate scenes and songs tied together by a dual narration by two Christmas "reporters." As they present the case for examining the meaning of Christmas well beyond what Luke 2 describes, we see an extension from the modern day celebration all the way back to the first millennium before the birth of Jesus. The action shifts between a chorus positioned on stage left, to a puppet stage in the center rear, to the two narrators at stage right. The puppet stage is a six foot wide frame of PVC pipe with dark curtains screening the puppeteers. At the rear of this stage is a backdrop showing the "skyline" of ancient Bethlehem. The two narrators are positioned behind two foamcore panels labeled "Joy S. Tydings" and "Gloria N. Excelcis," which hide their music stands. The rest of the action takes place in front of the puppet stage. The chorus can enter and exit left, while soloists can change into costume and retrieve props from behind the puppet stage. The other soloists and players enter from stage right.

## List of Props

| | | |
|---|---|---|
| 2 narrator panels (30X40) | two music stands | Bethlehem backdrop |
| 5 prophet panels | "Live from Bethlehem" sign | dog puppet |
| Bible panel for storyteller | rocking chair | Animal panels (on handles) |
| styrofoam "manger" | "No Vacancy" sign | sleighbells |
| 12 "gift" panels | halos | "News" panels |

costumes for: prophets, storyteller, astronomer royal, guards, king, shepherd, mouse, Mary, lambs

## Director's Introduction

Each year, much of the Peace and Good Will explicit in the Christmas season, seems to be obscured by the frenetic rush of postal deadlines, crowded stores, back-ordered items, travel delays, demanding children, frustrated parents, weather concerns and overly commercial considerations. Oh sure, there is the traditional music of Christmas... but even that seems to get pushed aside by Frosty the Snowman, Santa Claus is Coming to Town, Rudolph and all the rest.

Even those who can concentrate on Jesus tend to forget that 500 years before His birth, the prophets gave 45 separate prophecies detailing many aspects of His life and ministry. Mathematicians have calculated that the probability of any one person fulfilling those prophecies is one in ten to the $157^{th}$ power (that's a one with 157 zeros). More simply, if you limit that to the eight major messianic prophecies, the probability of any one person fulfilling them is one in one hundred quadrillion. The probability of Jesus getting lost in the annual seasonal hype is at best even...if not heavily weighted the other way.

On the commercial side, businesses taking advantage of the season, easily drown out those who try and give voice to Christmas' real meaning. In short, the commemoration seems overwhelmed by the decoration. The simplicity of celebrating the lowly birth of our Savior and rejoicing in the fulfillment of God's ancient promise to man, just doesn't seem to have priority.

The eight different reports of Christmas you will witness tonight are aimed at having Jesus finish this annual race ahead of Santa Claus... if only by a step. And maybe, just maybe, Bethlehem can be seen as just a bit more important than Toys R Us; perhaps "Hallelujah" will displace "bah humbug" as the expression of choice; and the shepherds, wise men and angels will be treasured ever so slightly more than Barbie, Beanie Babies and the latest action figure. Luke's gospel might even enthrall readers more than Harry Potter.

Then, who knows... we might even celebrate Christmas for its real meaning rather than for its impact on the economy.

Glory to God!

## REPORTS OF CHRISTMAS

**CAST:**

| | |
|---|---|
| JOY S. TYDINGS | Our Christmas reporters |
| GLORIA N. EXCELCIS | |
| MR. &MRS. SHOPPER | Hassled participants |
| STORYTELLER | Reader of "The Coming King" |
| THE PROPHETS | Jeremiah, Isaiah, Zechariah, Micah and Daniel |
| NARRATOR | For the annunciation |
| MARY | Silent dancer |
| THE ASTRONOMER ROYAL | By appointment to Herod |
| GUARDS | Herod's musclemen |
| SHEPHERD | Witness of a bright new star |
| KING | Another star witness |
| LAMBS | Testifiers of the Good Shepherd |
| WOOF-WOOF BLITZER | On-the-spot newshound |
| THE MOUSE | Who "saw it all" |
| LUKE | Quoter of Chapter 2 |

**MUSICAL NUMBERS:**

| | |
|---|---|
| OVERTURE | The orchestra |
| BLESSED REPORTS | Joy, Gloria & Chorus |
| THE COMING KING | Storyteller |
| THUS SAITH THE LORD | The Prophets |
| MARY | Mary & Narrator |
| THE ASTRONOMER ROYAL | Himself |
| BRIGHT NEW STAR | Shepherd, King, Joy & Gloria |
| MY GOOD SHEPHERD | The Lambs |
| AND THE GOOD NEWS IS | Joy, Gloria & Chorus |
| THE MOUSE WHO SAW IT ALL | The Mouse & Chorus |
| GIFTS OF GOD | The Chorus |
| GLORY TO GOD | Joy, Gloria & Chorus |

The chorus of "animals" and the "Mouse Who Saw It All"

Sarah dances the part of Mary

The storyteller reads,
"The Coming King"

*The stage is set in three parts; on the left is the chorus area; in the rear center a puppet stage with a backdrop depicting the skyline of ancient Bethlehem; on the right two narrator stations labeled JOY S. TYDINGS and GLORIA N. EXCELCIS. After the Overture, the announcer comes on from the right.*

**ANNOUNCER**

And now...our special Christmas reporters: Joy S. Tydings and Gloria N. Excelcis!

*Two young ladies in formal attire come on from the right and take their places behind each one of the labeled panels.*

**JOY & GLORIA** (*sing*)

EACH YEAR, WE HEAR
ALL SORTS OF REPORTS
AS CHRISTMAS DRAWS NEAR:

**JOY** (*sings*)

SHOPPING REPORTS

**GLORIA** (*sings*)

TRAVEL REPORTS

**JOY** (*sings*)

POSTAL REPORTS

**GLORIA** (*sings*)

AND REPORTS OF SANTA AND HIS NINE REINDEER

**JOY** (*sings*)

(SHE'S COUNTING RUDOLPH).

**JOY & GLORIA** (*sing*)

BUT WHERE IS THE CHRISTMAS
WE SHOULD KNOW SO WELL? –
THE BLESSED REPORT OF THAT FIRST NO-EL

*The piano begins a music box type introduction as the chorus assembles. Some children are carrying cutouts on handles depicting a star, angels, a shepherd, wise men, a dove. As each item is mentioned in the first stanza of the song, the icon is raised. In the second stanza, as the locations are mentioned, a pointer comes up from the puppet stage indicating that particular location on the backdrop.*

**CHORUS**

A STAR IN THE EAST
ANGELS ON HIGH;
SHEPHERDS AND WISE MEN
WITH WONDER DRAW NIGH;
A MESSAGE OF PEACE
COMES DOWN FROM THE SKY:
BLESSED REPORTS OF CHRISTMAS.

THE JUDEAN HILLS,
BETHLEHEM THERE;
SMALL VILLAGE INN
THAT HAS NO ROOM TO SPARE
A STABLE, A MANGER
ANIMALS SHARE:
BLESSED REPORTS OF CHRISTMAS.

JESUS IS BORN
LOVELY AND LOWLY
JESUS IS LORD;
HUMBLE AND HOLY

GLAD TIDINGS OF JOY
GOSPEL GOOD NEWS
GOD'S WORD MADE FLESH
AND THE PROPHETS' PREVIEWS;
REPORTS TO RE-TELL,
RE-HEAR AND RE-USE:
BLESSED REPORTS OF CHRISTMAS
BLESSED REPORTS OF CHRISTMAS!

*The chorus stays in place during the following scene with the shoppers, singing the last half of their song to end the scene.*

**JOY**

There seems to be a slight discrepancy here;
Between the events of that midnight clear...
And what currently passes for Christmas cheer...

**GLORIA**

A poll is what we ought to do
To sample some pertinent points of view
Now here's a couple that might have a clue
Excuse me – what is Christmas to you?

*A man and a woman laden with wrapped Christmas packages, and wearing red stocking caps, come on from the right. She is bustling, he is trailing behind under his load. She stops and he runs into her, dropping some packages. Sleigh bell rhythm starts as he picks up his packages.*

**MR. SHOPPER**

Well, Christmas to me is the food –
Roast turkey, roast goose,
Prime rib au jus
And desserts - chocolate mousse

**MRS. SHOPPER**

That's why your waistband is no long loose!

**MR. SHOPPER**

It shrunk.

**MRS. SHOPPER**

You grew.

**MR. SHOPPER**

Well, that's <u>your</u> point of view!

**MRS. SHOPPER**

Christmas for me is the music...

**MR. SHOPPER**

Some of which drives me insane, Dear;
Like re-runs of Rudolph the Red Nosed Reindeer;
And if I hear that one refrain again, Dear
I'll turn that North Polar denizen, into venison...stew
That's <u>my</u> point of view!

**MRS. SHOPPER**

Well, Christmas is to shop and decorate...

**MR. SHOPPER**

Two things I particularly hate!
Between decking the halls and trekking the malls
The ooohing, the ahhhing.. The fa-la-la-la-la-ing
Who needs a monogrammed Fisher-Price spinet
Or a thousand piece swing set, put up in "a minute"
Or even a pear tree with a partridge in it?

**MRS. SHOPPER**

Well, that's <u>your</u> point of view!

**MR. SHOPPER**

Your Christmas is wrapped up in ribbon and twine
And standing in some endless check-out line!

**JOY**

Wait.
Food and shopping and music are fine
But
Whatever happened to God's design?

**GLORIA**

Christmas is not
Just a gift list, Miss;
It's so much more...
Think what the star, the angel and the manger are for...

**CHORUS** *(sings)*

JESUS IS BORN
LOVELY AND LOWLY
JESUS IS LORD
HUMBLE AND HOLY

GLAD TIDINGS OF JOY,
GOSPEL GOOD NEWS,
GOD'S WORD MADE FLESH,
AND THE PROPHETS' PREVIEWS;
REPORTS TO RE-TELL,
RE-HEAR AND RE-USE:
BLESSED REPORTS OF CHRISTMAS
BLESSED REPORTS OF CHRISTMAS!

*The shoppers exit with their packages (to the right) as the chorus exits to the left. The piano plays a little of the Blessed Reports music to cover this action. Then Joy & Gloria resume their reporting.*

**JOY**

...and speaking of shopping, we've been shopping around for a few special Christmas reports that might give you all a better picture of what Christmas is all about.

**GLORIA**

I know that a lot of people look at this season from the point of view of retail profits – well, here is a report about an earlier sort of PROPHETS - ones that had a lot more to do with Christmas!

*While Gloria was speaking, Joy goes behind the puppet stage and changes into the grandmotherly Storyteller, complete with shawl and glasses. She emerges from behind the puppet stage bringing with her a rocking chair and Bible panel. She settles into the rocking chair as the chorus enters from the left and sits around her with their backs to the audience, listening attentively as she begins to read. The piano plays softly under.*

**STORYTELLER**

T'was the millennium before the first Christmas eve
And God's word occurred that men might receive,
And publish glad tidings for all to believe...
In the coming king, the Messiah.

Seed of woman, thru Abraham, Isaac and Jacob, this son
This branch from Judah and Jesse would run;
Priest, prophet, Lord - this anointed one...
Is the coming king, the Messiah.

But how would our God prepare, make aware, every heart?
What vessel to use for this news to impart?
Five prophets would name and proclaim, for a start...
The coming king, the Messiah.

Though they knew they might be rejected, or killed;
With faith they inscribed what God had willed:
Prophesies miraculously, completely fulfilled...
By Jesus, who is the Messiah.

His lineage, birthplace, the titles He'd hold,
His ministry, suffering - it all was foretold;
Even the price for which His betrayal was sold...
This coming king, the Messiah.

The extent of these prophesies therefore require
A degree of fulfillment that couldn't be higher;
Remember these prophets lived five hundred years prior...
To the coming king, the Messiah.

So all because of Isaiah and Zechariah,
Micah, Daniel and Jeremiah,
The world knew salvation could only come via...
        The coming king, the Messiah.

Now, imagine five prophets are speaking to you;
Words full of hope, so wonderfully true;
Many seasons before this blessing is due...
        This coming king, the Messiah.

And that's what we mean when we say, "good news"
Traced back to these five's prophetic clues,
And leading to Jesus, our savior who's...
        The coming king, the Messiah.

And the best news of all –
Though we don't know just when;
Is, this coming king...
        Is coming again!

*At this, from amongst the youngsters seated on the floor, five stand up identified by the names on their T-shirts as Jeremiah, Isaiah, Micah, Zechariah and Daniel.*

**GLORIA** *(sings)*

THOSE ANCIENT PROPHETS IN ANCIENT DAYS
WHEN THE HOPE OF MESSIAH THEY WOULD RAISE,
THEY FILLED THEIR PROPHESIES AND THEIR PRAISE,
WITH THE PHRASE...
        THUS SAITH THE LORD.

**CHORUS** *(sings)*

THUS SAITH THE LORD
THUS SAITH THE LORD
THUS SAITH THE LORD
THUS SAITH THE LORD

**JEREMIAH** *(sings)*

BEHOLD THE DAYS ARE COMING
WHEN I WILL MAKE A NEW COVENANT WITH
THE HOUSE OF ISRAEL;
I WILL FORGIVE THEIR INIQUITIES,
REMEMBER THEIR SIN NO MORE;
AND I WILL RAISE FROM DAVID A RIGHTEOUS BRANCH
AND HE SHALL BE CALLED:
THE LORD, OUR RIGHTEOUSNESS.

**CHORUS**

THUS SAITH THE LORD
THUS SAITH THE LORD
THUS SAITH THE LORD
THUS SAITH THE LORD

**ISAIAH**

A VIRGIN SHALL CONCEIVE
AND BEAR A SON
AND CALL HIS NAME:
EMMANUEL;
FOR UNTO US A CHILD IS BORN;
UNTO US A SON IS GIVEN;
HE BORE THE SIN OF MANY,
MADE INTERCESSION FOR US ALL;
ARISE SHINE - FOR THY LIGHT IS COME!

**CHORUS**

THUS SAITH THE LORD
THUS SAITH THE LORD
THUS SAITH THE LORD
THUS SAITH THE LORD.

**MICAH**

AND THOU, BETHLEHEM EPHRATA,
OUT OF THEE SHALL COME,
HE THAT IS TO BE
RULER IN ISRAEL;
AND HE SHALL STAND
IN THE STRENGTH OF THE LORD,
AND HE SHALL BE GREAT
TO THE ENDS OF THE EARTH;
AND THIS MAN,
SHALL BE – THE PEACE.

**CHORUS**

THUS SAITH THE LORD
THUS SAITH THE LORD
THUS SAITH THE LORD
THUS SAITH THE LORD

**ZECHARIAH**

REJOICE, DAUGHTER OF ZION;
BEHOLD THY KING COMETH UNTO THEE;
HE IS JUST AND HAVING SALVATION,
AND HE SHALL SPEAK PEACE
TO THE NATIONS.

**CHORUS**

...THE NATIONS...
THUS SAITH THE LORD
THUS SAITH THE LORD
THUS SAITH THE LORD
THUS SAITH THE LORD

**DANIEL**

I AM COME FORTH
TO GIVE THEE UNDERSTANDING;
SEVENTY WEEKS ARE DETERMINED
TO FINISH TRANSGRESSION,
MAKE AN END OF SINS,
MAKE RECONCILIATION
TO BRING IN EVERLASTING RIGHTEOUSNESS
AND TO ANOINT THE MOST HOLY.

**CHORUS**

THUS SAITH THE LORD
THUS SAITH THE LORD
THUS SAITH THE LORD
THUS SAITH THE LORD

**ALL**

THUS SAITH THE LORD!

*The chorus, prophets and the storyteller exit as the piano echoes the music of Thus Saith the Lord. The rocking chair is replaced behind the puppet stage. Joy resumes her place next to Gloria.*

**GLORIA**

Most people think of Christmas, and automatically associate it with Bethlehem. However, nine months before that first Christmas, the dateline was Nazareth...where the angel Gabriel was delivering a miraculous report to a very awestruck young girl.

**JOY**

Luke, who many believe personally interviewed Mary while the Apostle Paul was imprisoned in Caesaria, put down in his gospel, this very special Christmas report.

*Luke enters and takes Joy's place to narrate the story of Mary. The piano begins Mary's theme as Mary enters from the right and dances while the words are spoken.*

**LUKE**

And the angel said:
"Fear not, Mary,
For thou...
Hast found favor with God
And now...

So shall it be,
That the hope of glory
Will be borne by thee."

And she said of the miracle
Of which she heard:
"I am the Lord's; so be it
According to thy word."

"My spirit rejoices
For blessed am I;
The Lord, my soul, doth magnify."

Accepting the burden,
The wonder, the loss;
By faith she would bear
And always be there;

From the side of the manger
To the foot
Of the cross.

*Mary finishes her dance and exits right, as Luke exits behind the puppet stage. Joy resumes her place while the piano repeats Mary's theme underneath.*

**JOY**

Deuteronomy says: "there shall come forth a star out of Jacob;" Amos also prophesied about "the star of your God;" and both Peter and John referred to Jesus as "the bright and morning star."

**GLORIA**

How fitting then, that our Lord's birth should have been heralded by a star - a very special star. For the shepherds, that star certainly was a herald; for the wise men, that star was a guiding light; and for a weary world, that star was a sign from God. For King Herod, however, that star was a cause for concern.

**JOY**

So here is a star report - from all of these viewpoints.

*The astronomer royal enters at the piano introductory music. He is dressed as an astrologer/wizard type with a conical hat; purple robe with stars, comets etc. emblazoned on it. He is pompous and ridiculous with exaggerated motions and a bombastic style. He comes to the center of the stage. The chorus is still in place to the left.*

**ASTRONOMER** *(sings)*

I'M THE ASTRONOMER ROYAL

**CHORUS**

BY APPOINTMENT TO HEROD THE KING

**ASTRONOMER**

EXAMINING OMENS
FOR KING AND THE ROMANS,
THAT CELESTIAL PHENOMENA BRING:
    AGITATIONS, TRIBULATIONS AND TURMOIL
    ALL DETECTED BY
    THE ASTRONOMER ROYAL

**CHORUS**

BY APPOINTMENT TO HEROD THE KING

**ASTRONOMER**

I'VE INSIDE TIPS ON EACH ECLIPSE
PROPHETIC TALES FROM COMET TRAILS;
AND I'VE DISCUSSED HOW COSMIC DUST
AFFECTS THE YEARS OF BOOM AND BUST.
I'M THE ASTRONOMER ROYAL...

**CHORUS**

BY APPOINTMENT TO HEROD THE KING.

**ASTRONOMER**

VERY LEARN-ED AND DISCERN-ED AND QUITE LOYAL
THAT'S THE VERDICT ON
THE ASTRONOMER ROYAL

**CHORUS**

BY APPOINTMENT TO HEROD THE KING

**ASTRONOMER**

MOUNTAINS QUAKING, VALLEYS SHAKING,
OCEANS BOIL;
THAT'S WHEN THEY CALL UPON
THE ASTRONOMER ROYAL.

**CHORUS**

BY APPOINTMENT TO HEROD THE KING

*Two of Herod's guards enter from the right. They have ancient helmets, spears and breastplates. They go to either side of the Astronomer, as if to drag him off left.*

**GUARDS**

The king needs you!

**ASTRONOMER**

AND WHEN THE STARS ARE IN ALIGNMENT
I CAN TELL YOU WHAT THE SIGN MEANT

*His speech is cut off as the Guards drag him off. The music continues, but fades off as two shepherds enter from the left and a king (Magi) enters from the right. They position themselves apart from each other.*

**SHEPHERDS** *(sing)*

I SEE
A BRIGHT NEW STAR
SHINING IN THE EASTERN SKY;
HERALDING A BIRTH, AND PEACE ON EARTH,
AND GLORY TO GOD ON HIGH.

**KING** *(sings)*

I SEE
A BRIGHT NEW STAR
SPARKLING LIKE A ROYAL GEM;
AND IT SEEMS TO SAY, "THIS IS THE WAY
TO THE GOOD NEWS IN BETHLEHEM."

**JOY & GLORIA** *(sing)*

NOT ON ANY CHART,
THIS STAR ISN'T PART
OF ANY KNOWN CONSTELLATION;
BUT IT'S VERY CLEAR
TO THOSE FAR AND NEAR
THAT THERE IS ONLY...ONE EXPLANATION...

**SHEPHERDS & KING** *(sing)*

WE SEE
A BRIGHT NEW STAR
SHINING THROUGH THE DAY AND NIGHT;
COMING FORTH A SIGN
OF GOD'S DESIGN
AND PRAISING HIM WITH ALL ITS LIGHT
PRAISING HIM WITH ALL ITS LIGHT
THIS BRIGHT NEW, BRIGHT NEW
STAR!

*The shepherds and the King exit to the music's refrain.*

**JOY**

Sheep are certainly the most prominent animals in the Bible. They are mentioned 742 times.

**GLORIA**

Did you really count them all?

**JOY**

I tried - but I kept falling asleep. (Pause) Sheep were important for food, clothing and sacrifice. For as long as anyone can remember, the Christmas story is almost always illustrated with sheep and lambs.

**GLORIA**

...but the lamb depended on the shepherd - another central character in the Christmas story.

**JOY**

So, in our next report, here's a little testimony - or lambs' eye view.

*As the piano plays an introduction of a Christmas carol, several "lambs" enter from the left. They are dressed with white floppy ears, a white fluffy shoulder covering, and go to center stage.*

**THE LAMBS** *(sing)*

HE LEADS ME
HE FEEDS ME
HE CALLS ME BY NAME;
HE TENDS ME,
BEFRIENDS ME
HE'S ALWAYS THE SAME.

HE CALMS ME
HE PSALMS ME
HE SHOWS ME THE WAY;
HE PROTECTS ME
COLLECTS ME
WHEN I'VE GONE ASTRAY.

HE'S MY SHEPHERD, MY GOOD SHEPHERD
DAY AND NIGHT GIVING CARE;
AND LIKE ANY GOOD SHEPHERD,
HE'S ALWAYS RIGHT THERE.

LIKE DAVID
LIKE AMOS,
HE'S PROPHET AND KING;
MY GOOD SHEPHERD KNOWS JUST WHAT I AM;
BECAUSE HE'S THE ONE
WHO'S BOTH...
SHEPHERD AND LAMB.

*The lambs exit left. As they do, the chorus re-enters with each carrying a "news" panel showing alternately (when displayed) a TV screen or a newspaper front page on the other. On the flip side, there is a picture of an open Bible. As the scene unfolds, the chorus members hold the "news" panels to hide their faces. When they start to sing, they flip to the Bible side and hold it up.*

**JOY**

Now, as we all know, reports can sometimes be technically accurate, but miss the point entirely. TV news is a frequent example of this.

**GLORIA**

To illustrate the point, suppose CNN (let's call it the Covenant News Network), sent its top on-the-spot newshound to cover the developing Christmas story in Bethlehem one night nearly two thousand years ago.

**JOY**

Doggedly pursuing this story is our own, Woof-Woof Blitzer.

**GLORIA**

Woof-Woof...are you there?

*A sign in the center of the front of the puppet stage is flipped over, saying "Live from Bethlehem." At the same time up comes a dog puppet, complete with reporter's hat and Press tag. As he nonchalantly gives his report, he is blissfully unaware of any of the movement behind him.*

**WOOF-WOOF**

Right here – Woof-Woof Blitzer in Bethlehem – where there are three big stories: taxes, taxes and taxes.

Word on the street is that Augustus is just another "tax and spend" Caesar!

First, the traffic report: the roads are jammed with people coming from all over Judea to register here in Bethlehem for this tax.

All the inns - actually, there is only one - are booked solid.

*Behind him a "NO VACANCY" sign pops up, then disappears.*

**WOOF-WOOF**

...not a pad to be had. Guess you would say that a lot of people have reservations about this tax!

This just in - there are reports of a strange new light, and some voices, in the sky.

*Behind him, a star appears and a panel with some angels.*

**WOOF-WOOF**

In Jerusalem, Herod's palace is refusing comment on the usual rumors about a rival king.

No confirmation of anything - except the taxes. That's pretty much it from here - not much to report.

By the way, Gloria – what does "in excelcis deo" mean?

*Woof-Woof drops down behind the stage. The signs against the backdrop also disappear. The chorus is hiding their faces behind the news panel as the narrators start to sing.*

**JOY** *(sings)*

AND NOW FOR THE GOOD NEWS:
THE WORD IS MADE FLESH;
GOD'S PROMISE IS THERE NOW,
KNOWN AND SHOWN AS A CRECHE.

**GLORIA** *(sings)*

SO GET THE REPORT OF
THE WHOLE CHRISTMAS STORY;
AND KNOW WHY WE ALL SING:
TO GOD BE THE GLORY.

**JOY & GLORIA**

AND THE GIFT FOR US ALL
THAT FIRST CHRISTMAS MORN'
BEGINS WITH OUR HOPE
AND OUR SPIRIT RE-BORN.

*On the last note of this introduction, the chorus flips their news panels to the Bible side and holds them over their heads.*

**CHORUS**

AND THE GOOD NEWS IS:
JESUS IS LORD;
AND THE GOOD NEWS IS:
I AM REDEEMED AND RESTORED.

EVERLASTING LIFE,
FORGIVENESS TOO;
I HAVE RIGHTEOUSNESS,
ALL THAT IS IN ME IS NEW:

NEW SPIRIT, NEW HOPE,
NEW SONG, NEW CREATION,
NEW POWER, NEW PURPOSE,
AND A NEW DESTINATION.

THAT IS WHAT I CHOOSE:
ALL THIS GOOD NEWS;
AND SO MINE IS NOW THE VICTORY
AND THE GLORY HIS;
AND THAT'S WHAT THE GOOD NEWS IS!
HALLELUJAH!

*At the end of their song, the chorus exits left. They change their news panels for a collection of individual panels depicting various barnyard animals: a donkey, a lamb, a camel, sheep, goats, and a dove (among others). With these new panels, the chorus re-enters towards the end of Joy's introductory poem.*

**GLORIA**

Many artists have painted scenes showing what they think that Bethlehem stable looked like that night so long ago. There's Mary and Joseph, of course, usually surrounded by cattle, sheep, maybe a camel and sometimes a dove. But here's a report by one small creature who probably had the best view of all – only no one noticed her.

**JOY**

Now, if you were a mouse
You'd know that it mattered,
To be in a place
Where grain is scattered.
Now here is a mouse
Who, thus is no stranger
To the rain of the grain
Found round a manger.

*At this, the Mouse emerges from behind the puppet stage. She places a small manger in the center, towards the front of the stage. The chorus, with their animal panels, comes on and takes their places.*

**JOY**

In a Bethlehem stable
In ancient Judea,
She was a witness
Though no one could see her.
So here is her testimony,
Her part of the story
Of the night that God gave us
The hope of glory.

*As the music begins, the Mouse takes her place to the right of the manger.*

**THE MOUSE** *(sings)*

THE DONKEY WAS THERE
AND SO WAS THE LAMB,
AND ALSO THE CAMEL, NAMED ABRAHAM,
SOME SHEEP AND SOME GOATS,
AND A DOVE, I RECALL;
AND ME - THE MOUSE WHO SAW IT ALL.

OUTSIDE IN THE SKY
THE ANGELS WERE HEARD
GIVING ALL OF THE SHEPHERDS THE WONDROUS WORD,
A BRIGHT STAR ABOVE
WITH BEAMS THAT WOULD FALL
ON EVEN THE MOUSE WHO SAW IT ALL.

**THE MOUSE**

A BABY WAS BORN
THAT COLD WINTER NIGHT
AND INTO THE DARKNESS CAME A GREAT LIGHT;
FILLING THE STABLE
FROM MANGER TO STALL,
AND HELPING THE MOUSE TO SEE IT ALL.

*The chorus sings this next stanza, and as they do, the mouse turns toward the manger and drops to her knees in an attitude of prayer.*

**CHORUS**

AND GLORY TO GOD
AND PEACE BE ON EARTH;
AND WITNESS FOR ALL THAT SPECIAL BIRTH;
AND IF YOU LOOK CLOSELY
IN THE STRAW NEAR THE WALL
THERE WAS THE MOUSE WHO SAW IT ALL.
THERE WAS THE MOUSE WHO SAW IT ALL.

*As the piano continues with the music for this last stanza, the chorus exits left; the Mouse goes behind the puppet stage, taking the manger with her.*

**JOY**

Glory is certainly a "Christmas" word. You find it in almost every Christmas carol.

**GLORIA**

The most common definition of "glory" is: the presence of God.

**JOY**

...and "presence" - if you spell it ending in a T-S, certainly comes close to what most children think of when you speak of Christmas.

**GLORIA**

So, no report of Christmas would be complete without talking about "presents" - in the gift sense.

**JOY**

I feel a song coming on.

**GLORIA**

So do I... but I've been reading ahead.

*The chorus now comes back on. Each child is carrying (facing the audience) a gaily wrapped "gift" panel complete with bows and ribbon. On the back of these panels is one of 12 words, and as they sing the chorus they flip the panels in turn revealing the "gift" and holding it high.*

**CHORUS**

WE'VE RECEIVED
OUR PRESENTS FROM GOD;
AND WE'RE HERE TO SAY:
THAT HIS GIFTS, HIS PRECIOUS GIFTS
ARE ALL WRAPPED UP IN CHRISTMAS DAY.

GIFTS OF GOD, GIFTS OF GOD
ARE ALL WRAPPED UP IN CHRISTMAS DAY

*Now, as each sings the "gift" word, they sequentially flip their gift panel, revealing their word. This repeats when they sing this list the second time.*

**CHORUS**

JOY, PEACE, MERCY AND LOVE;
FAITH, HOPE, FORGIVENESS, SALVATION;
HIS WORD, HIS GRACE, HIS PROMISE IN JESUS;
THESE ARE THE GIFTS OF GOD.

GIFTS OF GOD, GIFTS OF GOD
ARE ALL WRAPPED UP IN CHRISTMAS DAY.

*Now, the children have re-flipped their panels to the gift (wrapped) side.*

**CHORUS**

SEEK YE FIRST
THE KINGDOM OF GOD
AND HIS RIGHTEOUSNESS;
AND THESE GIFTS WILL ALL BE YOURS;
TO USE, TO SHARE AND OTHERS BLESS.

GIFTS OF GOD, GIFTS OF GOD
ARE ALL WRAPPED UP IN CHRISTMAS DAY.

JOY, PEACE, MERCY AND LOVE,
FAITH, HOPE, FORGIVENESS, SALVATION
HIS WORD, HIS GRACE, HIS PROMISE IN JESUS;
THESE ARE THE GIFTS OF GOD.

GIFTS OF GOD, GIFTS OF GOD
ARE ALL WRAPPED UP IN CHRISTMAS DAY
ALL WRAPPED UP IN CHRISTMAS DAY!

*The chorus exits left. They drop off their gift panels and, re-enter (now wearing halos) during the following dialogue.*

**JOY**

Except for the story of the wise men in Matthew, we rely on Luke's gospel for most of the details of the Christmas story. Six verses in the second chapter of Luke contain the most familiar rendition of what happened on that blessed night so long ago.

**GLORIA**

Apart from Handel's "Messiah," there is no music associated with Christmas that uses actual words of scripture. So here is a song, with lyrics by Luke, that epitomizes our report of Christmas.

**CHORUS**

GLORY TO GOD
IN THE HIGHEST
AND ON EARTH, PEACE
GOOD WILL TO MEN
GLORY TO GOD
AND ON EARTH, PEACE
GOOD WILL TO MEN

**JOY** *(recites against the music)*

And it came to pass that in those days
There went out a decree from Caesar Augustus
That the world should be taxed, and so they went...
Every one to his own city.

**GLORIA**

...each and every one.

**CHORUS**

GLORY TO GOD
IN THE HIGHEST
AND ON EARTH, PEACE
GOOD WILL TO MEN

GLORY TO GOD
AND ON EARTH, PEACE
GOOD WILL TO MEN

**GLORIA** *(recites)*
And Joseph went up from Galilee
To the city of David, called Bethlehem
To be taxed with Mary, his espoused wife;
His wife being great with child...

**JOY**
...so very great with child.

**CHORUS**
GLORY TO GOD
IN THE HIGHEST
AND ON EARTH, PEACE
GOOD WILL TO MEN
GLORY TO GOD
AND ON EARTH, PEACE
GOOD WILL TO MEN

**JOY** *(recites)*
And so it was, while they were there
The days were accomplished that she brought forth a son
And laid him in a manger, because there was..
No room for them in the inn.

**GLORIA**
...no room in the inn.

**CHORUS**
GLORY TO GOD
IN THE HIGHEST
AND ON EARTH, PEACE
GOOD WILL TO MEN
GLORY TO GOD
AND ON EARTH, PEACE
GOOD WILL TO MEN.

**GLORIA** *(recites)*
And there were in that same country then,
Shepherds abiding in nearby fields;
Keeping watch over their flock by night...and lo...
The angel of the Lord came down.

**JOY**

...with the glory of the Lord.

**CHORUS**

GLORY TO GOD
IN THE HIGHEST
AND ON EARTH, PEACE
GOOD WILL TO MEN
    GLORY TO GOD
    AND ON EARTH, PEACE
    GOOD WILL TO MEN.

**JOY** *(recites)*

And the angel said: "fear not for I
Bring you good tidings of greatest joy;
For unto you is born this day:
A savior which is Christ, the Lord"...

**GLORIA**

...a savior, Christ the Lord.

**CHORUS**

GLORY TO GOD
IN THE HIGHEST
AND ON EARTH, PEACE
GOOD WILL TO MEN
    GLORY TO GOD
    AND ON EARTH, PEACE
    GOOD WILL TO MEN.

**GLORIA** *(recites)*

And suddenly, there was with the angel
A multitude of the heavenly host,
Praising God, and saying:

**CHORUS**

GLORY TO GOD
IN THE HIGHEST
AND ON EARTH, PEACE
GOOD WILL TO MEN
    GLORY TO GOD
    AND ON EARTH, PEACE
    GOOD WILL TO MEN

GLORY TO GOD; GLORY TO GOD; GLORY TO GOD!

# Reports Of Christmas

Clark Tyler
*Arranged by Andrew Bell*

# Blessed Reports

Clark Tyler
*Arranged by Andrew Bell*

28 A A7 F Dm G G7
sta - ble, a mang - er an - i - mals share bless - ed re - ports of Christ -
8va
35 C F Dm Gm B♭ F Gm
mas. Je - sus is Lord, love - ly and low - ly. Jes - us is Lord, hum - ble and
(8)
44 G C G Dm
rit.
ho - ly. Glad ti - dings of joy, gos - pel good news; God's word made
rit.
8va
51 G C A A7 F
flesh and the pro - phets pre - views; re - ports to re - tell, re - hear and re - use,
8va

58 Dm G G7 Am7
bless - ed re - ports of Christ - - mas,
(8)
62 Dm G G7 rit. C
bless - ed re - ports of Christ - - mas,
rit.
(8)

# Thus Saith The Lord

Clark Tyler
*Arranged by Andrew Bell*

# Thus Saith The Lord - Jeremiah

Clark Tyler

20
G
C
D
ness.
Thus sa - ith the
Lord,
thus sa - ith the
Lord,
25
D6/F♯
Em
thus sa - ith the
Lord,
Thus sa - ith the Lord.

# Thus Saith The Lord - Isaiah

Clark Tyler
*Arranged by Andrew Bell*

G rit. G
A vir-gin shall con - ceive and bear a son,
6 D D7 G Am7 G C
and call His name E - man - u - el for un-to us a child is born,
11 G D7 G D G
un-to us a son is giv en; He bore the sin of man-y, made
16 D D7 D6 D7 G Gsus G D7
in - ter - ces - sion for us all; a - rise, shine for thy light is

21
G
C
D
come!
Thus sa - ith the Lord,
thus sa - ith the Lord,
26
Em
B7
Em
thus sa - ith the Lord,
Thus sa - ith the Lord.

# Thus Saith The Lord - Micah

Clark Tyler
*Arranged by Andrew Bell*

21
C
G
C
be The Peace.
Thus sa-ith the
26
D
Lord, thus sa - ith the
Lord, thus sa - ith the
30
Em
B7
rit.
Em
Lord,
Thus sa - ith the Lord.
rit.

# Thus Saith The Lord - Zechariah

Clark Tyler
*Arranged by Andrew Bell*

# Thus Saith The Lord - Daniel

Clark Tyler
*Arranged by Andrew Bell*

No Chord
Em
I am come forth to
7 C7 Em D
give thee un - der -stand - ing.
Sev-en-ty weeks are de-ter-mined to fin-ish trans
3
12 Em Am7 B7 Em D7
gres- sion. Make an end of sins; make re-con-cil-i - a tion. And bring in
17 B7 Em B7 Am C
ev - er - las-ting righ-tous- ness; and to an - noit the most ho - o -

22
D
Em
C
D
-o - ly;
Thus sa-ith the Lord,
thus sa-ith the Lord,
thus sa-ith the
3
28
Em
Lord,
Thus sa - ith the Lord.
Thus sa-ith the Lord.

# SCENE: Mary's Theme

Clark Tyler
*Arranged by Andrew Bell*

# A Bright New Star

Clark Tyler
*Arranged by Andrew Bell*

22 G7 C7 F F C F CHORUS:
I've dis-cussed how cos-mic dust af - fects the years of boom and bust. I'm the as-tron o mer roy - al; by ap-
26 Gm7 C7 F SOLO: Dm C7 Dm
point-ment to Her-od the king. Ver-y learn-ed and dis-cern-ed and quite loy- al; that's the ver-dict on the as-
32 C7 F CHORUS: Gm7 C7 F SOLO: Dm
tron-o-mer roy - al; by ap-point-ment to Her-od the king. Moun-tains shak- ing val-leys quak -ing, oc-eans
38 C7 Dm C7 F CHORUS: Gm7 C7 F
bo - il; that's when they call up-on the as - tron-o-mer roy - al; by ap-point-ment to Her-od the king.

# A Bright New Star (Part 2)

Clark Tyler
*Arranged by Andrew Bell*

25
B♭7
D♭
A♭
D♭
B♭m7
those far and near that there is on-ly one ex plan - a - tion. We see a bright new star;
31
E♭m7
A♭7
D♭
G♭
shin-ing through the day and night; com-ing forth a sign of God's de - sign; and
35
E♭m
A♭7
D♭
rit.
E♭m
A♭7
prais-ing Him with all its light; rit. prais ing Him with all its
38
B♭m7
G♭
A♭
A♭7
D♭
light; this bright new, bright new star.
Ped.
Ped.
Ped.

# My Good Shepherd

by Clark Tyler
*Arranged by Andrew Bell*

F C7 F C7 F C7
Voice
He leads me, He feeds me, He calls me by name; He tends me, be - friends me, He's al - ways the
Piano
3
8
F C7 F C7 F C7 F
Voice
same. He calms me, He psalms me, He shows me the way; He pro-tects me, col-lects me, when
Pno.
16
C7 F B♭ F Gmin7 C7 F
Voice
I've gone a - stray; He's my shep-herd, my good shep-herd day and night giv-ing care; and like an - y good
Pno.

B♭ F C7 F C7 F Dmin Gmin7
23
Voice
shep- herd, He's al- ways right there; like Da- vid, like A- mos, He's pro- phet and king; my good shep- herd knows
Pno.

C7 F C7 F C7 B♭ F C7 F
31
Voice
just what I am; be - cause He's the one who's both shep-herd and lamb.
Pno.

# And The Good News Is

Clark Tyler
*Arranged by Andrew Bell*

Tempo = 130
Upbeat Swing
21
A7
D
be-gins with our hope
and our
spir it re - born.
26
D7
And the good news is...
Je-sus is
Lord.
And the good news is
31
A7
D
I am re-deemed and re -
stored.
Ev-er last-ing
life,
35
D7
A7
for-give-ness
too,
I have right-eous-ness

40
D
A7
all that is in me is new.
New spir- it, new hope, new song, new
45
E
D7
D
cre - a - tion. New pow - er, new pur - pose and a new des - tin - a - tion.
51
D7
That is what I choose all this good news. And so mine is now
56
A7
D
G
the vic - tor - y and the glo - ry His and
60
D
A7
D
that's what the good news is.

# The Mouse

Clark Tyler
*Arranged by Andrew Bell*

B♭min F B♭min F E♭min A♭maj
Voice
The don-key was there and so was the lamb and al-so the ca - mel named
Piano
9 D♭maj F7 B♭min F B♭min F E♭min
Voice
A - bra - ham. Some sheep and some goats and a dove I re - call and me the
Pno.
16 A♭ F B♭min F7 B♭min F B♭min F
Voice
mouse who saw it all. Out - side in the sky the an-gels were heard giving
Pno.
24 E♭min A♭maj D♭ F B♭min F B♭min
Voice
all of the shep-herds the won - drous word. A bright star a - bove with beams that would
Pno.

31 F E♭min A♭ F B♭min D♭
Voice
fall on even a mouse who saw it all. A ba-by was born that
Pno.
39 C Fmin B♭6 C B♭min
Voice
cold win ter night and in - to the dark ness saw a great light. Fil - ling the sta - ble from
Pno.
p mf f mp
47 Fmin D♭ Fmin C Fmin B♭min
Chorus:
Voice
man - ger to stall and help-ing the mouse to see it all. And glo-ry to
Pno.
54 F B♭min F E♭min A♭ D♭ F7 B♭
Voice
God and peace be on earth and wit-ness for all that spe - cial birth. And if you look
Pno.

62
F B♭min F E♭min A♭ F
Voice
close - ly in a straw near the wall there was the mouse who saw it
Pno.
68
B♭min E♭min A♭ F B♭min
Voice
all. There was the mouse who saw it all.
Pno.

# The Gifts Of God

Clark Tyler
*Arranged by Andrew Bell*

22 C Dm G G7 C C
word, His grace, His pro-mise in Je-sus; these are the gifts of God. Gifts of God;
3
27 F C G 1. C C
Gifts of God; are all wrapped up in Christ-mas Day. Christ-mas Day.
32 G C
all wrapped up in Christ - mas Day.

# Glory To God

Clark Tyler
*Arranged by Andrew Bell*

25 Em A D G G A D
Glo-ry to Go - d in the high - est
32 G D A D D7 Bm7 D G D
and on earth, peace good will to men. Glo-ry to God and on earth, peace good
39 A D G A7
rit.
will to men. Glo-ry to God. Glo-ry to God. Glo-ry to
rit.
Coda
44 - D- D G A7 D
God.
Spoken: "And suddenly there was with the angels a multitude of heavenly hosts praising God and saying:"
*Repeat Chorus to end.

## Chapter 3 - AN ARK FULL OF WITNESSES?

Teaching doctrine is not my bag. First, I don't really feel that kids can absorb it; second, most Christians tend to lapse into jargon, making the explanation even more unintelligible. However, the concepts of redemption and salvation are so important to our faith that I felt it was critical for my kids to understand them. The problem was those particular words.

In my mind, what was needed was a graphic illustration of what these words really meant and how they related to real world experience and circumstances that the children were likely to encounter. If this stumbling block could be overcome, I could visualize the class having a powerful impact on adults, especially in the nursing homes. That word, "overcome" stuck in my mind as I thought about the problem and I was drawn to that verse in the book of Revelation - "we overcome by the blood of the lamb and the word of our testimony." I decided to start by teaching the kids about testimony.

The day we started, there was a new little boy in our class. His name was Max. He was Russian and he had a friend with him who spoke no English. I explained to the class what testimony was, and that this was the way we told others what God was doing in our lives...how He answered our prayers. I gave a few examples and then asked if anyone had a personal example. No hands went up – except for Max. When I called on him, he stood up and said: "I prayed and asked God to help get my cousin out of Russia...and here he is!"

Wow! I couldn't have scripted a better scene! All of a sudden, there were lot of hands in the air and the "testimonies" flowed. I have always felt that such personal experiences are much more meaningful to others than all the structured evangelical explanations that are taught in seminaries. The challenge would be to translate this type of thing into a musical presentation that these kids might make before an adult audience. But first, I needed to have them understand "salvation."

A child aged 6 to age 11 has a more distant perception of what happens at the end of earthly life. Everlasting-ness is not really something they can put a high priority on. So I decided to concentrate on the idea of being saved FOR something; not just being saved FROM something. The example I used was baseball. If you hit a single and were trying to stretch it into a double, and slid safely into second base - you were SAFE, or saved. But the important point was that your "safety" was not just an end in itself, you were saved for a reason. You were expected to continue on, advance and score. You, in effect, were being enabled and empowered. You had a role to play by dint of your being "spared."

The story of Noah and the flood seemed a perfect example of this. I asked the class if Noah and his family, and all those animals, were saved just to give them a nice boat ride. Were they all supposed to do something once the flood was over? Why did God save them? As I pondered this, along with the children, I could visualize a series of testimonies by some of the Ark's animals as to what their post-flood task might be.

We began by making a list of some of the more notable animals in scripture. The list got fairly long and even included some animals such as llamas, rabbits, woodpeckers, monkeys, hamsters, dragons, dinosaurs and several others whose relationship to scripture was tenuous if not nonexistent. The list was therefore culled down to: lions, camels, donkeys, lambs, whales, locusts, snakes and doves. One little girl suggested the bee because Israel was a land of milk and honey. I didn't have the heart to explain that the honey mentioned was made from dates, so I included the bees anyway. To round out a list of ten, I added a mouse since this play would be presented around Christmastime and I could see a scene of a mouse who hid under the manger and told of what she saw (this was later also used in Reports of Christmas).

As the class concentrated on this batch (or herd) of animals, we tracked down each mention of each animal in the Bible. The blackboard got filled up each week as we did this, and choices had to be made as to what particular "testimony" each animal was to have. The idea was to have the character of Noah act as a kind of Master of Ceremonies on a cruise ship, introducing each animal testimony as to what key role that animal was to play in later scripture.

Now certainly one animal that had to be included in our roster of witnesses was the sheep. One of my sourcebooks even noted that this animal was mentioned 742 times in the Bible (I did not actually check this!). My problem was that that I had some actual experience with sheep and that gave me a bias that I had to overcome. Years ago, I had a small farm-like property that had a back acre that I grew very tired of mowing. My wife suggested we get some sheep to do the "mowing" for us. Great idea! However, we got just 2 sheep and they were forever getting out and roaming all over the neighborhood (delighting the children and annoying the grown-ups).

The person who sold us the sheep rather "sheepishly" explained that sheep were a herd animal, and that our 2 sheep were escaping because they were looking for other sheep! Having gotten real tired of chasing and rounding up our mini-herd on almost a daily basis, I doubled our flock to 4 and that solved the problem. Amazingly, none of the 742 sheep mentions in the Bible addressed this problem... so I had to research another approach.

The answer came (like so many others) from the kids in my class. When I asked them what they knew about sheep in the Bible, one child was quick to quote two Psalms: first, "we are the sheep of his hand (Psalm 95); and "the Lord is my shepherd" (Psalm 23). Another child added John the Baptist's description of Jesus: "behold the Lamb of God." Another produced a picture of Jesus carrying the "lost sheep" (from the parable).

But the shepherd seemed to be the answer. So, in class we talked about David's psalms and the fact that he was a shepherd. I asked the children what it was that a shepherd did. Interestingly, most had heard the 23rd Psalm primarily at funerals and so answered that the application was that Jesus, as our shepherd, would guide us to heaven. Not wanting to tackle the theology of ***that*** assumption, I decided to have the kids put together a kind of job description of the shepherd. <u>Another</u> list on the blackboard:

He protects the sheep against wolves
He finds the ones who have wandered off
He gets them food
He keeps them together (assuming there are more than 2!)
He knows each one
He takes them to "green pastures" (not heaven)
He cares for them
He watches over them at night

Luckily, no mention of guiding them to heaven! Now, when we all said, "The Lord is my shepherd," this comprehensive resume came into play. If the sheep were going to give a testimony of gratitude for the shepherd, here it was:

He leads me
He feeds me
He calls me by name;
He tends me,
Befriends me
He's always the same

He calms me
He psalms me
He shows me the way
He protects me
Collects me
When I've gone astray.

When I finished writing the song, encapsulating all of our shepherd's resume, making it a hymn of praise for The Good Shepherd, I decided the words were so critical that I didn't want to submerge them in any music. The lyric would be recited instead. This was passable, but for a later revised production of this play, I added a gentle waltz tune and it worked even better. It took away the sing-song nature of a bland recitation and made the testimony more natural. Of course, I made sure that the song would be sung by four little lambs - I remembered what happened when there were just two!

As we progressed with our witness list, I could see that each child was already visualizing what animal they wanted to be. Anticipating that no one would want to be a snake, for instance, I decided to ask the class what sort of personality they thought each animal would have. As we started down this road, the snake problem was solved when little Jessica said that she thought the snake would be sad that everyone was afraid of it and it didn't have any friends. It was easy to imagine Noah counseling a low self esteem problem and pointing out the two parts of scripture where snakes played a major faith role.

Now let's not see all the same hands! Did you guess the story of Moses in front of Pharaoh and the story of a shipwrecked Paul at the campfire on the island of Malta? Jessica became my snake and she was wonderful. Several years later, when Megan played the snake we ended her song with the tag line:

"Everyone's gladder to subtract an adder;
No Hilton or Statler has room for a rattler;
Not even Noah wants hugs from a boa...I can't take
Being a snake!"

It was a showstopper.

As each animal character was given its own special personality, the kids really got into the testimony angle. Josh, and later, Jason, were both large-sized boys and they really took to being the whale who would tell the story of Jonah from the whale's point of view. Jason, who was age 7 at the time, faithfully read the book of Jonah several times and really concentrated to articulate several very difficult words like, obedience, repentance, Nineveh etc. When the chorus sang of how Jonah exited the whale, Jason delivered his last verse:

"No worse for the wear - just a wee bit pale
He puts his foot on the Nineveh trail;
Praising God and thanking the whale -
Thanking the whale."

Jason took his bow and shook his attached fluke-like whale tail to the great delight of the audience. Jason wasn't much of a singer, but what an actor!!

As any experienced teacher will tell you, the job is full of unexpected challenges. Having only come recently to such challenges, I was not totally prepared when the unexpected came up. My "camel" posed such a challenge. Tiffany was going to be the camel. She was a little reserved and withdrawn, not really sure she wanted to be part of this edification/ silliness/testimony bit. I had the feeling she might have thought it was not dignified enough, or maybe even beneath her. She seemed to be rightl for the proud, haughty and reserved camel. When you see a camel at the zoo (or in Israel where I watched my wife ride one), the animal always looks like it knows something, but is not sure that it should tell you. Its personality is that it knows it is clearly unique, but will not deign to seek acclaim, attention, much less conviviality. Now try and impart all that to Tiffany, give her some rhyming verses that embody it and have her do it straight while wearing camel ears and having a large styrofoam "hump" jammed into the back of her tan sweatshirt. While to me that was a daunting assignment, for Tiffany it turned out to be a natural. Her opening lines were delivered with aplomb, conviction and self-assured dismissiveness:

"A plague on comedians, who think they're so witty
And say I'm a horse designed by committee;
I dismiss such nonsense and try to ignore it;
My design is unique And I praise God for it!"

While the chorus behind her sang of the camel being the "perfect desert mammal," the look Tiffany gave said it all. I had the distinct feeling that Tiffany had spent hours at the zoo, studying camel expressions.

Our church had merged with another church, swelling our Sunday School ranks considerably. Since I now had a swarm of both little kids (aged 6 and below) as well as middle schoolers, I needed to have in our musical productions some sort of vehicle for the added participants. Insects seemed to lend themselves to this solution, so "Take a Rainbow Cruise" naturally had to include both bees and locusts. Remember that the bees had been suggested because of the land of milk and honey, therefore the nation of Israel became a player. The resulting character of the Queen Bee pointed out to Noah that bees were responsible for one of Israel's greatest triumphs. When Noah scratched his head to think this through, the bee's reply of "The Maccabees," got the Pun of the Year Award and the biggest audience groan ever.

But the bees also gave us a chance to utilize the littlest kids in a hora-type dance that punctuated the Queen Bee's song. It also gave the author a chance to stay up until three in the morning crafting ten sets of tissue paper and wire coat hanger bees' wings! Now for the locusts.

The lady who choreographed my bees dance also helped put together the other insect jamboree by designing a clever Rube Goldberg kind of motion sequence whereby seven locusts delivered a series of "messages" to Pharoah. Borrowing the music from The Flight of the Bumblebee (there was no locust version of that), we made sure that each locust got a chance to deliver a plague-style message to Pharoah in limerick format (such as):

"Dear hard-hearted Pharoah, get focused;
Or **your** land gets covered with locust;
Just do it our way, and give way to Yahweh;
Your gods have you hokus-pokused."

Several years later, when we reprised this play, there was a small 8 year old girl in the class who was an accomplished gymnast. Substituting the faster "Sabre Dance" music for the "Flight of the Bumble Bee," little Marlayna became a frenetic one person swarm. She delivered the messages to Pharaoh by coming on and going off in a series of backflips, cartwheels, hand stands and somersaults. Plagues never looked so good!

Since this play contained more programmed movement than many of the others, it took a little more rehearsing and logistical planning. We divided the cast into two groups - one for stage left and one for stage right. Each group had an assistant director who would stage manage and cue the right person at the right time. This also kept the chatter and the fooling around to an absolute minimum. Masking tape labels applied to the stage in various color codes told each "animal" where they should be, either as a soloist or as part of a mini chorus. Props were assembled, numbered and put in order on each side of the stage for use at the appropriate time. Amazingly, it all came off with a certain degree of precision.

One of the hardest things to control came in the opening chorus (the title song, “Take a Rainbow Cruise”). After the animals were introduced by using little couplets, and Noah re-enters now dressed as a ship’s captain (replacing his Patriarchal get up in the first scene), the song was to end with a gimmick. Each child was to carefully bend down and pick up a small round, tightly packed colored streamer. Then, making sure one end was secured, they were to throw it at the audience they way you see passengers on a cruise ship do when the boat pulls away from the dock. The effect was obviously enhanced if everyone threw their streamer at the same time. Luckily these multiple rolls of streamers were not expensive, since we had to practice this a lot! I’m sure that the school our church rented is still finding little bits of streamers in strange places and wondering, “what were those Christians into?”

Rather than rely totally on complicated and definitive animal costumes, we decided to use some limited materials to just give a hint of the animal involved. Instead, we relied on face painting, much to the delight of the kids. I will always remember the picture of some of our “locusts” (whose face paint looked slightly demonic) praying with some of the older residents at the nursing homes we went to with this play. Holding the hand of a “snake,” “bee,” or “camel” didn’t seem to bother the patients one bit. They probably would have enjoyed having their faces painted as well!

Postscript:

As an interesting addition to the “Rainbow Cruise” story, here is an example of how a seed was planted that took several years (and a wild change of venue) to sprout. One of our church elders – the one who had urged me to write these plays – had a young son who was a featured player in several of my earlier efforts. Since that time, he had grown up, gone to college, and had entered the Army… and was on his way to Iraq.

His unit was part of the famous Rainbow Division, and their insignia/patch was a rainbow. In his unit there developed a spirited discussion as to whether the rainbow symbol was as military or as macho as some of the troops thought it should be. When my ex-student participated in these discussions, he wrote about all this to his father.

The father e-mailed him back, pointing out the biblical significance of the rainbow, and how it was a signal of God’s covenant to Noah that would protect mankind from future harm. To emphasize the point, the father quoted the lyrics to the Dove’s song, “Under the Rainbow.”

> “We’re under the rainbow
> Covered by what God above sent;
> A covenant his word and love sent,
> Under the rainbow.

We're under the rainbow,
Where we'll find the light of Jesus;
And where we'll find the truth that frees us –
Under the rainbow."

As my ex-student witnessed all this to his fellow war-fighters, the consensus developed that maybe the rainbow was a pretty good symbol after all.

The seed sprouted!

## Format

This play is all about salvation and testimony. The Ark, as a cruise ship Captained by Noah, is the context for ten animal testimonies on their individual role in scripture. While we first meet Noah in his patriarchal role, he is transformed into a kind of testimonial master of ceremonies to introduce us to ten animals of scripture who reveal their importance in God's plan. While costumed as the ship's Captain, he stands in the office of prophet to make the point that while the Ark is symbolic of refuge and shelter from the storm (much like Jesus), the real job for the passengers begins when they (and we) must go out from the Ark and spread the gospel.

Costumes should be minimal, limited to suggestions of the animal portrayed, plus a little face paint. A basic headband with ears attached does wonders. The emphasis should be on the personality of each animal as they detail their role in God's plan: the proud camel, the snake with low self esteem, the grateful lambs, the confident whale, the awestruck mouse etc. The major setting is a large rainbow backdrop, a ship's wheel to screen Noah's script stand, and a cutaway of the Ark's prow on each side of the stage. Minimal choreography can be used for the locusts' delivery of messages to Pharaoh and a hora-type dance for the chorus of bees.

## List of Props

- label (with handle) to identify each animal
- ship's wheel to screen Noah's music stand
- Bees' wings
- Crown for Queen Bee
- tree with red rope for donkey
- camel's hump
- whale's fluke/tail
- Israeli flag
- message envelopes for locusts delivery
- King Tut-type mask for Pharaoh
- manger for Mouse scene
- headbands for ears/antennae
- tails for lions, donkey, camel & mouse

## Director's Introduction

Bearing witness, or giving testimony, is one of the most important spiritual tasks. In examining this, Sunday School classes are all too often taught the doctrine of salvation and redemption. This is sometimes difficult for young children to understand. However the example of the animals on the ark giving testimony about why they were "saved" is something that children can relate to. There are a number of animals on the ark who had some glorious adventures in later scripture. This is the stuff of which wonderful testimony is made. By extension, the point is made that the real job of those given salvation comes after the act of being saved. In that sense, we are saved ***for*** something... not just ***from*** something.

Now if you were choosing a selection of the ark's "passengers" to illustrate all this, you might not choose locusts, a snake or bees... on the other hand if you were to choose the cockatrice, the cankerworm or the oyster you might spend a lot of frustrating time with your concordance and merely end up staring at a blank sheet of paper. In any event, here are ten not-quite-randomly selected testimonies that I hope will show you something useful about God's plan for all of us.

We will now meet Noah, who was 600 years old when God first spoke to him - that tells us something valuable about righteousness, hearing and the ability to act upon God's Word.

## TAKE A RAINBOW CRUISE

**CAST:**

THE LORD.......................................Unseen voice
NOAH..............................................Patriarch & cruise ship Captain
THE LIONS......................................Two young whelps with vivid anticipations
THE CAMEL.....................................Proud symbol of wealth
THE SERPENT.................................Self-pitier with an esteem problem
THE QUEEN BEE.............................Troubadour of the promised land
THE LAMBS.....................................Witnesses of the Good Shepherd
THE WHALE....................................Minstrel of a major role with minor prophet
THE DOVE.......................................Spiritual navigator
THE LOCUSTS.................................Annoying swarm of Pharaoh plaguers
PHARAOH.......................................Silent receiver of the locusts' messages
THE DONKEY..................................Bearer of the triumphant Lord
THE MOUSE.....................................Small witness of the manger scene

**MUSICAL NUMBERS:**

OVERTURE.....................................The orchestra
TAKE A RAINBOW CRUISE.............Noah and the animals
THE LION........................................The Lion whelps
THE CAMEL.....................................The perfect desert mammal & chorus
BECAUSE I'M A SSSNAKE..............The Serpent and Noah
BRING ON THE BEES.......................Queen Bee & the hive
THE GOOD SHEPHERD....................The Lambs
A TALE OF A WHALE.......................The Whale and chorus
UNDER THE RAINBOW...................The Dove
DEAR PHARAOH..............................The Locusts
THE LORD HATH NEED OF ME......The Donkey and chorus
THE MOUSE WHO SAW IT ALL.......The Christmas Mouse and chorus
IN THAT DAY....................................Noah and chorus

The Queen Bee complains to Noah

The Lion cubs testify

Finale

*After the Overture, Noah enters in front of the main curtain. He is robed as a patriarch, and when he hears the unseen voice of God, he stops and instinctively looks up.*

**THE LORD**

Noah!

**NOAH**

Here I am, Lord.

**THE LORD**

I've got some good news and some bad news, Noah.

**NOAH**

What's the good news, Lord?

**THE LORD**

I'm going to save you and your whole family.

**NOAH**

Thank you, Lord....save us from what?

**THE LORD**

That's the bad news.... the important thing is that I have plans for you, Noah.

**NOAH**

Thank you, Lord... that I, your unworthy servant, should be even a small part of your strategic purpose for all mankind...that I....

**THE LORD**

The plans I have for you are right there at your feet

*Noah looks around, then notices a large role of paper down on the floor. He picks this up, unrolls it and looks at its contents.*

**NOAH**

This is a plan... for a boat!

**THE LORD**

...it's an ARK, Noah – a really big boat....like a cruise ship.

**NOAH**

For just my family, Lord??

**THE LORD**

...and a few pets... But remember, Noah, while I am saving you **from** something, I am also saving you **for** something.

**NOAH**

Why, Lord?

**THE LORD**

Let's just call it a "Christmas" present.

**NOAH**

What's a "Christmas present?"

**THE LORD**

You'll see....you'll see.

*As Noah exits, there is a loud sound effect of thunder, lightning and a sustained rain storm. The curtains open to reveal the children dressed as various animals, standing in two rows. Behind is a large backdrop of a rainbow. To the left is a ship's wheel.*

**CHORUS** *(sings)*

WELCOME
TO THREE THOUSAND B.C.
TAKE A RAINBOW CRUISE;
GOD'S PLAN:
TO SAVE EVERY SPECIE,
TAKE A RAINBOW CRUISE!

COME DO THE OLD TWO BY TWO BIT
EMBARK ON THE ARK;
COME FILL UP EVERY LAST CUBIT.

IT'S HIGH WATER TIME
FOR THE GREATEST OF BIBLICAL ZOO'S
TAKE A RAINBOW, TAKE A RAINBOW CRUISE!

WELCOME ABOARD
TRUST IN THE LORD
YOU CAN AFFORD GOOD NEWS
TAKE A RAINBOW, TAKE A RAINBOW CRUISE!

*At this point the musical beat changes to a three-quarter tempo and continues underneath as four of the animals in the back row have pop-up promotional couplets spoken against the rhythm.*

**LION**

Our cruise ship will be (it's worth noting)
The finest (and only) thing floating.

**BEE**

If we had an ad or a brochure
It would say that our meals are all kosher.

**DONKEY**

Our crew is all righteous (God love 'em)
They're great, but there's only eight of 'em.

**LOCUST**

So come, the barometer's falling;
Come running, come hopping, come crawling.

**CHORUS** *(sings)*

HERE'S YOUR CHANCE TO GO AWAY
AS PASSENGER OR STOWAWAY

*Noah re-enters from the left and goes to the ship's wheel station. He is now dressed in maritime regalia with a captain's hat. As he enters, he shouts/sings his rhyming line.*

**NOAH**

RIDE OUT THE FLOOD THE "NOAH WAY!"

**CHORUS**

TAKE A RAINBOW, TAKE A RAINBOW CRUISE.
IT'S HIGH WATER TIME
FOR THE GREATEST OF BIBLICAL ZOO'S
TAKE A RAINBOW, TAKE A RAINBOW CRUISE.

*The same four animals as before now sing a progression of modulated musical phrases*

**LION**

CANKERWORMS AND KANGAROO'S

**BEE**

CROCODILES AND COCKATOO'S

**DONKEY**

KATYDIDS AND CARIBOU'S

**LOCUST**

GORILLA'S, GAZELLES AND GNU'S

**CHORUS**

TAKE A RAINBOW, TAKE A RAINBOW CRUISE
WELCOME ABOARD
TRUST IN THE LORD
YOU CAN AFFORD GOOD NEWS
TAKE A RAINBOW, TAKE A RAINBOW CRUISE

TAKE A RAINBOW, TAKE A RAINBOW CRUISE!

*As the chorus repeats this last line they reach down and pick up multi-colored"bon voyage" streamers and on the last "CRUISE" throw them out at the audience (holding on to the end).*

*At the end of the song, the animals break and half go to the stage left side and half to the stage right side. This must be worked out in advance with entrances and exits for soloists and chorus members.*

*On each side of the stage, there will be placed five signs on short handles with each of the ten animal names (the Lion, the Camel, the Serpent, the Lambs etc). Two of the smaller kids playing Bees should be selected to march across the stage, just behind Noah, as he introduces each "testimony." There should be one Bee/sign bearer on each side so they alternate crossing with the appropriate animal sign on cue. The signs should be labeled with 3-inch high letters for maximum visibility.*

*As the chorus breaks to the appropriate side, Noah stays in place to give his rhyming soliloquy. After the chorus exits, he pauses, indicating a change of pace and looks out over the audience.*

**NOAH**

I'm not really sure why I bother to steer
There's nothing to hit and nothing that's near;
    But the Lord set my course, and that is that;
    Til we dock on the rock at Mount Ararat.

In the meantime, we're saved, and the flood rages on;
It'll be more than a year til the water's all gone.
    So we're here on the Ark – cannot get off it,
    And I'm going to stand in the office of Prophet;

Revealing to you as we go on our way
The critical roles our passengers play;
    In scripture beyond just Genesis 8,
    With testimony they can't wait to relate;

For, we are His instruments, that's for sure;
Whether with scales, skin, feathers or fur;
    For the point is God saved us all with a plan;
    Animals too, in addition to man.

The mighty, the meek, the small and the tall
Whether they fly, swim, gallop, slither or crawl.
    Our refuge, salvation, symbolized by the Ark;
    But our real job starts when we disembark!

We all have a role...and a very good reason
To give thanks to HIM - especially this season.

*Now begins the pattern on one of the Bees crossing the stage with a scene sign that displays the specie name of the animal giving the testimony. In this case, the sign holder bee has a sign saying: THE LIONS. He crosses to Noah as Noah is speaking. When Noah doesn't notice him, the Bee impatiently tugs at Noah's sleeve...*

**NOAH**

Now, as a prophet, I know a little something about fulfillment, and....

*Responds to the Bee's tug and looks down at him.*

...Oh yes... the Lions. Well, they are going to be telling you something about fulfillment... of Psalms 34, verse 10: "the young lions do lack... but they that seek the Lord shall not want any good thing."

*The two lion cubs enter and go to two stools placed at center stage.*

**NOAH**

Now these two lion cubs may be small... but they have, as you will see, vivid anticipations.

**THE LIONS**

STRONG, FIERCE, MAJESTIC AND BOLD
THAT'S WHAT I'LL BE WHEN I AM OLDER;
BIG, FAST, CUNNING AND SHREWD,
PROUD TO BE THE SYMBOL OF THE TRIBE OF JUDAH.

BRAVE, FAST, FEROCIOUS AND STRONG;
(SO IT WILL BE A WEE BIT LONGER)
KING, CHIEF, RULER, THE CHAMP;
ONLY GOT SUBDUED BY DAVID AND SAMPSON!

I'M A LION'S WHELP
THOUGH I NOW NEED HELP
I'LL ROAR NOT YELP – YOU'LL SEE
I'LL GROW AND GAIN
HAVE A DOMAIN,
WITH A MIGHT AND A MANE ALL OVER ME;
I'M...

GREAT, SMART, PART OF GOD'S PLAN
IF YOU DON'T BELIEVE ME, JUST ASK DANIEL
LOVED, PRIZED, CHISELED IN STONE
TREASURED AS THE PETS IN SOLOMON'S
THRONE ROOM.

I'M IN GOD'S PROVISION
EZEKIEL'S VISION
AND I'VE MADE A DECISION TO BE
ZION'S BEST LION
THAT'S ME!! (roar)

*The Lion cubs exit, taking the stools with them. Noah, then returns to his Master of Ceremonies role.*

**NOAH**

No one was sadder to see the dry land disappear than the camel - the animal most associated with the desert. In the Bible, camels are also associated with great wealth. As a measure of his wealth, Job had 3,000 camels. Abraham also had many camels. There are many interesting things about camels - they can outrun a horse, for instance, and they can actually smell water before an oasis is even sighted. But they are very sensitive - so don't laugh at them...and never, ever mention their H-U-M-P!

*As Noah is saying this, a sign holder emerges and crosses behind him. The sign says "The Camel," but as soon as he gets to the edge of the stage, he turns the sign around revealing that the other side says: "The Hump." The Bee then mischievously exits as Noah says:*

**NOAH**

No. No... no...don't laugh!

*The Camel enters looking back at the sign holder, sternly. The Camel has a large hump under her sweat shirt. Behind the Camel are four members of a chorus who stand to one side. The Camel is proud, haughty and very serious.*

**THE CAMEL**

A plague on comedians, who think they're so witty,
And say I'm a horse, designed by committee;
I dismiss such nonsense and try to ignore it
My design is unique, and I praise God for it!

**CHORUS** *(sings)*

THE CAMEL
THE CAMEL
THE PERFECT DESERT MAMMAL;
YOU CAN'T DO BETTER THAN
HAVING THEM IN CARAVAN,
MAKING YOU A WEALTHY MAN;
LIKE JOB AND ABRAHAM
LIKE JOB AND ABRAHAM.

**THE CAMEL**

Four hundred pounds I can pack in a wink
And go on for days, without food or drink;
You can drink my milk and turn it to cheese;
what I am, do and have is meant to please.

My hair makes clothes, and tents, and coats;
Much finer and better than you get from goats!
Warriors ride, astride of me;
You can even make shoes from the hide of me.

I eat and drink and never run empty,
Because of the storage in my H-U-M-P.

**CHORUS**

THE CAMEL
THE CAMEL
THE PERFECT DESERT MAMMAL
YOU CAN'T DO BETTER THAN
HAVING THEM IN CARAVAN
MAKING YOU A WEALTHY MAN:
LIKE JOB AND ABRAHAM
LIKE JOB AND ABRAHAM

**THE CAMEL**

When a threatening force is what he saw
Thirty of me, Jacob gave to Esau;
I brought Sheba's queen to Jerusalem,
And I took three Kings to Bethlehem;

Following that star with reverence;
Carrying their gold, myrrh and frankincense.
I'm swift and sure and I always come through
But there is one thing I cannot do:

No matter how much I wiggle and wheedle
I can't pass through the eye of a needle!

**CHORUS**

THE CAMEL
THE CAMEL
THE PERFECT DESERT MAMMAL
YOU CAN'T DO BETTER THAN
HAVING THEM IN CARAVAN
MAKING YOU A WEALTHY MAN
LIKE JOB AND ABRAHAM
LIKE JOB AND ABRAHAM
-- THE CAMEL!

*When one member of the chorus says "The Camel," she bows, making sure her hump shows.*

**NOAH**

...and when God restored Job's wealth... he ended up with six thousand camels! I feel I'm lucky to just have two! ... well, well, well....what's this?

*As he says this, Noah turns to stage left as The Serpent enters, sobbing. The Serpent goes to a stool at the center., as the sign holder emerges from the opposite side with a "The Serpent" sign. As soon as the Bee signholder sees who it is, he makes an exaggerated detour around the serpent to carefully exit. Noah moves toward the Serpent to comfort her.*

**NOAH**

There, there... what seems to be the matter?

*Noah starts to put his hand out to re-assure her, but then thinks better of it, and quickly pulls his hand back.*

**SERPENT**

<u>That</u>'s what's the matter! See, you do it too. Everybody is afraid of me...I'm just plain repulsive.

**NOAH**

You're not plain at all; you're...ahh... very pretty. Let's talk about it; maybe I can help. You may be just too wrapped up in yourself....oops...sorry.

**SERPENT**

...even hissing is associated with a bad performance.

*Noah goes back to his position as the music starts; the Serpent begins her song.*

**SERPENT**

BECAUSE I'M A SSNAKE
I DON'T HAVE A HAND THAT YOU'D WANT TO SHAKE
AND WHAT'S MORE,
I SLITHER AROUND ON THE GROUND AND THE FLOOR.

WHAT AN ACHE
TO BE A SSNAKE
I CAN'T TAKE
BEING A SSNAKE!

BECAUSE I'M A SSNAKE
I OFTEN THINK GOD MIGHT HAVE MADE A MISTAKE;
AND IT'S SAID:
WHAT CHILD WOULD TAKE A STUFFED ME INTO BED?

WHAT AN ACHE
TO BE A SSNAKE
I CAN'T TAKE
BEING A SNAKE!

BECAUSE I'M A SSNAKE
WHEN PEOPLE SEE ME THEY REACH FOR A SHOVEL OR RAKE
AND TO BOOT,
JUST NOBODY THINKS THAT MY BABIES ARE CUTE!

WHAT AN ACHE
TO BE A SSNAKE
I CAN'T TAKE
BEING A SSNAKE!

NO HILTON OR STATLER
HAS ROOM FOR A RATTLER;
EVERYONE'S GLADDER
TO SUBTRACT AN ADDER;
NOT EVEN NOAH
WANTS HUGS FROM A BOA

I CAN'T TAKE
BEING A SSNAKE!

**NOAH**

Oh, come on – you're just looking at the downside!

**SERPENT**

That's what I have the best view of… It all started with that business in the Garden of Eden – it's all Satan's fault!

**NOAH**

Forget Satan. You should know what happens to him! *(Sings):*

'CAUSE HE WAS THAT SNAKE
OLD SATAN GETS CAST IN A FIREY LAKE
SO FOR HIM:
A SIZZLING CHANCE TO ETERNALLY SWIM...
BOIL AND BAKE
SO MUCH FOR THAT SNAKE!

**SERPENT** *(sniffs)*

Really?

**NOAH**

You need to know that two of the mightiest men of God in the whole Bible used snakes to bring great glory to God.

**SERPENT**

They did? ...how?

**NOAH** *(sings)*

BECAUSE OF A SNAKE
A PHARAOH WAS SHOWN HIS MAGICIANS WERE FAKE;
MOSES' ROD
TURNED INTO A WITNESS FOR THE POWER OF GOD.
IT WOULD TAKE
THE FORM OF A SNAKE.

Just as God had promised, Moses threw down his rod and it turned into a snake - a snake that devoured all of the other snakes conjured up by Pharaoh's magicians. Pharaoh got the point!

**SERPENT**

Gee.... maybe I don't need a PR consultant.

**NOAH**

And in the New Testament, Acts 28 tells us this: *(sings)*

BECAUSE OF A SNAKE
SAINT PAUL SHOWED A FAITH THAT NOTHING COULD SHAKE
THE BITE OF AN ASP
MADE ALL OF HIS SHIPMATES, MARVEL AND GASP;
FAITH WOULD MAKE
THE MOST OF A SNAKE!

**SERPENT**

I'm a symbol of faith?

**NOAH**

So, you've got no reason to feel sorry for yourself...try smiling... Then maybe you can even help me counsel the cockroaches...and the tarantulas.

**SERPENT**

You're right – I could reach out to others!

**NOAH**

...ahhh...maybe you'd want to practice that a bit, first – kind of...let them know you're coming.

*The serpent feels better already. She straightens up with a new found confidence, puts her shoulders back and sings her song with a little more gusto than whine.*

**SERPENT**

I'M GLAD I'M A SSNAKE
I KNOW NOW THAT GOD DIDN'T MAKE A MISTAKE –
HE GAVE ME A BREAK!

THOUGH LEGLESS AND ARMLESS
WE'RE ALL MOSTLY HARMLESS;
THOUGH I'M ONE THAT YOU MAY SHUN -
I'M STILL GOD'S CRE-ATION

FOR HIS SAKE:
WELCOME THE SNAKE!

*After the applause, the Serpent exits and, referring to the applause, she calls over her shoulder to Noah.*

**SERPENT**

See!

**NOAH**

Boy, these low self-esteem cases are tough! .... now what?

*As he says these last words, he sees the Queen Bee who enters and determinedly marches over to confront Noah. She stamps her foot as one of the Bee signholders crosses with THE BEES sign.*

**NOAH**

Yes, Miss Bee?

**QUEEN BEE**

**Queen** Bee!

**NOAH**

You wanted to see me?

**QUEEN BEE**

My quarters are not sufficient!

**NOAH**

What's the problem?

**QUEEN BEE**

Well, the hive is wedged right between the cankerworms and the kangaroos...and right across the way are the crocodiles and the cockatoos – we really deserve something better!

**NOAH** *(looks at plan)*

Well....let's see...

**QUEEN BEE**

After all, we Bees play a very important role in Israel's history.

**NOAH** *(looks up)*

Really?... I don't seem to recall any prominent bees...

**QUEEN BEE**

One of Israel's greatest triumphs belongs to us...

**NOAH**

Now, wait a minute...

**QUEEN BEE**

The MaccaBEES!

**NOAH**

I think I've just been stung... why don't you give your testimony why I try to re-locate your hive.

*Noah exits with the plans. The Queen Bee watches him go, and then starts for the stool at the center as the klezmer beat of the music begins. She starts to sing as she sits on the stool.*

**QUEEN BEE** *(sings)*

THE NATION OF ISRAEL IS COMING
AND THEN THIS LAND
WILL REALLY BE HUMMING;
WITH VINEYARDS AND GARDENS AND TREES
BRING ON THE BEES
BRING ON THE BEES

*At this last phrase, the musical beat changes to a slower tempo and four little bees emerge from each side in single file doing a studied leg over hora-type dance; they cross in front of the Queen Bee, as she sings her chorus*

**QUEEN BEE**

WHEN GOD PLANNED A LAND
OF MILK AND HONEY;
ONE OF THE KEYS
WAS BEES!
GET MILK FROM COWS
ON A THOUSAND HILLS;
GET HONEY FROM A ZILLION ME'S

**CHORUS OF BEES**

GET MILK FROM COWS
ON A THOUSAND HILLS;
GET HONEY FROM A ZILLION ME'S!

**QUEEN BEE**

THE DESERT IS VERY DRY AND BARREN
BUT IT WILL BLOOM
LIKE THE ROD OF AARON;
WITH POLLEN RIGHT UP TO OUR KNEES
BRING ON THE BEES
BRING ON THE BEES!

*Again, the chorus of Bees crosses single file doing their little dance.*

**QUEEN BEE**

WHEN GOD PLANNED A LAND
OF MILK AND HONEY
ONE OF THE KEYS
WAS BEES.
GET MILK FROM COWS
ON A THOUSAND HILLS;
GET HONEY FROM A ZILLION ME'S!

**CHORUS OF BEES**

GET MILK FROM COWS
ON A THOUSAND HILLS
GET HONEY FROM A ZILLION ME'S!

GET MILK FROM COWS
ON A THOUSAND HILLS
GET HONEY FROM A ZILLION ME'S!

*As the chorus repeats their lines, two of them hold up a pole from which is hanging down a flag of Israel.*

**QUEEN BEE** *(shouts)*

SHALOM!

*The Bees all finish their number and exit as Noah comes back on and resumes his position.*

**NOAH**

Now, all animals are valuable – but the one prized more than any other in Israel was the sheep ... not only as a source of food and clothing, but because of its value as a sacrifice. The sheep, or lamb, is mentioned more than any other animal in the Bible – 742 times.

**QUEEN BEE** *(shouts from side)*

Did you really count them?

**NOAH**

I tried... but every time, I kept falling asleep!

*The Queen Bee stamps her foot in disgust and goes off.*

**NOAH**

Now, I hasten to add - especially after that line about the Maccabbees - that one of those 742 times is **not** LAMBentations!

*The Queen Bee stamps her foot again as one of the Bee signholders crosses with a sign saying: THE LAMBS.*

**NOAH**

Our on-board lambs have asked to give a different kind of testimony - not about their role in scripture, but about someone the whole flock depends on..

*As the music begins, a mini-flock of Lambs comes on and takes their place at the center.*

**THE LAMBS**

HE LEADS ME
HE FEEDS ME
HE CALLS ME BY NAME;
HE TENDS ME
BEFRIENDS ME;
HE'S ALWAYS THE SAME.

HE CALMS ME
HE PSALMS ME
HE SHOWS ME THE WAY
HE PROTECTS ME
COLLECTS ME
WHEN I'VE GONE ASTRAY.

HE'S MY SHEPHERD, MY GOOD SHEPHERD
DAY AND NIGHT GIVING CARE;
AND LIKE ANY GOOD SHEPHERD,
HE'S ALWAYS RIGHT THERE.

LIKE DAVID
LIKE AMOS
HE'S PROPHET AND KING

BUT MY SHEPHERD KNOWS JUST WHAT I AM
BECAUSE HE'S THE ONE
WHO'S BOTH
SHEPHERD AND LAMB.

*The lambs finish their song and exits. Noah is back at his station.*

**NOAH**

Now, here's a mighty tale for you. Only one animal was mentioned by name in the story of creation in Genesis 1. (*Looks off stage)* No, it was **not** the Queen Bee! Genesis 1, verse 21 says: "And God created great whales." Our next witness has been swimming alongside - it was his choice. Unlike some, he had no problems with whatever quarters we might assign him.

*One of the Bee signholders crosses with THE WHALE sign, as the Whale enters along with three other animals who will form a chorus for his song.*

**NOAH**

Here he is to tell us about one of his descendants who played a major role with one of the minor prophets..... and it was no fluke!

**THE WHALE** (*sings)*

I'VE A WHALE OF A TALE TO SING TO YOU;
A TALE OF A WHALE TO BRING TO YOU;
IT'S A TALE WHOSE MAIN INGREDIENTS
ARE: JONAH, REPENTANCE AND OBEDIENCE.

**CHORUS**

A TALE OF A WHALE
AND A MAN WHO'D FAIL
TO PUT HIS FOOT ON THE NINEVEH TRAIL...
(NINEVEH TRAIL).

**THE WHALE**

JONAH HEARD FROM HIS GOD 'BOUT THE SIN OF A...
BAD CROWD IN A TOWN CALLED NINEVEH
GOD SAID; "GO EAST," BUT WEST HE WENT
SAYS THE 32ND BOOK, OLD TESTAMENT

**CHORUS**

A TALE OF A WHALE
A SAIL THROUGH A GALE
AND WHOOSH GOES JONAH OVER THE RAIL;
(OVER THE RAIL).

**THE WHALE**

AND SO GOD SENT A WHALE TO FOLLOW HIM;
AND OBEDIENTLY TO SWALLOW HIM
PRAISE GOD THAT HE'D PROVIDE A ME
FOR A THREE DAY JOURNEY INSIDE OF ME.

**CHORUS**

A TALE OF A WHALE
WHOSE MAJOR DETAIL
WAS TO PUT OLD JONAH IN A WHALE-SIZED JAIL
(WHALE SIZED JAIL)

**THE WHALE**

JONAH, THERE IN THE DARK, THEN SAW THE LIGHT
AND PRAYED THAT HE'S COME OUT ALRIGHT;
AND GET TO WHERE HE'D FIRST BEEN SENT;
AND GET THOSE NINEVANS TO REPENT.

**CHORUS**

A TALE OF A WHALE
A PRAYER TO AVAIL,
SO OUT CAME JONAH ON THE NEXT EXHALE
(NEXT EXHALE).

NO WORSE FOR THE WEAR
JUST A WEE BIT PALE;
HE PUTS HIS FOOT
ON THE NINEVEH TRAIL
PRAISING GOD AND THANKING THE WHALE

**THE WHALE**

THANKING THE WHALE!

*After his bow, the Whale and the Chorus exits. Noah continues.*

**NOAH**

Just as God is my rudder, He is also my navigator... but I do have some help. – the Dove. The Dove made two very important appearances in scripture: in the gospels, and here in the story of the flood. After all, it was the Dove that came back to tell us exactly where we were.

*As a signholder crosses with THE DOVE sign, the Dove enters and hands Noah an olive branch. She then goes to the center of the stage and sings:*

**THE DOVE**

WE'RE UNDER THE RAINBOW
COVERED BY WHAT GOD ABOVE SENT
A COVENANT HIS WORD AND LOVE SENT
UNDER THE RAINBOW

WE'RE UNDER THE RAINBOW
READY TO REFLECT GOD'S GLORY
AGROUND ON HOLY TERRITORY
UNDER THE RAINBOW.

FOR EACH OF US CAN
BE PART OF GOD'S PLAN
THAT'S HIS PROMISE;
HIS MERCY AND GRACE,
BROUGHT US TO THIS PLACE,
SAVING LOCUSTS, AND LIONS, AND LLAMAS.

WE'RE UNDER THE RAINBOW
WHERE WE'LL FIND THE LIGHT OF JESUS
AND WHERE WE'LL FIND THE TRUTH THAT FREES US
UNDER TH RAINBOW...

A MESSAGE OF
HOPE, PEACE AND LOVE,
DELIVERED BY ONE SMALL DOVE
...AND A RAINBOW.

*The Dove exits. Noah resumes.*

**NOAH**

Now, you may be wondering where the rest of our crew is – well, to tell the truth, I've assigned a 24-hour watch to the carpenter ants, the termites and the woodpeckers... just to make sure they have enough to eat.... without freelancing on my ship!

*A signholder with the sign: THE LOCUSTS, rushes on and hands Noah an envelope. He opens it.*

**NOAH**

I've just been handed a message that a swarm of one of our insect groups wants to witness. Just to prove that the Dove wasn't the only messenger in the Bible, here are the Locusts to show how an important message was delivered to a hard-hearted Pharaoh.

*Five locusts enters and line up as a silent Pharaoh (with a King Tut-type mask) stations himself near Noah with a guard next to him. As the music of Rimsky-Korsakov's "The Flight of the Bumblebee," begins, the Locusts go through a series of sequential turns and motions, each time ending up with the placing of a 5 X 6 card in the hand of the guard. Each time the guard reads the message to Pharaoh.*

**GUARD** *(reads)*

1. Dear Pharaoh, we're coming to plague you
Right after the frogs, hail and aigue;
And we won't behave, til you've freed every slave;
Don't wait for Moses to beg you.

2. Dear hard-hearted Pharaoh, get focused
Or your land gets covered with locust
Just do it our way, and give way to Yahweh
**<u>Your</u>** gods have **<u>you</u>** hokus-pokused.

3. Dear Pharaoh, please listen to Moses
His power's not what you supposes;
Your manner empirical's, no match for his miracles,
As Exodus 14 discloses

4. Turn now to John's Revelation
When 5th angel trumps tribulation
I'll give you a clue; from the pit comes guess who?
My dozens of cousins to cause devastation.

*After each of the four messages is delivered and read, the Locusts, Pharaoh and the Guard exit.*

*Next, a signholder crosses with THE DONKEY sign. The Donkey enters, goes to a tree in the center and ties his red cord to it.*

**NOAH**

Throughout scripture, the lowly donkey is a kind of symbol of humility. The horse was used in warfare, but the donkey was basically a pack animal – very used to bearing burdens. Donkey, I hope you're not going to re-hash that Balaam business... and how he beat you.

**DONKEY**

No, I have forgiven him for that - and forgotten it, as we are told to do.

**NOAH**

Good for you. What is your testimony?

**DONKEY**

It's about my servant's role and how I was called to it by the Lord Jesus Himself. It was a spring day in the year 30 AD. I was tied to a tree in a yard in Bethany.

*As the Donkey prepares to sing his testimony, a four person chorus comes on to back him up.*

**DONKEY** *(sings)*

WHEN JESUS WENT UP FROM GALILEE
TO OLIVET AND BETHANY
HE SENT THE WORD THAT SET ME FREE:
THE LORD, THE LORD HATH NEED OF ME

DISCIPLES WERE SENT TO FIND AND SEE
THAT WHICH WAS TIED BESIDE A TREE;
I WENT WITH THEM TO CARRY HE
WHO WAS THE LORD WITH NEED OF ME

**CHORUS**

WHAT A WONDERFUL THING
TO SAY THAT HE
THE LORD, MY LORD, HATH NEED OF ME.

**DONKEY**

A PROPHET ONCE SAID THAT THIS WILL BE:
SALVATION'S CALL, REJOICE ALL YE;
BEHOLD THY KING COMETH UNTO THEE
PRAISE GOD, MY LORD HATH NEED OF ME.

THAT BURDEN WAS LIGHT, AND ALL COULD SEE
THEY CRIED: "HOSANNA, BLESSED BE HE;"
HE ENTERED THERE TRIUMPHANTLY
BECAUSE THE LORD HATH NEED OF ME.

**CHORUS**

WHAT A WONDERFUL THING
TO SAY THAT HE
THE LORD, MY LORD HATH NEED OF ME
THE LORD, MY LORD HATH NEED OF ME!

*The Donkey and the chorus exit as Noah resumes his introductions. A signholder crosses with THE MOUSE sign.*

**NOAH** *(recites)*

Now, if you were a mouse
You'd know that it mattered
To be in a place where
Grain is scattered;
    Now here is a mouse
    Who thus is no stranger
    To the rain of the grain
    Found round a manger

In a Bethlehem stable
In ancient Judea
She was a witness
Though no one could see her.
    This is her testimony
    He part of the story
    Of the night that God gave us
    The hope of glory.

*As Noah recites these last two stanzas, the Mouse comes from stage right and places a manger at the center. At the same time, all of the animals come on and take their place as a chorus to the left.*

**THE MOUSE** *(sings)*

THE DONKEY WAS THERE
AND SO WAS THE LAMB
AND ALSO THE CAMEL, NAMED ABRAHAM;
SOME SHEEP AND SOME GOATS
AND A DOVE, I RECALL;
    AND ME, THE MOUSE, WHO SAW IT ALL.

OUTSIDE IN THE SKY
THE ANGELS WERE HEARD
GIVING ALL OF THE SHEPHERDS THE WONDROUS WORD
A BRIGHT STAR ABOVE
WITH BEAMS THAT WOULD FALL
    ON EVEN THE MOUSE WHO SAW IT ALL.

A BABY WAS BORN
THAT COLD WINTER NIGHT,
AND INTO THE DARKNESS CAME A GREAT LIGHT;
FILLING THE STABLE
FROM MANGER TO STALL
    AND HELPING THE MOUSE TO SEE IT ALL

*The mouse turns to the manger, drops to her knees and assumes an attitude of prayer.*

**CHORUS**

AND GLORY TO GOD
AND PEACE BE ON EARTH;
AND WITNESS TO ALL THAT SPECIAL BIRTH;
AND IF YOU LOOK CLOSELY
IN THE STRAW NEAR THE WALL
    THERE WAS THE MOUSE WHO SAW IT ALL
    THERE WAS THE MOUSE WHO SAW IT ALL.

*The mouse leaves the manger and takes her place with the chorus. Noah re-enters, and is no longer costumed as a ship's captain, but is wearing the Patriarchal robe he had on at the beginning. He looks up.*

**NOAH**

Lord, now I know what a "Christmas" present is - and we all thank you for it. We know that the gift of the Lord Jesus isn't just something for the season, but He's always there for us. We also know, from scripture, that He is coming back very soon.

Isaiah, Ezekiel and Hosea all prophesied about a special day which is coming - a day when there will be a new heaven and a new earth... and a new covenant of Peace. In that day, they said, there would be a sign of peace among men as well as among the animals.

And the best part of that day would be that: "the earth shall be full of the knowledge of the Lord; as the waters cover the sea."

Now, that's something our passengers know something about!

**NOAH** (*sings*)

THE WOLF SHALL DWELL WITH THE LAMB
IN THAT DAY;
THE LEOPARD LIE DOWN WITH THE GOAT;
AND THE CALF AND THE CUB TOGETHER WILL PLAY
AS A LITTLE CHILD LEADS THE WAY.

**CHORUS**

AND THE EARTH SHALL BE FULL
OF THE KNOWLEDGE OF THE LORD
AS THE WATERS COVER THE SEA
    AND THE EARTH SHALL BE FULL
    OF THE KNOWLEDGE OF THE LORD
    AS THE WATERS COVER THE SEA.

**NOAH**

THE COW SHALL GRAZE WITH THE BEAR
IN THAT DAY
THE LION EAT STRAW LIKE THE OX;
AT THE SERPENT'S DEN, NO HARM NOR FEAR
WHEN THE SMALLEST OF CHILDREN GOES NEAR.

**CHORUS**

AND THE EARTH SHALL BE FULL
OF THE KNOWLEDGE OF THE LORD
AS THE WATERS COVER THE SEA
AND THE EARTH SHALL BE FULL
OF THE KNOWLEDGE OF THE LORD
AS THE WATERS COVER THE SEA.

**NOAH**

A PROMISE OF PEACE SHALL BE
IN THAT DAY;
A NEW EARTH AND HEAVEN TO COME;
WITH THE BEASTS OF THE FIELD; THE BIRDS OF THE AIR
AND THE THINGS ON THE GROUND TO DECLARE:

**CHORUS**

AND THE EARTH SHALL BE FULL
OF THE KNOWLEDGE OF THE LORD
AS THE WATERS COVER THE SEA
AND THE EARTH SHALL BE FULL
OF THE KNOWLEDGE OF THE LORD
AS THE WATERS COVER THE SEA.

***CURTAIN.***

# Take A Rainbow Cruise

Clark Tyler
*Arranged by Andrew Bell*

Voice
Pno.
Caug C F Gmin7
ev - ery last cu - bit. It's high wa-ter time for the great-est of Bib-lic-al
ev - ery last cu - bit.
F F/B♭ C7 F F
zoos. Take a rain- bow, take a rain-bow cruise. Wel-come a- board.
Gmin7 C7 F F C7 F
Trust in the Lord. You can af-ford the news. Take a rain- bow. take a rain-bow cruise.
Tempo = 200
F C7 F

47
F
C7
Voice
Our cruise ship will be it's worth noting The finest and on-ly thing
crew is all right-eous God love'em. They're great but there's on-ly eight
Pno.
54
F
C7
1.
floating. If we had an and or a brochure it would say that our
of 'em. So come the bar - o-met-er's fall-ing.
61
C7
Cdim
meals are all Ko-sher.
Our Come run-ning, come hop-ping, come crawl -
68
C7
F
C7
F/A
Bm
F
ing Here's your chance to go a-way as pass-en-ger or stow-a-way. Ride out the flood the

74
Gmin7
F
C7
F
Voice
No-ah way! Take a rain- bow. take a rain-bow cruise. It's__ high wa-ter
Pno.
80
Gmin7
F
F/B♭
C7
F
rit.
Voice
time for the great-est of Bib-lic-al zoos. Take a rain- bow, take a rain-bow cruise.
rit.
Pno.
86
A
slower swing
Dmin
Gmin
Voice
Can-ker worms and Kan-ga roos__ Croc-o-diles and Cock-a- toos__
Pno.
91
Am
C7
F
Voice
Ka-ty-dids and Car-i- bous,__ Go - ril- las, Ga-zelles, and G - nus. Take a rain- bow.
Pno.

96
C7
F
F
Gmin7
Voice
take a rain-bow cruise.
Wel - come a-board. Trust in the Lord.
Pno.
101
C7
F
F
C7
F
Voice
You can af-ford the news
Take a rain- bow. take a rain-bow cruise.
Pno.
106
F
C7
F
Voice
Take a rain- bow. take a rain-bow cruise.
Pno.

# The Lions

Clark Tyler
*Arranged by Andrew Bell*

21
C F Gm
Voice
On-ly got sub- dued by Dav-id and Samp- son. I'm a Li - on's whelp,
Pno.
26
C F
Voice
I now need help. I'll roar not yelp, you'll see. I'll
Pno.
31
Gm F C F
Voice
grow and gain, have a do - main, with a might and a mane, all o - ver me. I'm great, smart,
Gm
Pno.
36
C F Dm Gm
Voice
part of God's plan, if you don't be-lieve me just ask Dan- iel. Loved, prized, chis-led in stone,
Pno.

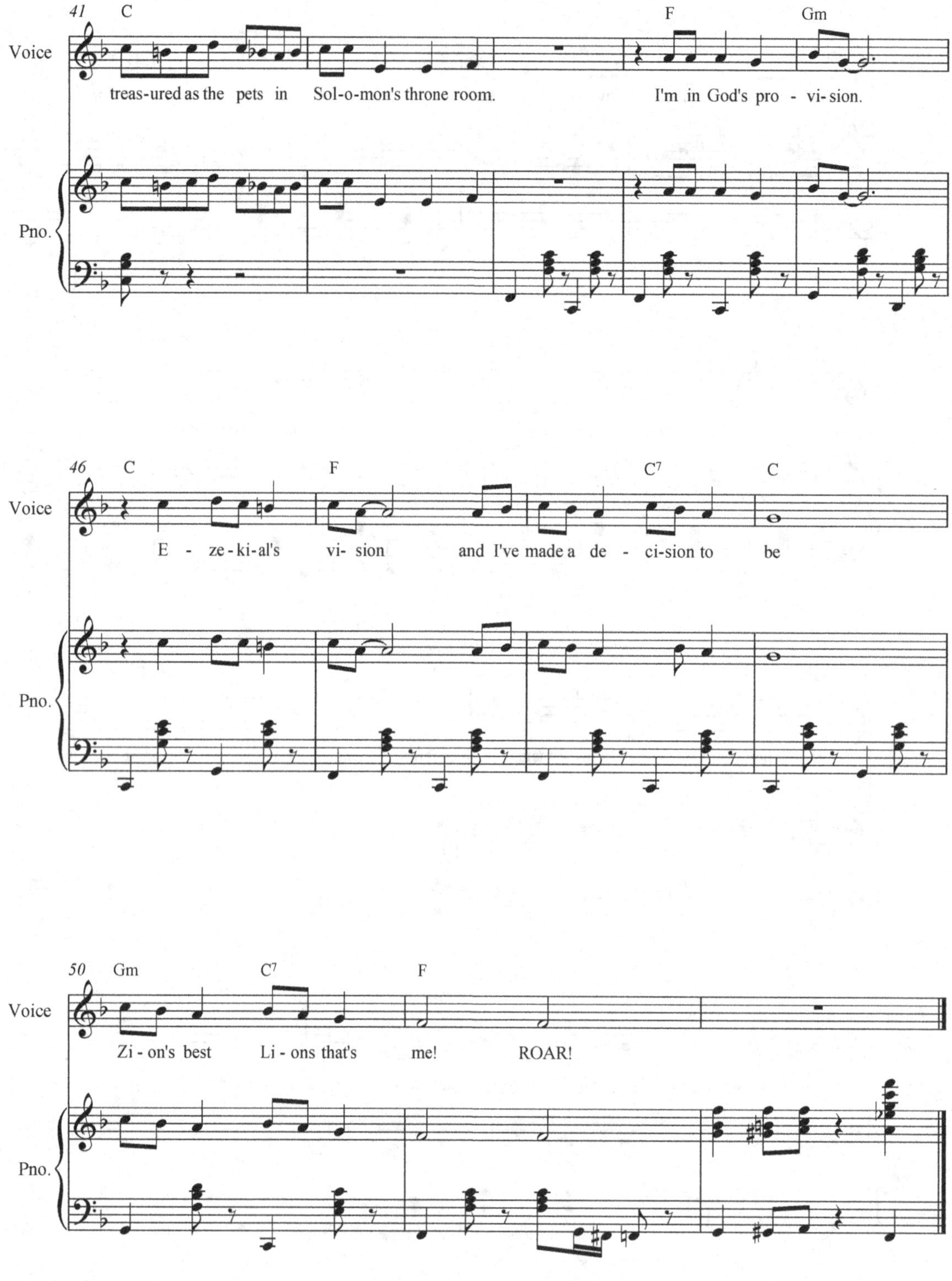
41
C
F
Gm
Voice
treas-ured as the pets in Sol-o-mon's throne room.
I'm in God's pro - vi- sion.
Pno.
46
C
F
C7
C
Voice
E - ze - ki - al's vi- sion and I've made a de - ci-sion to be
Pno.
50
Gm
C7
F
Voice
Zi - on's best Li - ons that's me! ROAR!
Pno.

# The Camel

by Clark Tyler

*Arranged by Andrew Bell*

Voice
Piano
Pno.
F Dmin7 B♭7 F
The cam-el the cam - el the per - fect des - ert mam - mal
6 Cdim7 Gm
You can't do bet - ter than them in your car - a - van mak - ing you a weal - thy
9 Dmin B♭ C F B♭ C F
man like Job and Ab - ra - ham like Job and Ab - ra - ham.

# The Snake

by Clark Tyler
*Arranged by Andrew Bell*

♩= 120
Voice
Piano
B♭
E♭
Be - cause I'm a snake I don't have a
Be - cause I'm a snake I often think God
Be - cause I'm a snake When people see me
5 Dmin
F
B♭
hand that you'd want to shake. And what's more I
might have made a mis - take. And it's said
they reach for a shovel or rake. And to boot Just
Pno.
9
3
sli - ther a - round on the ground and the floor. What an ache
what child would take a stuffed me in to bed.
no - body thinks that my bab - ies are cute.
12 F
to be a snake. I can't take

17
F
B♭
Cm7
E♭
Cmin
F
Dmin7
Voice
be-ing a snake.
No Hil ton or Stat-ler has room for a rat-tler
Pno.
22
E♭
Cmin
F
Dmin7
E♭
Cmin
F
Dmin7
Voice
eve-ry-one's glad-der to sub-tract an ad-der. Not ev-en No-ah wants hugs from a bo-a.
Pno.
26
F
F
B♭
Voice
I can't take
be-ing a snake.
Pno.
Ped.

12
F
Eb
Cm
F
Cm/Eb
Voice
so much for that snake.
the form of a snake.
the most of a snake!
Don't be a flake and just give me a break and you'll
*stop after each
verse and resume
after spoken dialogue
Pno.
17
F
Bb
Voice
make
a real - ly great snake.
Pno.
Ped.

# The Bee

by Clark Tyler
*Arranged by Andrew Bell*

Voice
Piano
Pno.
Em B7 Em
The Na-tion of Is-ra-el is com-ing. And
The Des-ert is sal-ty dry and bar-ren, but
7 D Em D7add6 Em D
then this land will real-ly be hum-ing with vine-yards and gar-dens and trees.
it will bloom like the rod of Aar-on. With pol-len right up to our knees.
14 D G C G
Bring on the bees, Bring on the bees.
D/F♯ Em B7
21
Em B7 Em B7 Em B7 Em B7 B

27
Voice
Pno.
Em
D
(Hum)
When God planned a land of milk and
34
Em B7 Em G Am7
hon ey one of the keys was bees. Get milk from cows on a
41
G C D7sus D G Am7
thou - sand hills get hon-ey from a zil - lion bees. Get milk from cows
48
G C
on a thou - sand hills get hon - ey from a
52
Dsus D7 G
1.
2.
zil - ion mes.

# My Good Shepherd

by Clark Tyler
*Arranged by Andrew Bell*

Voice
Piano
Pno.
F C7 F C7 F C7
He leads me, He feeds me, He calls me by name; He tends me, be - friends me, He's al - ways the
8
F C7 F C7 F C7 F
same. He calms me, He psalms me, He shows me the way; He pro-tects me, col-lects me, when
3
16
C7 F B♭ F Gmin7 C7 F
I've gone a - stray; He's my shep - herd, my good shep-herd day and night giv-ing care; and like an - y good

23
B♭ F C7 F C7 F Dmin Gmin7
Voice
shep- herd, He's al- ways right there; like Da- vid, like A- mos, He's pro- phet and king; my good shep- herd knows
Pno.

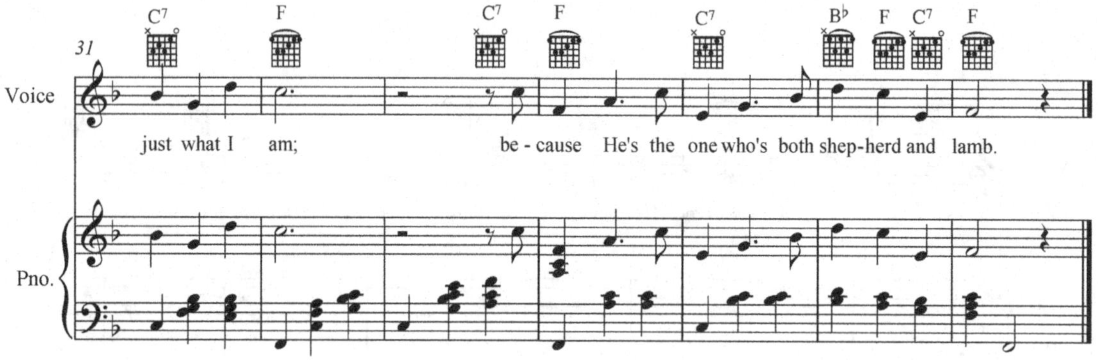
31
C7 F C7 F C7 B♭ F C7 F
Voice
just what I am; be - cause He's the one who's both shep- herd and lamb.
Pno.

# The Whale

by Clark Tyler
*Arranged by Andrew Bell*

In A Sea Shanty Style
Voice
Piano
Dm C G7
1. I've a whale of a tale to sing to you. A tale of a whale to bring to
2. Jo - nah heard from his God 'bout the sin of a crowd in a town called Ni - ne
3. And so God sent a whale to fol - low him, and o - be - dien - tly to swal - low
4. Jo - nah there in the dark then saw the light. And prayed that he'd come out al-
4 C C7 F C
Pno.
you. It's a tale whose main in - gre - di - ents are Jo - nah, re - pen - tence and o-
veh. Go east, but west he went says the 32 - nd Book old
him. Praise God that he'd pro - vide a me for a three day jour - ney in -
right. and get to where he'd first been sent. And get those Ni - ne - vehs
1.2.3.
8 F C7 F C F rit.
be - di - ence. A tale of a whale and a man who'd fail to put his foot on the Nin - e - veh trail.
test - ta - ment. A tale of a whale a sail thru a gale and plop goes Jo - nah o - ver the rail.
side of me. A tale of a whale whose ma - jor detail was to put old Jo - nah in whale size jail.

molto rit.
13
4.
F C7 F
Voice
(Nin - e-veh trail) to re-pent. A tale of a whale, A prayer to av-ail, So
(o - ver the rail)
(whale size_ jail)
Pno.
17
C F Dm C7
out came Jo - nah on the next ex-hale (next ex-hale) no worse for the wear just a
rit.
21
F C7 F
wee bit pail He put his foot on the Nin - e - veh trail.
24
C7 F F
Prais - ing God and thank - ing the whale. (Thank - ing the whale)

# Under The Rainbow

by Clark Tyler
*Arranged by Andrew Bell*

19
B♭ Dm Cm F
Voice
bow for each of us can be part of God's plan. That's his pro - mise his
Pno.
23
Cm Dm C7/E F7
mer-cy and grace brought us to this place sav-ing lo- custs and li- ons_ and lla- mas. We're
27
B♭ B♭M7 Gm C7 F7 B♭
un- der the rain - bow where we'll find the light of Je - sus.
31
Cm7 F7 B♭ F7/C B♭ F7 Gm
And where we'll find the truth that frees us. Un-der the rain - bow A

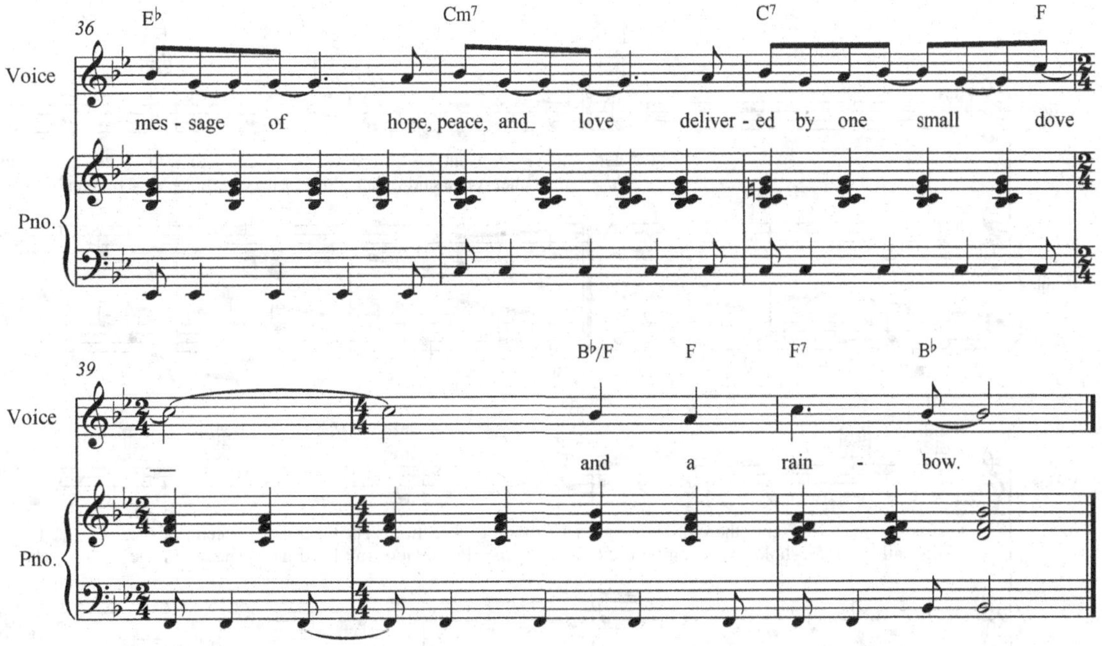
36
E♭ Cm7 C7 F
Voice
mes - sage of hope, peace, and love deliver - ed by one small dove
Pno.
39
B♭/F F F7 B♭
Voice
and a rain - bow.
Pno.

# The Donkey

by Clark Tyler

♩. = 60
Voice
Piano
B♭ E♭ F
1.When Je - sus went up from Ga - li-lee to O - li - vet and
2.A pro - phet once said that this will be Sal - va - tions call re-
6
E♭ B♭ E♭ B♭ F B♭
Be - tha - ny. He sent the Word th - at set me free. The Lord, The Lord hath need of me. Di-
joice all ye. Be - hold thy King com - eth un - to thee. Praise God my Lord hath need of me. That
Pno.
11
E♭ F E♭ B♭
sci - ples were sent to find and see that which was tied be - side a tree I went with them to
bur - den was light and all could see they cried Ho - san - nah, blessed be He. He en - tered there tri
16
E♭ B♭ F B♭ Cmin7
car - ry me. Who was the Lord with need of me. What a won - der - ful thing to
um - phant - ly be - cause the Lord hath need of me.

Dmin7
F
B♭
21
Voice
say that He the Lord my Lord hath need of me.
Pno.
F
B♭
24
Voice
Lord my Lord hath need of me.
Pno.

# The Mouse

Clark Tyler
*Arranged by Andrew Bell*

31
F E♭min A♭ F B♭min D♭
Voice
fall on even a mouse who saw it all. A ba-by was born that
Pno.
39
C Fmin B♭6 C B♭min
Voice
cold win ter night and in - to the dark ness saw a great light. Fil - ling the sta - ble from
Pno.
p mf f mp
47
Fmin D♭ Fmin C Fmin B♭min
Chorus:
Voice
man - ger to stall and help-ing the mouse to___ see___ it all. And glo-ry to
Pno.
54
F B♭min F E♭min A♭ D♭ F7 B♭
Voice
God and peace be on earth and wit-ness for all___ that spe - cial birth. And if you look
Pno.

62
F
B♭min
F
E♭min
A♭
F
Voice
close - ly in a straw near the wall there was the mouse who saw it
Pno.
68
B♭min
E♭min
A♭
F
B♭min
Voice
all. There was the mouse who saw it all.
Pno.

# In That Day

Clark Tyler
*Arranged by Andrew Bell*

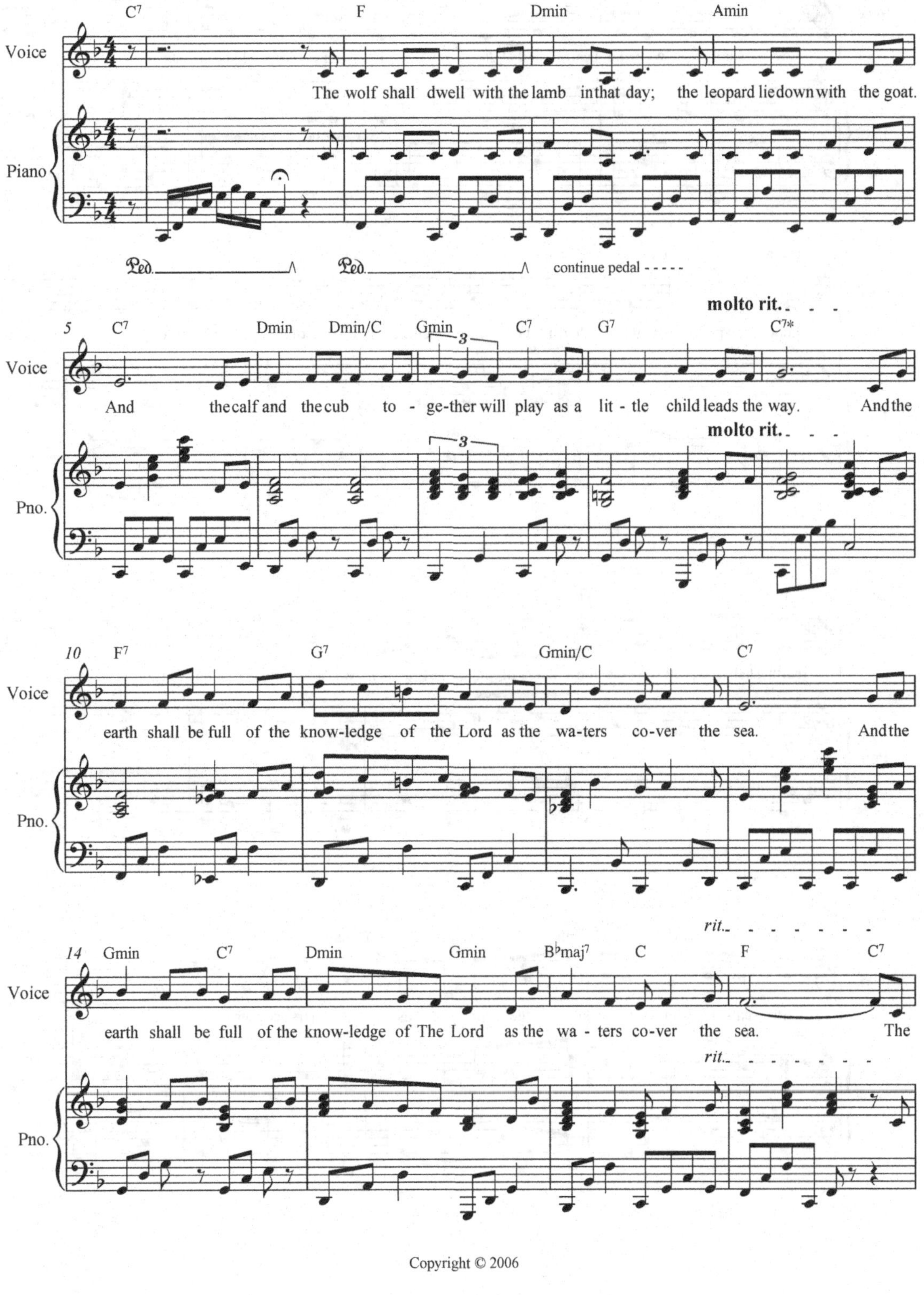

18 F Dmin Amin Gmin7 C7
Voice
cow shall graze with the bear in that day, the li - on eat straw like the ox. At the
Pno.
22 Dmin Dmin/C Gmin C7 Gmin C7
Voice
poor ser-pents den no harm, nor fear when the small - est of child - dren goes near And the
Pno.
3
26 F G7 Gmin/C C7
Voice
earth shall be full of the know-ledge of the Lord as the wa-ters co-ver the sea. And the
Pno.
30 Gmin C7 Dmin Gmin B♭maj7 C F C7
Voice
earth shall be full of the know-ledge of the Lord as the wa - ters co-ver the sea. A
Pno.

34 F Dmin Amin Gmin7 C7
Voice
pro - mise of peace shall be in that day. A new earth and hea - ven to come. With the
Pno.
38 Dmin Dmin/C Gmin C7 G7 C7
Voice
beasts of the field the birds of the air and the things on the ground to de - clare. And the
Pno.
3
42 F G7 Gmin/C C
Voice
earth shall be full of the know-ledge of the Lord as the wa-ters co-ver the sea. And the
Pno.
rit.
46 Gmin C7 Dmin Gmin B♭maj7 C F
Voice
earth shall be full of the know-ledge of the Lord as the wa - ters co-ver the sea.
rit.
Pno.

# Chapter 4 - SCRIPTURAL AEROBICS

(The Faith Hall of Fame)

Most Christians don't believe in coincidences; many say, instead, that God spoke to them through one way or another and showed them the way; I may not be as spiritual as these folks, or maybe it's just that I have a slight fear of being presumptuous. Being led by the Holy Spirit seems to be a gentler, more accurate way of deciphering those situations that bring handy ingredients together at a particular point in time. For instance, here is the background on a little musical play called, "Exercising Faith."

Several parents suggested to me one day that my Sunday School kids do some sort of presentation on Mothers' Day. My Pastor also thought this would be a good idea. Since Mothers' Day is not a major biblical event, I couldn't really start going through concordances and hope to find anything truly appropriate. However, at about this time, I heard a tape teaching on the book of Hebrews, chapter 11, and the phrase, "The Faith Hall of Fame" was used to describe those wonderful verses that cited all the heroes of faith. The one thing that struck me as I re-read this chapter was that most of the heroes were men - yes, Rahab was mentioned, but the impression was left that the men were the truly great faith champions.

I had been meaning to do a series of teachings in our little class on the subject of faith. Conveniently, in the back of my Bible were a number of messages by Kenneth Hagin on the subject of Faith. As I read these, I made a kind of checklist on the major points Rev. Hagin made about what faith is and, more importantly, how it works. The main point was that God gives us a measure of faith, but if we don't use it (or exercise it), that measure won't grow or do us any good.

So there were the three ingredients: Mothers' Day, the Faith Hall of Fame and exercise. Inducting a few more ladies into the Faith Hall of Fame, evening up the ratio of men to women seemed like something my little class could enthusiastically accept (there being a preponderance of girls in the class). Since many of the mothers of these kids were enrolled in aerobic exercise classes, I knew I would not lack for technical advisors.

Since the Mothers' Day idea hadn't arisen until after the holidays, that meant I had about a little less than three months to write this production and still have 7 Sundays to do rehearsals. I had learned that these productions had the prospect of being "ragged" unless we could actually do 6 run-throughs. So if everyone had a practice tape, and I could do a number of individual rehearsals, we might just make it.

Luckily (another coincidence??), I had to make a business trip during this formative time, and since it was a three hour flight, I decided to try and write all this into a relatively cohesive outline of the presentation. After takeoff, I got out my bible, my always-present yellow pad and my notes. As I worked, the man sitting next to me commented: "Excuse me, but I must say it is refreshing to see someone reading a bible on a plane." I explained

what I was trying to do...about the play, the kids and the idea of faith and its "exercise." The man explained that he was an Assistant Pastor in an Arizona Church and he was charmed with the whole idea. He encouraged me and gave me a number of very useful ideas - all of which I incorporated into the script. This little encounter saved me a great deal of time and provided just the right stimulus at precisely the right moment.
It was not a coincidence! As we parted, he gave me his business card and asked that I send him a tape or a script when it was all finished. I thanked him and said I would. Unfortunately I put his card in my shirt pocket and it didn't survive the wash. I console myself by thinking he might have been an angel anyway.

As a result of this encounter, I felt more confident and relaxed about how to stage this opus. I therefore concentrated on the particulars of getting the children involved in both the teaching and the rehearsing. Knowing that anxiety is bred by the pressure of having to memorize lines, I decided to use two puppets as joint impresarios. This meant that the "voices" of these puppets could read their parts behind the curtain without the pressure of having to perform in front of everyone. Now for the other components.

If you have ever witnessed the various Hall of Fame inductions for the various sports, then you know that as each person is inducted, a filmed scene is presented showing what their achievement is based on. This little film or tape is narrated so that what you are witnessing makes sense to the viewer. Not a bad format.

Now, to choose my "inductees. As we talked about this in class, a consensus developed around Rahab, Mary, Ruth, Hannah, the woman of Galilee who touched the hem of Jesus' robe, and (displacing Barak), Deborah. As a kind of culmination of these wonderful examples of faith, I visualized a championship faith event inspired by Paul's admonition in Ephesians 6:12 that "we wrestle not against flesh and blood but against the powers...of darkness." This was an unabashed excuse to have my little Miss Mustard Seed actually wrestle a hulking Power of Darkness... and win!

As each of these new heroines of faith were introduced, I decided to have a narrator read a simple verse depiction of each event while several of the children acted out, mime-style, what was being recounted. This eliminated the need for any memorizing as the narrator could read from the script on a music stand that was screened by a little signpost showing where that scene took place – Galilee, Mount Tabor, Moab, Nazareth, Jericho, Shiloh, and, for the wrestling match, the Spirit Arena.

After each one of these scenes, the Faith Aerobic Class would go through their routine while the two little puppets sang the title song, "Exercising Faith." I needed only to have some appropriate, and scriptural, names for my two puppets - the curator of the Faith Hall of Fame, and the exercise leader. The names, Sarah and Leah seemed just about right, but to signal the sense of fun woven into the presentation, the names became Sarah Phim and Leah Tard. To balance the engrafted fun with a certain degree of edification, an opening number was written which was nothing more than the first verse of Hebrews 11 - the classic definition of faith set to a simple waltz: "Now faith is the substance of things hoped for; and the evidence of things not seen." Memorizing that was, in my opinion, important for the class.

We reprised this production on at least three other Mothers' Days and always took it to a number of nursing homes. The children's enthusiasm for this play was always matched by the wonderful reception they got from the residents of the nursing homes. When little Miss Mustard Seed, in the final scene, faced the huge teenager (done up in red cape and black mask) playing the Power of Darkness, there was always an explosion of applause when she goes to the side and lugs back my large old family bible, plops it down on the floor and stands on it to flip her opponent in an exaggerated "defeat." It kind of gave a new meaning to the phrase, "standing on the Word."

To this day, the children in that class have a unique understanding of the stories of Hannah, Ruth, Deborah etc. and why their faith enabled them to triumph. And they can even still sing the songs!

# EXERCISING FAITH

## Lesson Plan

Hebrews 11 is the basic text for this series of teachings. Other key chapters are: James 2 and Romans 4 (for Abraham's faith). To these, I have added Proverbs 3:5 - "trust in the Lord with all thine heart and lean not unto thine own understanding." That has always seemed to be an excellent definition of faith, especially when coupled with the first verse of Hebrews 11. The Rev. Kenneth E. Hagin has written more about faith than any other Bible teacher, so what follows draws heavily on many of his lessons and devotions.

I. What is faith? Why is it important? What does God say about it? What are you supposed to do with it? Faith is one of the gifts of God. It's important because without it, you can't please Him. The faith chapters listed above detail the basics. As for what do you do with it, see 2 Thessalonians 1:3; Matthew 8:10 and 9:29. You must exercise faith and make it grow. The best way to remember these things is the following:

| | |
|---|---|
| **F** | Faith is like **Food. It is nourishing . See Matthew 4:4** |
| **A** | Faith requires **A**ction; acting on belief, being a doer of the word (James 1:22) |
| **I** | Four "**I**'s" : I say it, I do it, I receive it, I tell it (Mark 5:25-34) |
| **T** | T is for **T**rust in God's word (Proverbs 3:5) |
| **H** | **H**earing - faith cometh by hearing the word (Romans 10:17).<br>H is also for **H**eroes - who are the heroes of faith? |

II The faith heroes, all 30 of them are listed in Hebrews 11. But there are only one or two heroines listed (Sara and Rahab). What about other faith heroines. Shouldn't we induct some into the Faith Hall of Fame? Who? Rahab, certainly; but what about Ruth, Deborah, Hannah, Mary and the woman of Galilee who was healed by touching the hem of Jesus' robe. Chapter 1 of the Book of Ruth; Joshua 2 (Rahab); Deborah is in Judges: 4 & 5; Hannah is in I Samuel 1 and the woman of Galilee in Mark 5:25-34.

III Practice the definition of faith. Sing the "Faith" song and study the lyrics. What does it mean to have the evidence of things not seen. Are there things that are very real, but not seen? Of course. To illustrate the point, have two children take the parts in the skit on the next page. See how many real, but unseen, things are mentioned. Have the class count them.

IV Turn to I Timothy 6:12 and to Ephesians 6:12 and you will see that:

a. We are to fight the good fight of faith
b. We wrestle not against flesh and blood but against the powers of darkness.

If we are to have a good fight of faith, then the size of the wrestler doesn't matter. Someone as tiny as a mustard seed could easily beat the Power of Darkness. All they would have to do is..."stand on the Word." Imagine a wrestling match like that!

## Format

This mini-musical is a combination of songs, puppets, mime-type acting, recitation and aerobic style movements – all meant to dramatize the point that our faith is only as useful as our ability to act on it, or exercise it. Picking up on scripture in James 2, Romans 4 and Hebrews 11 (the so-called Faith Hall of Fame), six moments in the lives of great women of faith are depicted through verse, song and action. There are two puppet narrators, Sarah Phim, the curator of the Faith Hall of Fame, and Leah Tard, the faith exercise leader. Silent acting roles are Ruth, Rahab, the Woman of Galilee, Deborah, Mary and Hannah (with lesser acting roles for the two spies, Naomi, Jesus, Barak and Eli. A final scene shows a spiritual wrestling match between Faith and the Power of Darkness.

There are two chorus numbers, two alternating background themes for the mime scenes, and a solo song, "Exercising Faith," to which an aerobic style routine is performed. Musical score is written for piano and guitar.

## List of Props

7 scene signs (with handles)
Naomi's bundle
Rahab's red cord
two spy masks
Line of David sign (Boaz, Obed, Jesse)
Barak's sword
Power of Darkness mask & cape
Large family Bible
bell and mallet

Costumes include white robe with sash for Jesus, Mary's robe/shawl, Eli's robe & ephod and simple vests for other players.

## EXERCISING FAITH

### Cast:

SARAH PHIM ............................................Curator of the Faith Hall of Fame
LEAH TARD...............................................Aerobic exercise leader
Scene 1 - MOAB:
RUTH........................................................Widow of Moab
NAOMI .....................................................Ruth's mother-in-law
Scene 2 - Jericho:
RAHAB......................................................Citizen of Jericho
2 SPIES ....................................................Sent by Joshua
Scene 3 - Galilee:
WOMAN....................................................Healed by touching Jesus' robe
JESUS........................................................Savior, Lord, healer
Scene 4 - Mt. Tabor:
DEBORAH.................................................Judge of Israel
BARAK......................................................Army commander
Scene 5 - Nazareth:
MARY .......................................................Mother (to be) of Jesus
Scene 6 - Shiloh:
HANNAH..................................................Mother of Samuel
ELI.............................................................Temple Priest
Scene 7 - The Spirit Arena:
FAITH .......................................................Miss Mustard Seed
CHALLENGER ..........................................The Power of Darkness

*Each scene has a narrator who recites while the cast acts out the story.*

### Musical Numbers:

WELCOME TO THE FAITH HALL OF FAME .................All
NOW FAITH IS ...............................................................All
THEME FOR SCENES 1, 3, 5 ...........................................Piano
THEME FOR SCENES 2, 4, 6 ...........................................Piano
EXERCISING FAITH (6 versions) ....................................Sarah & Leah
NOW FAITH IS (reprise) ...................................................All

The faith "aerobics team"

Rehab, the "spies" and her genealogy

Deborah, the Judge and Barak, the reluctant warrior

*The stage is set with a large puppet stage set up on stage left. On top of it is a sign proclaiming "The Faith Hall of Fame." At stage right is a platform with a music stand. In front of the stand is a PVC pipe (about waist high) topped to look like a pillar or column. This "pillar" is the receptacle for the location signs that each narrator will carry on, placing the sign's handle in the top opening so that it fits snugly. In the center is a large open "exercise" area.*

**CHORUS**

OPEN YOUR BIBLES
TO HEBREWS ELEVEN,
FOR THIRTY EXAMPLES OF FAITH
(WE'LL JUST SHOW YOU SEVEN)

HERE IN THE FAITH HALL OF FAME
WELCOME TO
THE FAITH HALL OF FAME

FILLED WITH MEN AND WORKS
THAT WON GOD'S ACCLAIM;
OBEDIENCE AND TRUST COMBINED
ARE BEHIND EVERY NAME
ENSHRINED IN
THE FAITH HALL OF FAME.

WELCOME TO
THE FAITH HALL OF FAME
OPEN YOUR BIBLES
TO HEBREWS ELEVEN

*As the chorus stays in place (minus the two "voices" of the puppets which go behind the stage), a puppet comes up in the stage. This is Sarah Phim, the curator of the Faith Hall of Fame. She is prim, with a slight schoolteacher look. But she is bright and bouncy as she speaks in a series of rhyming couplets.*

**SARAH**

Welcome! I'm Sarah ... Sarah Phim
(You were expecting maybe a cherubim?)
Here at the Hall I'm curator and guide
For the heroes of faith that are just inside;
Plus, we have some special exhibits
Some Biblical tidbits that you can kibitz:
There's Jacob's ladder and young David's sling;
For Abraham, we've got a whole separate wing!

And today you'll see our new addition;
But first, a faith definition.
It's Hebrews eleven, verse number one
(And I'll be back right after they're done.)

*Sarah drops down into the well of the stage as the chorus sings*

**CHORUS**

NOW FAITH IS THE SUBSTANCE
OF THINGS HOPED FOR
AND THE EVIDENCE OF THINGS NOT SEEN
FAITH IS TRUSTING GOD
WITH ALL THY HEART
NOT LEANING ON THINE UNDERSTANDING

NOW FAITH IS ASSURANCE
GOD'S WORD IS TRUE
AND IT COMETH BY HEARING HIS WORD
YOU MUST ACT ON FAITH
LIKE ABRAHAM
BELIEVING AHEAD OF RECEIVING

*The chorus repeats this with half singing the counter melody against the first stanza*

NOW FAITH IS ASSURANCE
GOD'S WORD IS TRUE
AND IT COMETH
BY HEARING HIS WORD

NOW FAITH IS THE SUBSTANCE
OF THINGS HOPED FOR
AND THE EVIDENCE
OF THINGS NOT SEEN

FAITH IS TRUSTING GOD
WITH ALL THY HEART
NOT LEANING
ON THINE UNDERSTANDING

YOU MUST ACT ON FAITH
LIKE ABRAHAM
BELIEVING
AHEAD OF RECEIVING

**ALL**

NOW FAITH IS THE SUBSTANCE
OF THINGS HOPED FOR
AND THE EVIDENCE OF THINGS NOT SEEN..

*The puppet Sarah reappears, as the chorus disperses to each of the wings.*

**SARAH**

So, faith is something you have, that's true;
But faith is also something you do:
    Acting on faith; trusting God's word
    That's the message we want heard.
So here are some women in our newest section
Who exercised faith, taking God's direction;
    Making a choice and finding the truth
    What better example than the story of Ruth?

*As Sarah drops down, the two actors for Scene 1 take their place and freeze. A narrator crosses in front of them, holding a sign labeled "Moab." He puts this in the "pillar" and waits as the musical theme begins. As he speaks, the actors mime the story.*

**#1 NARRATOR**

For the young widow of Moab
A choice was at hand:
She could stay with her people
Or go...
Go with this woman, across mountain and sand,
And respond to a yearning
She did not understand.

    "Stay," said her mother-in-law,
    "For I can't provide;
    Go back to your family, and there abide."
    But Ruth would not leave
    The old woman's side ;
    There was just something there
    That made her decide:

"Whither thou goest
I will go;
Whatever thou sowest
I will sow;
For the God thou knowest,
I would know."

    Said Ruth,
    The young widow of Moab.

*As the musical theme concludes and the actors finish, puppet Sarah reappears. Actors exit*

**SARAH**

Now Ruth's descendants were in Jesus' lineage
Through Jesse and David and their kith-an-kineage;
    But that's enough from Sarah Phim
    Now, to our Faith Exercise gym!
And to help you, so it won't be too hard,
Here's your exercise leader – Leah Tard.

*Puppet Leah comes up beside Sarah. Leah is an active girlish type with pigtails. As she speaks, the six or eight members of the "aerobic exercise team" come out and take their positions to begin their routine when Leah sings.*

**LEAH**

Now, remember two things about faith: it's proved as you act on it; and it works for you as you exercise it. That's what I'll help you with. After all, nobody wants flabby faith! Here we go!

**LEAH** (*sings)*

WARMING UP AND WORKING OUT
EXERCISING MY FAITH;
AND I'M SHEDDING POUNDS OF FEAR AND DOUBT
EXERCISING FAITH
    LIFT THAT HEAD
    BEND THAT KNEE;
    EXERCISING FAITHFULLY
    I'M FLEXING MY
    AUTHORITY
EXERCISING FAITH

**LEAH & SARAH** (*sing)*

AND OF HIS WORD
I AM A DO-ER
AND WITH MY FAITH
I'M A FOLLOW THROUGH-ER
...AND I'M COUNTING ON GOD

**EXERCISE TEAM**

TWO, THREE, FOUR...

**LEAH & SARAH**

EXERCISING FAITH!

*After the song and the exercise routine, Leah drops down, leaving Sarah.*

**SARAH**

Now here's a story of spies and intrigue
And a woman of faith who is major league;
    At considerable risk, she made a stand
    To help open up the Promised Land.
You'll find it in Joshua's first few chapters:
Jericho falls to Hebrew captors.
    Down went the walls, the Canaanites lose;
    But Rahab's faith was the really big news.

*Sarah drops down as the actors take their places and the narrator walks across with the location sign: "Jericho," which he puts in place. The two "spies" and Rahab freeze until the narration and the theme music starts.*

**#2 NARRATOR**

"Send the scouts," said Joshua;
So, scouts were sent, and off they went
To Jericho;
And there they go,
To Rahab's house in Jericho,
Is where they go.

    And Rahab gives them help and hiding
    Plus an escape – all providing
    That when the city's defenses caved,
    Her whole family would be saved.

"I know," she said
"I know the Lord,
Has given you this land as your reward;
But spare this house
And hold your sword,
When you see my blood red cord."

    She moved by faith and it was done;
    And in time she had a son,
    Whose son would have a son to bring
    A son to be
    Anointed king.

*During this last line, one of the spies holds up a "family tree" which shows first, Boaz, then Obed, then Jesse, and finally David. The actors go, replaced by the exercise team as Leah comes up, joined by Sarah.*

**LEAH**

...and whether you're up against the walls of Jericho... or the gates of hell, you'd better have your faith in shape... C'mon team...

**LEAH** *(sings)*

SHAPING UP TO BUILD MY SCORE
EXERCISING MY FAITH
WINNING POINTS AND ALL BLUE RIBBONS FOR
EXERCISING FAITH
COACHED BY GOD, I'LL WIN THE GAME
COMING IN FIRST AND TAKING AIM
TO MAKE THE FAITHFUL HALL OF FAME
EXERCISING FAITH

**LEAH & SARAH**

AND IT'S BY FAITH
THAT I AM WALKING
AND IT'S MY FAITH
THAT DOES ALL MY TALKING
...AND I'M COUNTING ON GOD...

**EXERCISE TEAM**

TWO, THREE, FOUR...

**ALL**

EXERCISING FAITH!

*The team exits, Leah drops down and Sarah proceeds to introduce the next scene. As she does so, the #3 Narrator walks across holding the sign "Galilee" and puts it in place.*

**SARAH**

Fast forwards to a town in Galilee
At the time of Jesus' ministry
A woman in the crowd (we don't know her name),
Acted on faith; made a healing claim;
And the lesson of this part of the gospel? –
By faith in Him, all things are poss'ble.

*The actors come on: Jesus, first, then a small crowd of disciples with the Woman behind them.*

**#3 NARRATOR**

As always, the crowd
Was pressing around Him;
And that is how
**<u>She</u>** now found Him.

And the woman of Galilee
Said: "So,
If I may but touch His garment
I shall be whole, I know."

Her faith thus spoken
Moved her to feel
Just the hem of His robe;
and the power to heal?

He felt it go
Her faith made it real
This He could see
From her humble appeal.

For twelve years the plague
Had taken its toll
"Go in peace," she heard,
"Thy faith has made thee whole."

Go in peace, go in peace,
Thy faith has made thee whole

*As the theme music and the narration ends, the actors exit. Leah reappears from the stage.*

**LEAH**

There are four steps to exercising faith – you say it, do it, receive it and tell it. That's what the woman of Galilee did. Now, let's put it all together..

**LEAH** *(sings)*

GOING STRONG AND LONG PERHAPS
EXERCISING MY FAITH
'CAUSE IN LIVING WATER I SWIM LAPS
EXERCISING FAITH
CASTING MOUNTAINS IN THE SEA
MARK ELEVEN, TWENTY-THREE
THE WORD OF GOD IS WASHING ME
EXERCISING FAITH.

**LEAH & SARAH**

AND OF HIS WORD
I AM A DO-ER
AND WITH MY FAITH
I'M A FOLLOW-THROUGH-ER
...AND I'M COUNTING ON GOD

**EXERCISE TEAM**

...TWO, THREE, FOUR...

**ALL**

EXERCISING FAITH!

*The exercise team exits; Leah drops down and Sarah continues as the next scene unfolds.*

**SARAH**

When the Hebrews' faith had gotten slack,
The Canaanites took some real estate back
    But Deborah had a plan of attack;
    Her faith moved an army - along with Barak!
Exhortation was her special knack,
That won her a Faith Hall of Fame Placque.

*Narrator #4 crosses with the sign, "Mt. Tabor," as Deborah and Barak come on and freeze in place. Once the sign is in place, the theme music starts and the narration begins.*

**#4 NARRATOR**

Awake, awake, Deborah,
And utter a song;
Arise with Barak,
Take him along.

    Praise ye the Lord,
    Deborah, the judge
    Barak to battle!
    (He may need a nudge)

"Hear, oh ye kings,
Jabin and Sisera
This day is the Lord's
It couldn't be surer

Nine hundred chariots
Won't stand on this day
The torrent of Kishon
Will sweep them away.

Down from Mount Tabor,
Let His enemies perish;
This day is the Lord's,
Him will I cherish."

The militant faith of Deborah cheers;
So the land had rest for forty years.

*The actors exit as the narration ends. Puppet Leah comes back up and the exercise team comes on.*

**LEAH** (*sings)*
PRESSING ON WITH MY BEST SHOT
EXERCISING MY FAITH
BEATING EVERYTHING THAT SATAN'S GOT
EXERCISING FAITH
FLOORING HIM, I TAKE MY BOW
MUSCLES BOUND FOR GLORY NOW
I'M ALL PUMPED UP TO SHOW YOU HOW
(TO) EXERCISE YOUR FAITH.

**LEAH & SARAH**
AND IT'S BY FAITH
THAT I AM WALKING
AND IT'S MY FAITH
THAT DOES ALL MY TALKING
...AND I'M COUNTING ON GOD

**EXERCISE TEAM**
...TWO, THREE, FOUR

**ALL**
EXERCISING FAITH!

*The team exits and Leah drops down.*

**SARAH**

To Nazareth now for this little scene
The home of a girl, no more than a teen;
    Can you be trained; can you be taught,
    To handle the message the angel brought?
No, it depends on faith, in a new category
As Luke tells the Mother of Jesus' story.

*As Sarah finishes her lines, Narrator #5 crosses with the sign: "Nazareth" and puts it in place. A young girl enters from the right and stands as if listening to something. As the music and the narration begin, she does a simple dance.*

**#5 NARRATOR**

And the angel said:
"Fear not, Mary,
For thou
Hast found favor with God,
And now...

    So shall it be
    That the hope of glory
    Will be borne by thee."

And she said of the miracle
Of which she heard:
"I am the Lord's, so be it
According to thy word.

    My spirit rejoices
    For blessed am I;
    The Lord, my soul doth magnify."

Accepting the burden,
The wonder, the loss;
By faith she would bear
And always be there;
    From the side of the manger
    To the foot of the cross.

*Mary exits, as Leah comes up in the puppet stage.*

**LEAH**

Hebrews eleven also says that without faith, it's impossible to please God. Mary certainly had God-pleasing faith... and she was obedient to answer his call. She pleased God and she praised God – the best exercise of all!

**SARAH**

Faith is released by words that are said
And come from the heart; not just the head;;
    Faith makes you certain of what is to come,
    And this is a difficult concept for some...
But not Hannah, who was hardly surprised
By results of the faith that she exercised.

*Narrator #6 crosses the stage with the sign: "Shiloh," and puts it in place. Hannah and Eli, the priest come on and take their places, as the musical theme begins.*

**#6 NARRATOR**

Indeed
Wouldn't it be odd,
For faith to lead
To a bargain with God?

    A childless Hannah
    Prayed in the spirit;
    Made vow to God,
    Knowing He's hear it:

"Oh Lord of hosts, grant me a son,
And he shall be yours
To do what you
Would want done."

The child was delivered
By God, then by Hannah
To Eli, the priest, with praise and hosanna;
And the glory to God, his mother sings
Is for Samuel —
    Prophet...Judge...Anointer of Kings.

*The actors exit as Leah reappears.*

**LEAH**

Hannah trusted God; gave him the glory; and God blessed her with five more children! – way to go, Hannah!

*The exercise team comes back on and Leah starts her song.*

**LEAH** *(sings)*

PRAISING HIM WHO STRENGTHENS ME
EXERCISING MY FAITH
FOR HE'S GIVEN ME THE VICTORY
EXERCISING FAITH.
SHAKING OFF DEPRESSION'S DUST
IN MY GOD I PUT MY TRUST
NO SWEAT FOR ME BECAUSE I'M JUST...
EXERCISING FAITH.

**LEAH & SARAH**

AND OF HIS WORD
I AM A DO-ER
AND WITH MY FAITH
I'M A FOLLOW-THROUGH-ER
...AND I'M COUNTING ON GOD..

**EXERCISE TEAM**

...TWO, THREE, FOUR...

**ALL**

EXERCISING FAITH!

*As Sarah starts her next dialogue, the cast assembles on stage forming a ring around the center area. Narrator #7, with a sign saying: "The Spirit Arena" crosses and puts it in place.*

**SARAH**

Now if you are of a spiritual bent
You'll love this next sporting event
For exercised faith, it's a culmination,
A sort of final examination;
Because when we face spiritual warfare
The tests of our faith are neither simple , nor fair;
With the gospel, we must be a witness or vessel
And Paul said we all...should be ready to wrestle!

*The narrator this time speaks in the style of a ring announcer; excited and playing the crowd. The crowd around the ring cheers or hisses , as appropriate.*

**#7 NARRATOR**

Good afternoon, ladies and gentlemen. From the Spirit Arena - it's championship wrestling!!!

*Crowd cheers*

This is your announcer, First Timothy... here to cover the action as the pros fight the good fight of faith! First, the challenger - from the Pit of Hell... it's the Power of Darkness.

*Crowd boo's as the masked & red-caped hulk enters with a flourish.*

..and in this corner... measuring three cubits and representing faith... it's Miss Mustard Seed.

*Crowd goes wild with cheering. Power of Darkness makes dismissive gesture.*

The Power of Darkness is fresh from big outings all over the world... he's looking for the upset. Can Faith move this mountain???

*The ring bell sounds and the opponents start to circle each other*

Here comes the Power of Darkness... he seems to be going right for a soul slam...
Miss Mustard Seed waits - using her famous Scorpion Tread.... trained at the Jacob School of Wrestling, she knows her stuff!. But wait.... she's going back to her corner!
Is she retreating?

*Miss Mustard Seed goes to the side and gets a huge family Bible and lugs it to the middle of the ring.*

No... she's getting the Word.... now she heads for the Power of Darkness, and... shes...
**Standing** on the word... She has him....and.... down he goes!

*Miss Mustard Seed puts the Bible down on the floor, gets up on it and grabs the Power of Darkness, who makes an exaggerated tumble to end up flat on his back. She clasps her hands in triumph over her head.*

It's all over! Faith wins again.!

*Crowd goes wild with cheering as the bell sounds. With the match over, Leah comes back up. The whole "crowd" now becomes an exercise team.*

**LEAH**

James 2 says that even the devil and demons have faith in God... the difference is that we **use** our faith, act on it, exercise it and trust God so we can see the answer in spite of the circumstances. Now there is fitness of the spiritual kind.... right, Sarah?

**SARAH**

Yea and amen.
Again and again.

**LEAH** *(sings)*

BUILDING UP AND FEELING FIT
EXERCISING MY FAITH
I'M A WINNER 'CAUSE I NEVER QUIT
EXERCISING FAITH.
WRESTLING NOT WITH FLESH AND BLOOD
TRAMPLING DEMONS IN THE MUD
THE POWERS OF DARKNESS GO DOWN, THUD!
EXERCISING FAITH

**LEAH & SARAH**

AND IT'S BY FAITH
THAT I AM WALKING
AND IT'S MY FAITH
THAT DOES ALL MY TALKING
... AND I'M COUNTING ON GOD

**ALL**

.. TWO, THREE, FOUR...
EXERCISING F-A-I-T-H.... FAITH!!

*As they line up for a curtain call, the cast assembles into its positions for the opening chorus and sings the Hebrews 11 song, as at the beginning.*

NOW FAITH IS THE SUBSTANCE
OF THINGS HOPED FOR
AND THE EVIDENCE OF
THINGS NOT SEEN

NOW FAITH IS ASSURANCE
GOD'S WORD IS TRUE
AND IT COMETH
BY HEARING HIS WORD

FAITH IS TRUSTING GOD
WITH ALL THY HEART
NOT LEANING
ON THINE UNDERSTANDING

YOU MUST ACT ON FAITH
LIKE ABRAHAM
BELIEVING
AHEAD OF RECEIVING

NOW FAITH IS THE SUBSTANCE
OF THINGS HOPED FOR
AND THE EVIDENCE OF THINGS NOT SEEN.

# The Faith Hall Of Fame

Clark Tyler
*Arranged by Andrew Bell*

23
C B♭ C F C F
Voice
bined are be - hind ev-ery name en - shrined in The Faith Hall Of Fame.
Pno.
29
F B♭ C F
Voice
Wel-come to The Faith Hall Of Fame.
Pno.
34
F
Voice
O-pen your Bi - bles to He-brews e - le - ven.
Pno.

# Now Faith Is...

Clark Tyler
*Arranged by Andrew Bell*

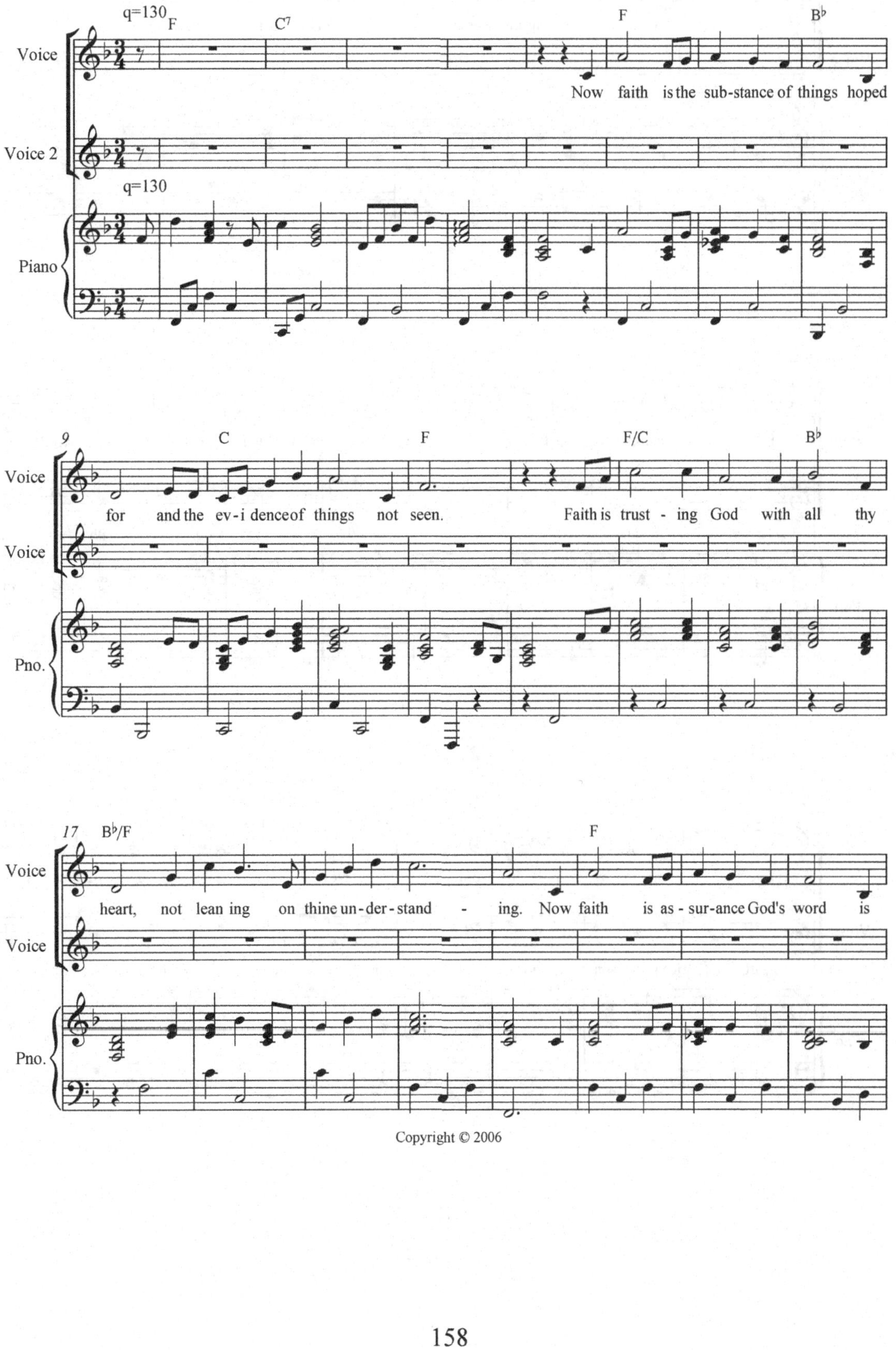

25
C
F
F7
B♭
Voice
true and it com eth by hear ing his word. Youmust act on faith like Ab - ra-
Voice
Pno.
Start Row
33
C
F
F
B♭
Voice
ham, be - liev ing a - head of re - cei - ving. Now faith is as - sur - ance God's word is
Voice
Faith is trust - ing God with all thy
Pno.
41
C
F
F
B♭
Voice
true and it com - eth by hear - ing his word. Now faith is the sub - stance of things hoped
Voice
heart, not lean - ing on thine un - der - stand - ing. You must act on faith like Ab - ra-
Pno.

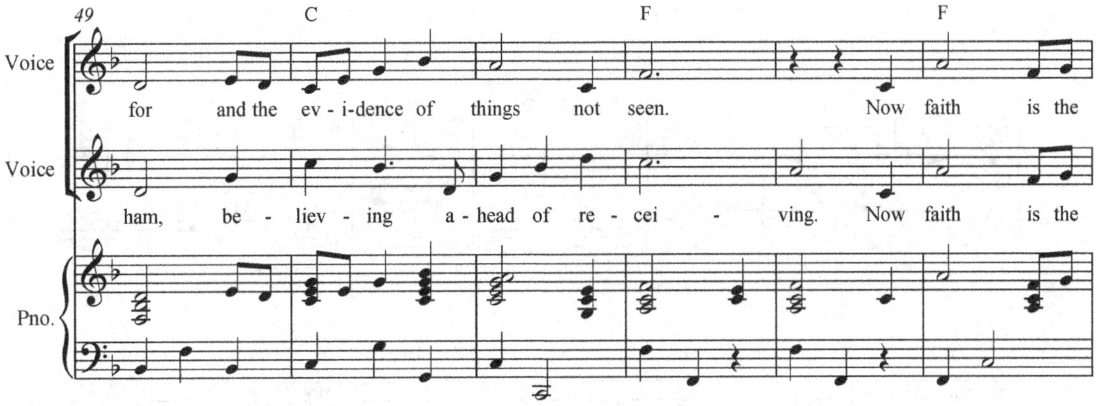
49
C
F
F
Voice
for and the ev - i-dence of things not seen. Now faith is the
Voice
ham, be - liev - ing a - head of re - cei - ving. Now faith is the
Pno.

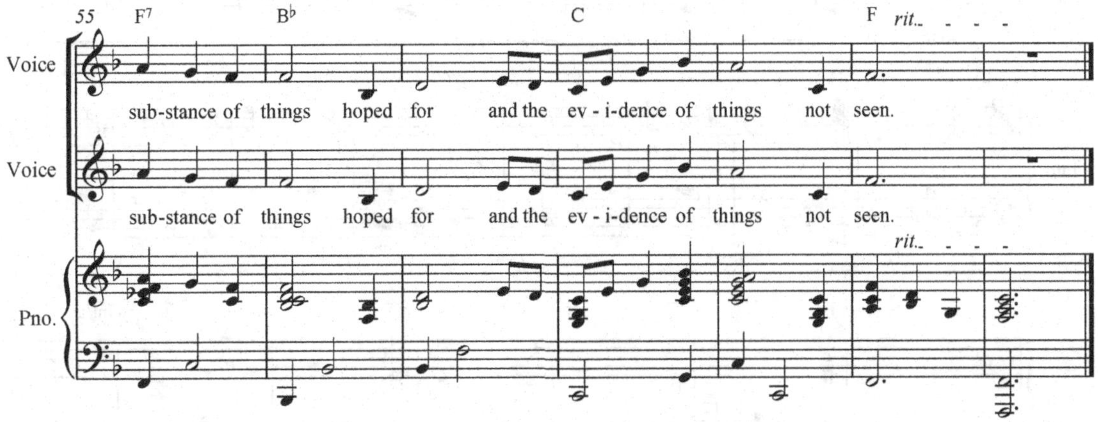
55
F7
B♭
C
F rit.
Voice
sub-stance of things hoped for and the ev - i-dence of things not seen.
Voice
sub-stance of things hoped for and the ev - i-dence of things not seen.
rit.
Pno.

# SCENES: Ruth, Woman of Galilee, Mary

Clark Tyler
*Arranged by Andrew Bell*

# SCENE: Rahab, Deborah, Hannah

Clark Tyler

*Arranged by Andrew Bell*

# Exercising Faith

Clark Tyler
*Arranged by Andrew Bell*

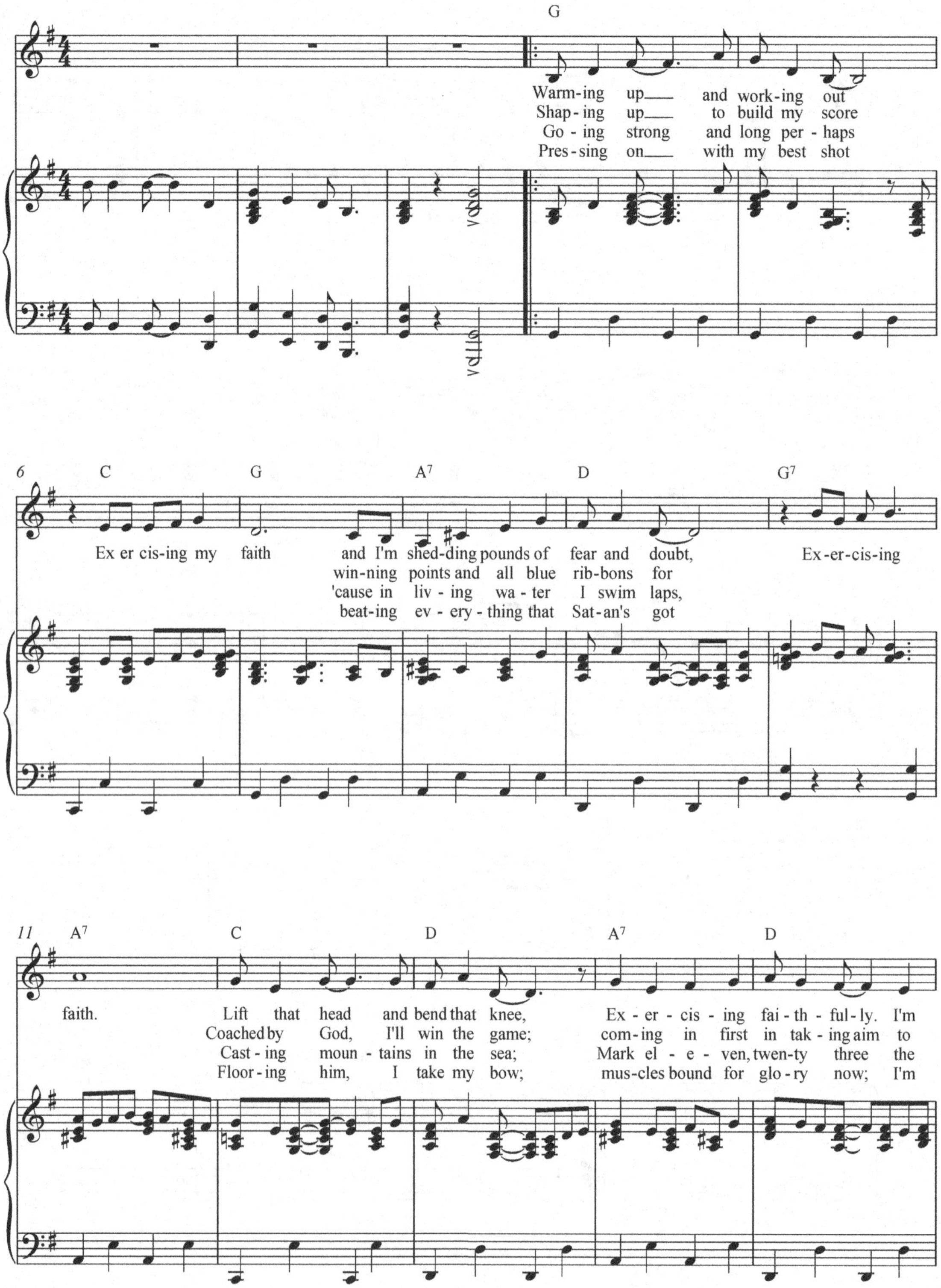
G
Warm-ing up___ and work-ing out
Shap-ing up___ to build my score
Go - ing strong and long per - haps
Pres-sing on___ with my best shot
6 C G A7 D G7
Ex er cis-ing my faith and I'm shed-ding pounds of fear and doubt, Ex-er-cis-ing
win-ning points and all blue rib-bons for
'cause in liv - ing wa - ter I swim laps,
beat-ing ev - ery - thing that Sat-an's got
11 A7 C D A7 D
faith. Lift that head and bend that knee, Ex - er - cis - ing fai - th - ful - ly. I'm
Coached by God, I'll win the game; com - ing in first in tak - ing aim to
Cast - ing moun - tains in the sea; Mark el - e - ven, twen-ty three the
Floor - ing him, I take my bow; mus-cles bound for glo - ry now; I'm

16 Bm A7 G G7
flex - ing my au - thor - i - ty, Ex - er - cis - ing faith. And of his
make the faith - ful hall of fame And it's by
word of God is wash - ing me.
all pumped up to show you how to ex - er - cise your faith.
21 C G D
word Sing times 1 and 3: I am a do - er and with my faith
faith Sing times 2 and 4: that I am walk - ing; and it's my faith
26 D13 G A7
I'm a fol - low through - er and I'm count - ing on God. 2 3 4
that does all my talk - ing
30 D13 D7 1. G G
Ex - er - cis - ing faith.
(last time only)
F - A - I - T - H Faith!

## Chapter 5 - LIFE BEGAN IN A GARDEN

...I jotted down those words which sprang out at me from the Pastor's message. He went on to speak of God's plan and spiritual growth... but those first five words kept echoing inside me. As it was spring, his message focused on gardens, the promise of seeds leading to a bountiful harvest...and there was something about the Garden of Gethsemane – but I was still back at "life began in a garden." After the church announcements were given and the offering taken, I glanced down at my "sermon notes" and saw what I had written:

Life began in a garden
A garden of God's own plan;
And from a tomb in a garden
Everlasting life began.

Our church had experienced growth and one of the fruits of that was to have a "family night" on Wednesdays, with a time for adult classes, prayer and, hopefully, something for the kids to do. I offered to come up with something for them and decided that they could help me write a new musical play about a Garden. I had often wanted to do a musical play that was an evangelical invitation, making a strong case for the power and growth that comes from a spiritual commitment. Given the fact that the nursing home audiences we visited always were receptive and hungry for these kind of biblical truths, it seemed an appropriate approach for the children to take.

On that first Wednesday night, I had 21 eager little saints show up in our rented school's combination cafeteria/auditorium. I had gotten a large two feet by three feet pad of white paper and had taped single sheets up on one long wall. I told the children that we were going to have a brainstorming session so they could help write our next musical presentation. Their job would be to suggest stories or incidents (or characters) in the Bible that had to do with gardens or growth. It could be flowers, trees, crops or anything else that had anything to do with botany, agriculture and growing things. One sheet was titled TREES, another was FLOWERS, a third was FOOD, another was GARDENS, another was WEEDS, another was PEOPLE, and I added a final one: HELPING THINGS GROW.

Of course the first suggestion was something that didn't fit on any of these sheets - it was "seeds." Little Laura had remembered the song that featured the parable of the sower and the seed, and this was her chance to hit a home run! Quickly, I put up a sheet titled: OTHER GARDENING STUFF, and the first entry was "seeds." That pulled the plug, and soon that sheet was filled with: "rake," "shovel," "watering can," "fertilizer," "clippers," "rain," "sunshine," "well," "fence," "wheelbarrow," "bug spray" and other even less edifying entries. Refocusing my class's exuberance, I explained that we needed to be able to relate each listing to something in the Bible (there went the clippers and the bug spray!). Time to re-group.

I explained that the point here was to be able to come up with an interesting, and fun, message for the people in the nursing homes who like to grow plants and have flowers. We needed to present a real invitation. We needed to be able to tell them that God wanted us all to grow - not just the little kids, but He wanted our spirits to grow in Him so that we became a kind of heavenly harvest. Nodding all around. I promised that when we finished filling up all these sheets of paper, I would take them and spend the summer writing songs and scenes about each and put it all in a new production which we would start rehearsing in the fall. "Come to the Garden" would be our "invitation."

Knowing how much the children loved to be a "character" I decided that we needed some character names so that they could visualize the fun part of the message. So the next week I added to the PEOPLE sheet the names: Rose Bloom, H. Basil Coriander, Professor Ivy LeVine, and a few others which I have thankfully forgotten. I explained that as our study progressed, there would be other people and characters to fill our "Garden." Some of the children might be trees, others could be seeds, and all would be some sort of denizen of this "floratorio." I explained what ***that*** meant.

As that first session closed, I gave each child a paper cup and a small bunch of different kinds of seeds. I told them that they should put some dirt in the cup and plant the seeds, not too deeply, and water them, not too much. Then after a couple of weeks, they should bring them to class and we could see how their mini gardens were coming along. Their other assignment was to start to find some things in the Bible that might be appropriate on one or more of those sheets on the wall.

As the weeks went on, our brainstorming sheets became filled with scriptural references and notations of such things as: the Cedars of Lebanon, the fig tree, the Rose of Sharon, the Garden of Eden, the Garden of Gethsemane, seeds (of course), the hanging gardens of Babylon (???), famine (??), the wheat and the tares, olives (and the Mount of...), vineyards, grapes, dates and one entry that posed quite a challenge – Manna. Manna dutifully went up on the FOOD roster, which of course meant that Moses had to go up on the PEOPLE list. I say "challenge" about manna because I had already begun to visualize a garden on stage with a wishing well type of screen around the puppet stage from which a couple of puppet "consultants" would pop out of. I just couldn't see how the story of manna would naturally fit into that setting. Oh well...

The seeds in the paper cups had indeed sprouted and the kids were thrilled. This set up a teaching about the power of seeds. I had seen an article in some publication about a scientific experiment where a bunch of scientists did a total chemical analysis of several seeds. Using all kinds of hi tech tools they were satisfied that they could completely duplicate all the components of a seed and produce a clone (if you will) of one. Triumphantly, they announced they had succeeded – only one problem...it wouldn't sprout! Looking at the children's little sprouts poking out of the dirt, we talked about this and related it to the parable of the sower and the seed. Since Jesus has given a detailed explanation of this parable to his disciples, the class' understanding enabled them to act out the parable.

Since "seeds" was the very first entry in this botanical sweepstakes, I knew I 'd better deliver a seed song or a seed scene - or both. I could fudge the "bug spray," but the seeds were a critical component. As these little plays evolved, I tried to meld each song into (or spring out of) a scene with its own little lesson. Remembering how the class had acted out the parable of the sower, I imagined a number of "seed" children, plus a sower character, birds, rocks, thorns and a burning sun – all giving animation to the parable. Since the seed thing was Laura's contribution, and there were three other little girls all the same size and age, it seemed a natural to have a singing group called the Four Seeds which would set up the acting out of the parable. Dressing kids up as birds, rocks, thorns and a sunburst would take some craft and artistic talents from some of the mothers.

The making of such props and costumes turned out to be a wonderful way of getting more people involved. This in turn provided a steady source of other creative contributions, not to mention the value of having built-in traffic control for all these children. I had learned this lesson from the aerobic class participants ("Exercising Faith"), the artistic guidance ("Picture the Kingdom"), and the face painting help ("Take a Rainbow Cruise"). The more elements that were added (mime, dance, backdrops, puppets), the more the lure of "showbusiness" added much needed assistance. Of course it took a lot of logistical support to take these little productions "on the road" to the nursing homes. This venue, in itself, proved to be a superb magnet as our church was constantly looking for outreach opportunities. The residents of these homes were the most receptive audience I could imagine... and very hungry for the things of God and the love of Jesus. Very often our congregational participation in these nursing home performances matched the number of performers.

Before our Wednesday night sessions were interrupted for the summer break and vacations, the seed song was completed and we had a chance to stage it and rehearse it a few times. The only thing that seemed to be missing was an appropriate ending to the acted out parable. As I studied the scripture, I kept looking at the concluding words, "but others fell on good ground; sprang up and yielded a crop a hundred fold." How to dramatize this critical point? The Baltimore Orioles (that's right, the baseball team) provided the answer. At one of their "giveaway" nights, fans were given a simple folding umbrella with the Oriole logo on it. The handle telescoped down so when you pushed a little button on the end, it sprang open. Carefully removing the umbrella fabric from the frame, we then made a "hundred fold" crop of little red apples (good old foamcore!) And attached them to the frame with twist ties.

At the conclusion of the seed scene, when the last two little "seeds" survive the birds, rocks , sun and thorns, one of the little girls reached down and carefully picked up the folded umbrella and at just the right moment, pressed the button. At the narrator's words, "yielded a crop a hundred fold," there, poof, was a dangling crop of little red apples. It never failed to cause a burst of applause. God's word wins again! The kids then sang the last stanza of the seed song, much to the delight of the audiences:

“I’m a seed
And it would be scriptural to follow my lead...
Everyone needs:
The power and determination,
(And of course the germination)
Of seeds like me...and me...and me...and me.!”

Over the summer, I enmeshed myself in gardening books and was lucky enough to see a five part program on the Discovery Channel called, “Gardens of the World” narrated by Audrey Hepburn. As a non-gardening, botanical novice, I at least became familiar with the terminology if not the practice. The pieces all seemed to be coming together as I plotted out both the script & songs, as well as the class teaching that would ensure the kind of understanding that tended to guarantee the children’s performance. I was always amazed at the fact that the more the class understood the message behind all the lyrics, lines and characters, the more their performance seemed to sparkle. Talent and repetition of rehearsing seemed to be secondary.

As all this came together, it became clear that there were two things missing: what to do about the “manna” idea, and how to design a finale to the play. As I sat in my hotel room in Dallas Texas, where I was attending a conference, I went over and over the script that I had. Somewhere deep within me, the question arose, “where is Jesus?” If indeed, the point of this play, now titled “Come to the Garden,” was to make Jesus the Lord of your life, then that was a very fair question. The answer came in the idea to stage a curtain call around a new song, “Jesus is my Garden.” The song summarized the main points of all the embedded lessons in the various scenes and brought the characters back out in sequence to be recognized.

But the “manna” thing still eluded me.

When we all got back together after Labor Day, there were two adorable little twin girls, age 5, who had joined our class. Their grandmother had asked if they could be a part of our production - usually children that small were unable to concentrate and take direction. However these two got a copy of the practice tape of all the songs and absorbed them like little blotters. In no time, they knew all the tunes and most of the lyrics and acted like little sparkplugs for the rest of the cast. I just had to find some way of using this matched set of angelic little girls.

Angels!... Perfect. The manna scene turned out to be a singing commercial for miraculous growth. Before Moses and Aaron came on to sing about the attributes of manna, we had the twins dressed as angels cross the stage scattering little styrofoam “peanuts.” Then on came the chorus wearing kaffiahs (the Hebrew headdresses) to pick up the “manna” and sing:

"It's manna;
Our daily delivery from heaven;
It's manna;
Not bad if you add.. A pinch or a tad,
Of pepper and salt, onions and garlic... and leaven."

When "Come to the Garden" was performed, we took it to three different nursing homes. One of these was in the District of Columbia and was a home for Medicaid recipients. I doubt if the staff or the residents had ever seen anything like what we presented. Certainly few churches had ever visited with anything more than a hymn sing-along or a traditional service. Seeing singing fig trees, marching Cedars of Lebanon, manna-scattering angels, puppet garden consultants, or a puffed Colonel O'Wheat in full regalia was certainly a first for this audience. Their reaction was memorable.

Seeds were certainly planted that day, prayers were shared, hugs were given and the joy of the Lord permeated that hall. It has remained one of the more special memories. And unlike one of the other nursing homes we visited with this play, no one tried to actually eat the scattered "manna."

...and I believe those seeds resulted in many needy people coming to "The Garden."

# COME TO THE GARDEN

## Lesson Plan:

This play is a collection of lessons about growth...a very important concept for children who may think that just accepting Jesus as Lord is enough. To drive home the point that God has a plan for each of us, the context of a garden is used. Genesis 2:8 says that after the creation, God's very first task was that "He planted a garden." He didn't just create it or speak it into existence - He "planted" it. Therefore the elements of growth, hard work, planning and providing are the things to emphasize as they all have a spiritual application. Having the children each plant some seeds early on in the class will graphically illustrate these points (especially if they nurture them properly so they sprout, grow and flourish!).

I. What is a garden? A source - to feed, to clothe, to heal, to please, to decorate, to teach. God planted a garden - Eden. It was the beginning of God's plan for Man. When Man disobeyed God and was sent out of Eden, there even was a provision - the Tree of Life. This was a way to get back. Jesus was God's provision for us - the way the truth and the life. Gardens of the Bible - Eden, Gethsemane, the Garden Tomb, and gardens of Kings (Nebuchadnezzar, Ahab, Xerxes, Solomon & David). What do Biblical gardens represent? – life, hope, knowledge, spirit, solitude/meditation & re-birth. Discuss the cycles and seasons in Ecclesiastes 3. Why is time important? (Growth). Besides plants, a garden has planning, purpose, care and results. Types of gardens: flower, vegetable, formal, country, cutting, orchards, vineyards, agricultural fields, greenhouses, window boxes.

II Growth - why is this important? Examples of growth: from baby to adult; savings - from pennies to dollars; intellectual - learning in school; from seed to tree; from small group to large crowd; bad growth - warts, tumors & weeds; multiplication (numerical) versus enhancement (quality); a garden versus a jungle. What is spiritual growth? Paul in Galatians 4:19 said "til Christ be formed in you." Luke 2:52 spoke of Jesus' growth. The rate of our growth depends on the choices we make - its up to us. Look at the example of the seed. It can be dormant for hundreds of years. It will only grow when it is planted, has water and sunshine... and care. Examine the process:

> preparing the ground; planting the seed properly; germination; care & nourishment; water, sun & weeding; vulnerability; sprouting; leaves, growth & pollination; from bud to blossom; from bloom to fruit; from fruit to seed – and what about pruning?

Why is time important? How is growth related to sharing the gospel and reaching others to "plant seeds?" Read the Parable of the Sower and the Seed (Matthew 13, Luke 8). Discuss what "good ground" means. Try the song: "I'm a Seed."

III The elements and rewards of growth:

| ELEMENTS | REWARDS |
|---|---|
| good ground | beauty |
| proper care/the right tools | satisfaction |
| hard work/help | harvest |
| weeding | blessing others |
| nourishing | wise use of resources |
| pruning | bees |
| sunshine | preventing erosion |
| rain/water | prosperity |
| good seed | nourishment |
| protection (tares) | continuity/regeneration |
| following instructions | preservation/reclamation |
| planning/preparation | enrichment/fulfillment |

What examples in the Bible might illustrate some of these? The Parable of the Fig Tree (Luke 13:6-9); the importance of wheat (and the seven species in Deuteronomy 8:7-8); the Cedars of Lebanon (II Chronicles 2:3,8); manna (Exodus 16:15).

IV Your garden. What would you plant in your garden if you were going to show someone God's Word and God's promises?

| | |
|---|---|
| "Apple" - Genesis 3:3 | myrrh - Genesis 43:11; Matthew 2:11 |
| mustard - Mark 4:30-32 | oak - Amos 2:9 |
| mint - Matthew 23:23 | onions - Numbers 11:5-6 |
| lentils - Genesis 25:34 | wheat (tares) - Matthew 13:24-30 |
| cotton - Esther 1:5-6 | reeds - Exodus 2:3 |
| papyrus - Job 8:11 | hyssop - Exodus 12:21; John 19:28 |
| willow - Leviticus 23:40 | millet - Ezekiel 4:9 |
| lily - Matthew 6:38-30 | myrtle - Isaiah 41:19 |
| bitter herbs - Exodus 12:8 | gourds - II Kings 4:39-40 |
| beans - II Samuel 17:27-29 | thorns - Judges 8:7 |

flowers - Isaiah 40:6; Song of Solomon 2:12; Matthew 6:28
almond - Numbers 17:8

V. Invitation. Remember that this play's title is an invitation - an invitation to share the joy of the Lord and the love of Jesus. Who do you know that would be happy to have such an invitation?

Note: While there are many books relating to gardens and Biblical plants etc., I am a big fan of the series of "Eyewitness" Books (Alfred A. Knopf). These are wonderfully laid out with easy to read text and great artwork. Three particularly are great for this teaching: "Farm" by Ned Halley; "Plant" by David Burnie; and "Tree" by David Burnie. Children love these books, as do I!

## Format

This is an invitation in a story format - not really a play, as there is no plot progression or character development. The idea is to showcase some scriptural truths in the context of a garden and to develop a message of spiritual growth. The idea of growing, bearing fruit - all as part of God's plan should be graphically illustrated by the use of decorative flowers, vines and Biblical examples. The stage can be bordered on three sides by a series of 1 inch PVC piping, anchored on 1 X 6 boards, and put together in a framework on which vines and flowers can be made to "grow" by means of a series of fishing lines which can be pulled up in the opening scene. The vertical pipes have holes in them to receive the stems of the flowers. Thus a seemingly bare stage will become a garden during the opening number. A well masks the puppet stage, set to the right, and the chorus carries a number of garden-type implements as they assemble - watering can, rake, hoe, trowel, etc. The Gardener's script station is a music stand masked by a foamcore cutout birdbath. When Colonel O'Wheat appears, this cutout is covered by a cutout of a classical stack of wheat sheaves.

## List of Props

Gardener's basket
Eden signs - NO LOITERING; GET THEE HENCE
large plastic red apple
hoe, rake, trowel, watering can
sunburst
skeletal umbrella for 100 fold fruit
seed pouch for sower
large papier mache rock
short branches for "Cedars"
styrofoam peanuts - Manna
large selection of artificial flowers, vines, fruits
string of cutout gold figs
birdbath screen
wheat sheaves screen
6 signs for fig parable: BE FRUITFUL; BE SUCCESSFUL; BE USEFUL;
BE LOVE-FUL; BE GRATEFUL; BE CAREFUL
Bible panel
Gardening Guide panel
3 puppets

## COME TO THE GARDEN

### Cast:

| | |
|---|---|
| THE GARDENER | Our guide from Eden to Gethsemane |
| THE SERPENT | Tempter in the Garden of Eden |
| ROSE BLOOM | Gardening consultant |
| H. BASIL CORIANDER | "Herb" - another consultant |
| THE FOUR SEEDS | Basic unit growth experts |
| THE SOWER | Of the parable |
| SEEDS, SUN, BIRDS, THORNS | Other parable characters |
| THE CEDARS | Of Lebanon fame |
| COL. O'WHEAT | Ancient crop expert |
| PROF. IVY LAVINE | Botanical expert on figs |
| THE FIG TREE | Silent witness of the parable |
| THE ANGELS | Manna scatterers |
| MOSES & AARON | Celebrity endorsers |

Plus chorus of gardeners, parable people, Israelites and botanists

### Musical Numbers:

| | |
|---|---|
| INTRO & OVERTURE | Violin & piano, guitar |
| LIFE BEGAN IN A GARDEN | The Gardener & chorus |
| COME TO THE GARDEN | Chorus |
| I'M A SEED | The Four Seeds |
| THE CEDARS OF LEBANON | Themselves |
| THE STORY OF WHEAT | Col. O'Wheat |
| PARABLE OF THE FIG TREE | Prof. LaVine, the Gardener & chorus |
| WHAT IS IT? | Moses, Aaron & Israelites |
| THE GARDEN OF GOD | The Gardener & chorus |
| THERE IS A TIME | The Gardener |
| JESUS IS MY GARDEN | All |

Opening chorus with the Gardener(r.)

The Manna angels

How to bring forth fruit
"a hundred fold"

*The stage is empty and dark. A framework of green PVC piping rims the stage. To the right is a "wishing" well which screens a puppet stage. A music stand is just to the left of this. A solo violin is heard with the melody of "Come to the Garden." At the last note of this, the piano seamlessly picks up and begins the overture. As the music develops, the lights come up. The Gardener enters followed by the other children. She is dressed in bib overalls, with a straw sun hat and white gardening gloves. Then the children enter down the center aisle and take their places as a chorus on the stage. They are in three rows on stage left. At the end of the Overture, the Gardener begins her song.*

**THE GARDENER** (*sings*)
LIFE BEGAN IN A GARDEN
A GARDEN OF GOD'S OWN PLAN
AND FROM A TOMB IN A GARDEN
EVERLASTING LIFE BEGAN.

**CHORUS**
LIFE BEGAN IN A GARDEN
A GARDEN OF GOD'S OWN PLAN
AND FROM A TOMB IN A GARDEN
EVERLASTING LIFE BEGAN

**GARDENER**
A GARDEN IS BEAUTY AND BOUNTY
A GARDEN PUTS ON QUITE A SHOW;
BUT A GARDEN IS ALSO A LESSON:
ON HOW TO TAKE ROOT
AND HOW TO BEAR FRUIT
AND MOST OF ALL...
HOW TO GROW.

**CHORUS**
A GARDEN IS BEAUTY AND BOUNTY
A GARDEN PUTS ON QUITE A SHOW;
BUT A GARDEN IS ALSO A LESSON:
ON HOW TO TAKE ROOT
AND HOW TO BEAR FRUIT
AND MOST OF ALL...
HOW TO GROW.

**GARDENER**
LIFE BEGAN IN A GARDEN.

*At the end of the song, the chorus moves to positions around the rim, under the framework. The Gardener moves to the music stand and puts the birdbath cutout in front of it as a screen. As the Gardener speaks, the chorus raises flowers and vines on strings and the frame is a garden.*

**GARDENER**

A garden...
What does it do?
Well, it sure can teach us about growth!

But there's a lot more to a garden:
For one thing, a garden is defined -
Usually by a wall, a fence, or a hedge.
So it's protected and cared for.

But a garden doesn't just happen...
It's planned.
What's there is there by design.

In the story of creation,
Genesis tells us that right after He made man,
God planted a garden... for man.

It was God's provision.
It was God's plan.
And even when man fell,
There was a provision -
The Tree of Life -
Representing God's way for man to come back...
Into His fellowship...
And into His garden.

God's plan started with Adam,
In the Garden of Eden...
And was fulfilled by Jesus
In the Garden of Gethsemane...
And in the garden of the empty tomb.

Our garden wants to tell you about all that.

*By now, all the flowers, fruits and vines are in place on the vertical poles and along the top horizontal poles. The well has been decorated with flowers at its base. Now, the chorus resumes its place in three rows to the left front. The music begins.*

**CHORUS**

THERE IS PEACE
THERE IS REST
THERE IS ALL OF GOD'S BEST
WHEN YOU COME,
WON'T YOU COME
TO THE GARDEN.

FROM THE SEED
THAT HE'LL SOW
COME AND LET YOURSELF GROW
WHEN YOU COME,
WON'T YOU COME
TO THE GARDEN.

**GARDENER**

NOW SOME COME FOR COMFORT,
AND SOME FOR COMMUNING;
SOME HOPE TO BLOSSOM,
BUT FIRST NEED A PRUNING!

**CHORUS**

THERE IS HOPE
IN THIS EARTH
THERE IS LIFE AND RE-BIRTH
AND FOR ALL OF YOUR SINS
THERE'S A PARDON

BY HIS GRACE YOU BECOME
AN ETERNAL GREEN THUMB
WHEN YOU COME,
WON'T YOU COME
TO THE GARDEN.

*The chorus exits to the sides - half to each. Focus now shifts to the Gardener and to the well, where a light comes on from the interior.*

**GARDENER**

I am the Gardener; I plant and I work here;
To weed out the thorns
And the pests that may lurk here:
And just so this tech talk
Won't make you at all tense;
We've called in a couple
Of garden consultants!

The first is Rose Bloom
And she is superb...

*Up from the well comes a puppet, Rose Bloom, who bows to the Gardener.*

**GARDENER**

...and H. Basil Coriander...

*Up from the well comes the second puppet,*

**HERB**

...call me "Herb."
A garden is hope, sprouting promises...
For even the most doubting of Thomases.

**ROSE**

At its greenest and growing-est and blossom-est,
A garden shows God at His awesome-est!

**HERB**

Admission is free to this botany;
You'll just need some faith... if you've got any.

*The Gardener starts to work her way, watering, off to exit at stage left.*

**HERB**

Come, follow the path from Eden to Gethsemane
You'll find some friends... and one enemy.

**ROSE**

Now with tools and seeds, and watering can,
We'll start where God did -
With a plan!

**HERB**

Right after creation, do I hear you all ask?
What was the Lord's very first task?

**ROSE**

He planted a garden, says Genesis two
With rivers, and trees... and you-know-who.

**HERB**

And into this garden, says the writer of Genesis,
Along comes mankind's continuing nemesis.

**ROSE**

Bringing temptation and lies to the premises.

*The puppets drop down into the well, as the Gardener re-enters, still watering or working with her rake... as she does so, she sees that a very slick character has entered and is now leaning up against the edge of the well. This is the Serpent, and he is casually tossing an apple up and catching it.*

**GARDENER**

Who are you?

**SERPENT**

Oh... I'm just... a serpent.

**GARDENER**

Wait a minute! Serpents are supposed to be crawling around down on the ground.

**SERPENT**

That's **after**... you're getting ahead of the story!

**GARDENER**

What are you doing here?

**SERPENT**

I'm a salesman.

**GARDENER**

and what are you selling?

**SERPENT**

Apple futures... and I intend to make a killing!. I just need to get someone to bite...
Can I tempt you?

**GARDENER**

I don't have time... here, help me with these.

*The Gardener has picked up two signs which she holds out to him, so the audience can see them: one says: NO LOITERING and the other says: GET THEE HENCE. The Serpent now sees this and turns to go, tossing his apple up and catching it. He calls back, as he exits..*

**SERPENT**

I'll be back. My next appearance is in the Book of Job.

**GARDENER**

I'm glad he's gone... he certainly has no place in this garden... But here's someone who does. Now, when you're talking about growth, you'd better start at the beginning - with the basic unit.

*The Gardener indicates the Four Seeds who enter as she leaves. The Seeds line up as their music begins.*

**SEEDS**

I'M A SEED
AND I HAVE INSIDE OF ME
THE POWER I NEED;
TO GROW UP AND BE
A FLOWER OR TREE
OR WHATEVER IT IS GOD HAS PLANNED FOR ME
BOUND TO SUCCEED
AS A SEED

I'M A SEED
AND MY SPROUT-ABILITY
HAS BEEN GUARANTEED
JUST GIVE ME GOOD GROUND
WITH NO BIRDS AROUND
AND NOT ANYWHERE NEAR WHERE THE THORNS ARE FOUND
THAT IS MY CREED
AS A SEED.

WE MAY SEEM LIFELESS AND DRIED UP
BUT WE REMAIN
READY TO SPRING INTO ACTION
AT THE FIRST RAY OF SUN
AND THE FIRST DROP OF RAIN
YES, INDEED...

I'M A SEED
AND IT WOULD BE SCRIPTURAL
TO FOLLOW MY LEAD;
EVERYONE NEEDS
THE POWER AND DETERMINATION
AND OF COURSE, THE GERMINATION
OF SEEDS LIKE ME...
AND ME... AND ME...AND ME... AND THEM!

*They indicate a bunch of smaller seeds who have come on at the right - along with a Sower, who is equipped with a seed pouch. At the same time, the Gardener has re-entered with a Bible panel. As she reads, the music of the song continues underneath as the action of the parable unfolds. A large papier mache "rock" has been placed at the center.*

**GARDENER**

Behold, a sower
Went out to sow his seed...

*In a choreographed sequence the sower starts across the stage in front of the Gardener. He is accompanied by two small "seeds." He sows them by spinning them off as he walks; they twirl to a stop, just left of center, and squat down.*

**GARDENER**

And as he sowed, some fell by the wayside;
And the birds of the air devoured them.

*Two "birds" come on and carry off the two protesting seeds - exit left. The Sower now starts on from the left and crosses to the right, accompanied as before by the two Seeds.*

**GARDENER**

Some fell on rocks, where
They did not have much earth...

*The Sower twirls the two seeds to a halt by the large rock - he continues on across to the right side.*

**GARDENER**

And when the sun was up, they were scorched...

*A child holding a large sunburst runs on and "scorches" the two seeds; they run off to the right, holding their rears.*

**GARDENER**

...and some fell among thorns;
and the thorns sprang up and choked them.

*The Sower now crosses again towards the left, twirling the two seeds to a halt by the rock. Hiding behind the rock is a "thorn" - a spiny costumed elf who reaches for the seeds as if to choke them.*

**GARDENER**

But others fell on good ground;
Sprang up and yielded a crop...
A hundred fold.

*Again, the sower crosses and twirls the two seeds to a halt at a green spot in front of the rock. A skeletal umbrella has been placed beside the green carpet piece; on cue, one of the seeds picks up the umbrella and presses the "open" button, at which, the frame expands revealing a "crop" of little apples that dangle down.*

**GARDENER**

He who has ears to hear, let him hear!

*The four seeds who had moved to the rear during this pantomime, now move forward to their singing position as the background music ends; the tempo picks up as all sing the last stanza of the Seed song:*

**ALL**

I'M A SEED
AND IT WOULD BE SCRIPTURAL
TO FOLLOW MY LEAD...
EVERYONE NEEDS,
THE POWER AND DETERMINATION -
AND , OF COURSE, THE GERMINATION
A SEEDS LIKE ME...
...AND ME...AND ME...AND ME...
AND... US!

*The seeds and the players exit as the Gardener goes back to her station by the well.*

**GARDENER**

The seed is really like life itself - a cycle of sprouting and growing and bearing fruit... and re-planting... and even dying. Jesus said He was like a seed... going into the ground and dying, but in so doing, bringing forth much fruit.

*The puppet, Rose and Herb come up from inside the well.*

**ROSE**

And you can't tell - looking at a seed - what it might become. It could grow into a Pomegranate or Poison Ivy; watermelon or... water lilies; a pine tree or a pineapple; crabgrass or crabapple...

**HERB**

Remind me not to use **<u>your</u>** seed catalogue!

**ROSE**

Well, the point is that from a tiny seed, a great and glorious thing could grow. Like a Cedar of Lebanon .... tall, straight, tough, majestic...

**HERB**

... and gone. There aren't any left!

**ROSE**

But we have some right here - who are going to give us their whole drill... like how they helped build Solomon's temple. King Hiram of Tyre sold the cedars to Solomon for 20,000 measures of wheat and oil... and it took 80,000 men to bring them all out!

**HERB**

Think what he could have saved if he'd just gotten the seeds... instead of the cedars!

**ROSE**

Enough! Time to log on... to the cedars.

*The two puppets drop down as the introductory music begins. Four "Cedars" march on. They are dressed with sprigs of leaves on them and are carrying some tree branches in each hand. They first line up to sing their song; then perform a drill with exaggerated precision motions as the music continues.*

**CEDARS**

WE ARE THE CEDARS OF LEBANON
HOLDING UP THE TEMPLE OF SOLOMON
PRIZED FOR OUR SIZE AND BOTANICAL BRAWN;
WE ARE THE TREE THAT GOES ON AND ON.

CAUSE WE ARE NOT
SUBJECT TO ROT,
OR TERMITE PLOT;
WHAT WE HAVE GOT
IS LONGEVITY... NOT BREVITY

*now they perform their drill as the music continues. When they finish, they are lined up in their beginning position, as the Gardener re-renters and sings:*

**GARDENER**

BUT IF YOU'RE A READER OF SECOND CHRON,
YOU KNOW WHAT THE LEADER OF BABYLON
DID TO THE CEDAR OF LEBANON...
AND TO THE TEMPLE OF SOLOMON
TIMBERRRRR.!

*At the shout of "Timberrrr" the cedars all fall down. As the Gardener returns to her station, the Cedars exit.*

**GARDENER**

Historical, archeological and Biblical evidence tells us that there is one crop that's been grown for over 9,000 years: WHEAT - very important in the Bible.

*The Gardener reaches behind the puppet stage (well) and gets the wheat sheaves screen which she places in front of the birdbath cutout. She then exits as Rose and Herb re-appear in the well.*

**HERB**

While we are still in military formation, it might be appropriate to bring out our own field officer - Colonel O'Wheat.

**ROSE**

...to tell you all the Story of Wheat.

**HERB**

Did you know that there's a species of wheat called Amaranthus - which has not only a flower, but its spinach-like leaves have medicinal properties; it is used as a herb and as an ornamental... and its seeds or kernels are ground into what is called Inca Wheat.

**ROSE**

Sounds like an all-purpose flower. But here's our very own kernel to sift through the whole wheat story for you.

*Colonel O'Wheat, in full military regalia, marches in as the music begins. He takes his place behind the sheaves as the chorus comes on and lines up to the left. The Colonel salutes.*

**HERB**

How did **he** get to be a Colonel?

**ROSE**

The same way General Mills got to be a Major producer – self promotion. He's one of the Puffed Wheats!

**HERB**

Enough.. with the wheat jokes - this is a serious presentation.

**ROSE**

Then what are **we** doing here?

*The puppets drop down into the well, as the chorus sings:*

**CHORUS**

THERE IS GLORY IN THE STORY OF WHEAT;
IT IS TOPS AMONG THE CROPS WE EAT;
IT'S THE GRAIN OF TRUTH
BRINGING BOAZ TO RUTH;
THERE IS GLORY IN THE STORY OF WHEAT...
WE REPEAT
THERE IS GLORY IN THE STORY
GLORY IN THE STORY... OF WHEAT.

**COLONEL** *(recites)*

Allow me to introduce myself: I am Colonel O'Wheat
With the chronicle of my family tree
From the Biblical elite.

We wheats crop up in arable land,
In parable and, in scriptural allegory
From Egypt to Canaan, and then again in
King Solomon's territory.

Now wheat was one of the seven crops -
The props of the Canaan economy;
The other six - the harvested picks -
Are listed in Deuteronomy.

There, chapter eight lists barley and date,
Olive and pomegranate;
Fig and vine – all God's design
For this special part of the planet.

Wherever hungry people are fed,
You'll find the wheats (most well-bred),
And ready to rise and meet
Any challenge to bear.. Be it famine or tare..
So there.. Is the stand of wheat.

**CHORUS**

THERE IS GLORY IN THE STORY OF WHEAT
IT IS TOPS AMONG THE CROPS WE EAT;
IT'S THE GRAIN OF TRUTH
BRINGING BOAZ TO RUTH
THERE IS GLORY IN THE STORY OF WHEAT

WE REPEAT
THERE IS GLORY IN THE STORY
GLORY IN THE STORY
GLORY IN THE STORY.. OF WHEAT.

**COLONEL**

Remember when Samson sought revenge
When the Philistines started to cheat;
His clever campaign, went against their grain
As his foxes fired their wheat.

And David to purchase the temple site
Where the angel put sword at his feet;
He paid without pressure, Ornan the thresher
Of all of the Jebusite wheat.

And when King Solomon sought to acquire
The temple's cedars from Hiram of Tyre;
This prime supplier (Hiram of Tyre)
Promptly wrote a receipt
To Solomon (buyer) an amount no higher
Than 200,000 bushels of wheat.

They sow, they grow, they winnow, they thresh;
They mill, they grind, they store...
Joseph, Gideon, Boaz and more...
Wheat by the omer, the ephah, the kor..

So when the Hebrews say: "B'tay avon"
(Which would probably mean something between,
"Let's eat" and "bon appetite")
The grain that graced the kosher terrain
Was a strain of the family of WHEAT.

**CHORUS**

THERE IS GLORY IN THE STORY OF WHEAT
IT IS TOPS AMONG THE CROPS WE EAT;
IT'S THE GRAIN OF TRUTH
BRINGING BOAZ TO RUTH;
THERE IS GLORY IN THE STORY OF WHEAT;
WE REPEAT:
THERE IS GLORY IN THE STORY
GLORY IN THE STORY
GLORY IN THE STORY.. OF WHEAT.

**COLONEL**

Now here.. Seedy characters enter the scene,
(We wheats have had our shares)
For instance, those fraudulent counterfeits,
The seedy, weedy TARES.

They peopled a parable, you'll recall
Catching the farmer unawares;
Disguised as wheat (which is no mean feat)
The strangled and tangled our roots in their snares.

But a happier ending quoth the Lord;
The tares are burned, the wheat is stored;
And the harvest time is sweet;
From the First Fruit's praise.. To Sukkot's days
We celebrate the wheat.

Yes, with consummate skill, we've been through the mill
With our bran and our germ, we're refined;
And I don't mean to gloat over rye, corn or oat,
But I am inclined to repeat:
That for nine thousand years
To eyes, hearts and ears,
The symbol of harvest... is WHEAT!

**CHORUS**

THERE IS GLORY IN THE STORY OF WHEAT
IT IS TOPS AMONG THE CROPS WE EAT;
IT'S THE GRAIN OF TRUTH BRINGING BOAZ TO RUTH
THERE IS GLORY IN THE STORY OF WHEAT.
WE REPEAT:
THERE IS GLORY IN THE STORY
GLORY IN THE STORY
GLORY IN THE STORY... OF WHEAT!

*The chorus marches off to the left; the Colonel salutes, then marches back, takes the sheaves cutout and marches off. The Gardener re-enters and takes her position as the puppets come back up.*

**ROSE**

Well, I vote for putting Boaz' picture on the Wheaties box - he was an ancestor of champions!

**HERB**

Right.... if it hadn't been for Boaz' wheat field, he might never have met and married Ruth...

**ROSE**

...and there would have been no Obed, the father of Jesse... who was the father of King David.

**GARDENER**

All because of a wheatfield in, of all places, Bethlehem. Quite a harvest!
... and speaking of harvests - there was nothing as productive as the fig tree. It produced fruit ten months out of every year... and would grow almost anywhere.

**ROSE**

The fig was called the "first fruit of summer."

**HERB**

It was also the source of honey - which is why Israel is called the land of milk and honey.

**ROSE**

Don't tell the bees. Next, you'll be telling me the milk came from coconuts!

**GARDENER**

Back to fig trees – growers planted them in their vineyards as insurance – in case the grape crop failed, they knew they could count on the fig tree to come through. Now you guys go get the Professor...

*The puppets drop down, as the Gardener continues.*

**GARDENER**

We need some scholarly help here to set the stage for a most remarkable citizen of our garden - the fig tree. So we've asked Professor Ivy LaVine to give us her famous fig lecture. Ivy?? Professor LaVine???

*The Gardener goes off calling as puppet Ivy LaVine (dressed appropriately) comes up from the well. She is wearing a white mortarboard, glasses and white jacket, plus a wreath of ivy, grape earrings and other similar adornments.*

**IVY** *(recites)*

The fig tree has every right to be proud;
In orchards and vineyards, it stands out from the crowd;
Its prolific nature has us botanists wowed...
Ah yes, the fig tree:

It’s more than viable
It’s reliable;
And mentioned 50 times in the Bible.

For starters, consider the fig tree’s leaves,
Providing the cool shade the gardener receives;
And the wardrobe that once was Adam’s and Eve’s
Ah yes, the fig tree:
Not only beautiful
But dutiful
And three times a year so fruit-iful

When King Hezekiah was with boils so sick;
What natural medicine did Isaiah pick?
A compress of figs would soon do the trick
Ah yes, the fig tree:
Always so willin’
To try and fill in
The gap that existed before penicillin.

But I digress
Let me address
The fig tree’s prowess
In land not so arable
There’s the point of the parable!
Ah yes, the fig tree!

*The fig tree enters (in tan sweatsuit covered with leaves) The chorus follows quickly as the Gardener re-enters, much like a troubadour to sing the Parable. Ivy watches, waiting for her line in the song’s chorus.*

**GARDENER** *(sings)*
HEAR THE PARABLE OF THE FIG TREE
JESUS TOLD IN LUKE THIRTEEN
I THINK YOU WILL SEE
YOU CAN LEARN FROM A TREE
AND ITS FIG PRODUCTIVITY:
(AND THAT’S THE KEY - FIG PRODUCTIVITY)

**CHORUS**
OH, IT TAKES THREE YEARS FOR A FIG TREE
TO HAVE ANY FIGS APPEAR;
BUT BEFORE IT IS DONE
YOU CAN FIGURE ON A TON
OF FIGS PER TREE, PER YEAR

**IVY**

FIGURATIVELY SPEAKING, IT'S ABUNDANTLY CLEAR
YOU CAN FIGURE ON FIGS RIGHT UP TO HERE.

**GARDENER**

NOW A CERTAIN MAN HAD A FIG TREE
PLANTED IN HIS VINEYARD WHEN
HE CAME IN PURSUIT
OF ITS VERY FIRST FRUIT
AND HE FOUND NONE THERE TO COMPUTE
(FROM TWIG TO ROOT - NOT A FIG THERE TO COMPUTE)

**CHORUS**

OH, IT TAKES THREE YEARS FOR A FIG TREE
TO HAVE ANY FIGS APPEAR
BUT BEFORE IT IS DONE
YOU CAN FIGURE ON A TON
OF FIGS PER TREE, PER YEAR

**IVY**

FIGURATIVELY SPEAKING IT'S ABUNDANTLY CLEAR
YOU CAN FIGURE ON FIGS RIGHT UP TO HERE.

**GARDENER**

THEN THE MASTER COMPLAINED TO THE GARDENER:
"I HAVE WAITED THREE LONG YEARS;
AND A FIG CAN'T BE FOUND
GO AHEAD, CUT IT DOWN
IT IS ONLY USING UP GROUND.
I NEED THE GROUND; THIS TREE IS FIREPLACE BOUND."

**CHORUS**

OH, IT TAKES THREE YEARS FOR A FIG TREE
TO HAVE ANY FIGS APPEAR
BUT BEFORE IT IS DONE
YOU CAN FIGURE ON A TON
OF FIGS PER TREE, PER YEAR.

**IVY**

FIGURATIVELY SPEAKING, IT'S ABUNDANTLY CLEAR
YOU CAN FIGURE ON FIGS RIGHT UP TO HERE.

**GARDENER**

BUT THE GARDENER REPLIED TO THE MASTER:
"WHY NOT GIVE IT ONE MORE CHANCE?
I'LL GIVE IT MORE CARE
FERTILIZER TO SPARE;
THEN IT BETTER HAVE FIGS TO BEAR!"

**FIG TREE**

AND I'M AWARE.. HIS AX IS JUST OVER THERE!

**CHORUS**

OH, IT TAKES THREE YEARS FOR A FIG TREE
TO HAVE ANY FIGS APPEAR
BUT BEFORE IT IS DONE
YOU CAN FIGURE ON A TON
OF FIGS PER TREE, PER YEAR.

**IVY**

FIGURATIVELY SPEAKING, IT'S ABUNDANTLY CLEAR
YOU CAN FIGURE ON FIGS RIGHT UP TO HERE!

**GARDENER**

Now what does this parable tell us?

**ROSE**

That we ought to give a fig for growth?

**GARDENER**

Yes, but it's clear, there are six lessons here
In the parable these verses quoth.
... and what are those lessons?

*Each time one of the puppets gives one of the lessons, a sign holder appears with the appropriate sign and lines up so that all six can fit with their signs held in front of them.*

**ROSE**

First... when it's time to bear fruit, you should bear it;
Whether you're a fig tree, a person or carrot!

*Sign holder with sign: BE FRUITFUL, marches to far left.*

**HERB**

Second.. Uselessness invites disaster;
In his kingdom, in His church, in His pasture.

*Sign holder with sign: BE USEFUL, marches next to the first one.*

**ROSE**

Third... If you're taking much more than you're giving
You're just using space while you're living.

*Sign holder with sign: BE LOVE-FUL, marches to join others.*

**HERB**

Fourth.. And this is the most consequential:
We must live up to our potential!

*Sign holder with sign: BE SUCCESSFUL, marches to join others.*

**ROSE**

Fifth... We've a champion who loves and oversees us
And will always plead our case - that's Jesus!

*Sign holder with sign: BE GRATEFUL, marches to join the others*

**HERB**

Sixth.. There's a limit to even God's patience;
We must answer his call and expectations.

*Sign holder with sign: BE CAREFUL, goes to join the others*

**GARDENER** *(sings)*

THAT'S THE PARABLE OF THE FIG TREE
JESUS TOLD IN LUKE THIRTEEN
NOW YOU CAN SEE
WHAT'S TAUGHT BY THAT TREE
'BOUT FIG PRODUCTIVITY.

**ALL** *(slowly)*

FIG PRODUCTIVITY!

*As all sing these last two words, the two angels come on the decorate the Fig Tree with a string of gold figs. Then the chorus and players exit. The Gardener has returned to her station.*

**GARDENER**

As we listen to the lessons of the fig tree
We should learn and discern - or both
Let's review what we've heard
From the garden and the Word
About the importance of growth

**HERB**

Well, the seeds showed that timing and conditions are treasured;

**ROSE**

The cedars, while impressive, got Nebuchadnezzar-ed!

**HERB**

And the Colonel saluted wheat as a new category...

**ROSE**

Of botanical marvel that brought glory to the story;

**HERB**

Though the figs were figments, the tree could be saved...

**ROSE**

Bearing timely fruit was all that was craved.

**GARDENER**

That's pretty good. Now remember what we said about a garden representing God's provision? Well, here's a scene about God's provision for the children of Israel when they were in the desert... and there was nothing to eat. In modern terms, this is a story about a new product introduction... to a very skeptical market. This is a commercial for trusting God - a singing commercial! And it's about a kind of growth we haven't seen before – miraculous growth. It's in Exodus, chapter 16 – the story of MANNA.

**HERB**

A word that means: "what is it?"

**ROSE**

When you're hungry, who cares?

**HERB**

Well, it depends on the seasons.

**ROSE**

Spring, summer or fall?

**HERB**

No, silly... salt, pepper, garlic and mustard!

**GARDENER**

Now in our little "what might have been" scene... we need something else. Like most new product introductions, it's good to have celebrity endorsements. In the case of Manna, Moses and Aaron are the obvious choices.

*The Gardener exits as the "orchestra" takes up a three quarter beat - to which two little angels enter with white bags. As the beat continues, they begin to scatter little white bits of "manna."*

*As the angels cross the stage scattering these, they exit to the left as the chorus, dressed as Israelites, with white desert headdresses. As they come on, they see the manna and each picks up a piece, looks at it quizzically, and mime comments to each other. Then on comes the Gardener and one other, similarly dressed. This is Moses and Aaron, who begin to sing:*

**MOSES/AARON**

IT'S SO LIGHT AND IT'S WHITE
AND IT COMES IN THE NIGHT;
WHAT IS IT? WHAT IS IT?
IT'S MANNA!

IT'S SO GRAND; SO IT'S BLAND
IT'S NOT FROZEN OR CANNED;
WHAT IS IT? WHAT IS IT?
IT'S MANNA!

**CHORUS**

IT'S MANNA!
OUR DAILY DELIVERY FROM HEAVEN
IT'S MANNA
NOT BAD IF YOU ADD
A PINCH OR A TAD.....
OF PEPPER AND SALT...
ONIONS AND GARLIC... AND LEAVEN.

**MOSES/AARON**

NOTICE THAT, IT'S BEGAT
WITH HIGH FIBER, LOW FAT
WHAT IS IT? WHAT IS IT?
IT'S MANNA.

NO ONE SHOPS OR GROWS CROPS
FOR THE RIGHT AMOUNT DROPS;
WHAT IS IT? WHAT IS IT?
IT'S MANNA.

**CHORUS**

IT'S MANNA
OUR DAILY DELIVERY FROM HEAVEN
IT'S MANNA
NOT BAD IF YOU ADD
A PINCH OR A TAD...
OF ONIONS AND GARLIC AND LEAVEN.

*At a cue from the "orchestra," Professor Ivy LaVine pops up from the well.*

**IVY**

BUT YOU SHOULD BE CAREFUL TO PLAN A...
MENU THAT TAKES ALL YOUR MANNA;
IF YOU STORE IT IN YOUR CABANA...
IT'LL ROT AND HAVE WORMS BY MANANA!

**MOSES/AARON**

IN THIS BIZ, IT'S A WHIZ
BECAUSE IT'S ALL THERE IS;
WHAT IS IT? WHAT IS IT?
IT'S MANNA.

THERE'S NO WASTE, (THERE'S NO TASTE)
BUT WE'RE BLESSED AND WE'RE GRACED
BY ITS VISIT; WHAT IS IT?
IT'S MANNA.

**CHORUS**

IT'S MANNA
OUR DAILY DELIVERY FROM HEAVEN
IT'S MANNA
NOT BAD IF YOU ADD
A PINCH OR A TAD
OF ONIONS AND GARLIC AND LEAVEN.

**MOSES/AARON**

IT'S COMPLETE - NOT TOO SWEET
AND IT'S NOT TOUGH LIKE MEAT
WHAT IS IT? WHAT IS IT?
IT'S MANNA.

HAVE NO FEARS, IT APPEARS
FOR THE NEXT FORTY YEARS
WHAT IS IT? WHAT IS IT?
IT'S MANNA

**CHORUS**

IT'S MANNA
OUR DAILY DELIVERY FROM HEAVEN
IT'S MANNA
NOT BAD IF YOU ADD
A PINCH OR A TAD
OF ONIONS AND GARLIC AND LEAVEN

**IVY**

YOU WON'T FIND MIRACULOUS MANNA
GROWING IN MAINE OR MONTANA
THEY GET NOTHING LIKE THIS FROM NIRVANA
IT'S UNIQUE AS A LEEK OR BANANA!

**CHORUS**

IT'S MANNA
OUR DAILY DELIVERY FROM HEAVEN
IT'S MANNA
NOT BAD IF YOU ADD
A PINCH OR A TAD
OF ONIONS AND GARLIC.....

*Moses and Aaron take over for an extended finish*

**MOSES/AARON**

...AND SHALLOTS AND CAPERS...
AND MUSTARD AND BASIL...
AND LEMON AND HONEY..
TABASCO AND CREAM CHEESE.

**ALL**

AND LEAVEN!!!

*The chorus and Moses and Aaron all exit as Rose and Herb come up in the well.*

**ROSE**

And I'll bet that you thought Miracle Gro was just about lawns and tomatoes!

**HERB**

I'll have you know that the Bible says manna was like Coriander seed – one of MY relatives.

**ROSE**

Yeah... "what is it?" would apply to your relatives!

**HERB**

Enough... here comes our Gardener with an important lesson.

*The Gardener, back in her costume, comes back on holding a panel that reads: "Gardening Guide." She comes to center stage as the chorus comes back on to their chorus position.*

**GARDENER** (*sings*)

PAGE SEVENTY THREE OF MY GARDENING GUIDE
TELLS ME ALL THAT I NEED
TO GET A FLOWER OR FRUIT
FROM EACH PLANT OR SHOOT;
OR TO GROW A TREE FROM A SEED...
    IT SAYS:
    YOU NEED SUN
    AND JUST ENOUGH RAIN
    AND LOTS OF LOVING CARE...

NOW THAT SOUNDS FAMILIAR
I'VE READ THAT SOMEWHERE
GROWTH IS A FACTOR OF SUN, RAIN AND CARE...
    THREE BASIC TOOLS
    AND THREE BASIC RULES:
    YOU'VE GOTTA HAVE SUNLIGHT
    WATER AND CARE.

**GARDENER**

WHERE HAVE I READ THAT?
SUNLIGHT AND RAIN
AND TENDER LOVING CARE....

Of course! It's the gardener's gospel, that growers count on...

IT'S ALL THERE IN MATTHEW
MARK, LUKE AND JOHN.

**CHORUS**

IT'S ALL THERE IN MATTHEW
MARK, LUKE AND JOHN!

OH IT TAKES LIGHT;
IT TAKES LOVE,
AND IT TAKES LIVING WATER
TO BLOOM IN THE GARDEN OF GOD;
SO LET THERE BE LIGHT, LOVE
AND A WELL OF LIVING WATER
AND I'LL GROW WITH THE FLOW
IN THE GARDEN OF GOD.

GARDEN OF GOD
GARDEN OF GOD
I'M GOING TO BE GROWING
IN THE GARDEN OF GOD

**GARDENER**

I'VE GOT THE SEED OF FAITH
THAT'S PLANTED BY HIS GRACE
THE LIGHT OF JESUS SHINES IN ME
AND, AS FOR LOVE, SUCH LOVE,
A SHOWER FROM ABOVE
HIS WORD WILL WASH AND WATER;
GLORY BE!

**CHORUS**

OH, IT TAKE LIGHT
IT TAKES LOVE
AND IT TAKES .LIVING WATER
TO BLOOM IN THE GARDEN OF GOD
SO LET THERE BE LIGHT, LOVE
AND A WELL OF LIVING WATER
AND I'LL GROW WITH THE FLOW
IN THE GARDEN OF GOD

GARDEN OF GOD
GARDEN OF GOD
I'M GOING TO BE GROWING
IN THE GARDEN OF GOD

**GARDENER**

I'M GROWING EVERY DAY
MY ROOTS ARE IN HIS WORD
THE LIGHT OF JESUS HELPS ME SEE
THAT MY NEW LIFE BEGINS
HE'S PRUNED AWAY MY SINS
I'M BRANCHING OUT TO FRUITFUL...
GLORY BE!

**CHORUS**

OH, IT TAKE LIGHT
IT TAKES LOVE
AND IT TAKES LIVING WATER
TO BLOOM IN THE GARDEN OF GOD
SO LET THERE BE LIGHT, LOVE
AND A WELL OF LIVING WATER
AND I'LL GROW WITH THE FLOW
IN THE GARDEN OF GOD

GARDEN OF GOD
GARDEN OF GOD
I'M GOING TO BE GROWING
IN THE GARDEN OF GOD.

**GARDENER**

WHEN HARVEST TIME IS NEAR
I'M HEAVY ON THE VINE
THE LIGHT OF JESUS BRIGHTENS ME
HE'S SHINED AWAY MY GLOOM
I'VE GONE FROM BUD TO BLOOM
I'VE RIPENED, GROWN AND BLOSSOMED...
GLORY BE!

**CHORUS**

OH, IT TAKES LIGHT
IT TAKES LOVE
AND IT TAKES LIVING WATER
TO BLOOM IN THE GARDEN OF GOD
SO LET THERE BE LIGHT, LOVE
AND A WELL OF LIVING WATER
AND I'LL GROW WITH THE FLOW
IN THE GARDEN OF GOD

GARDEN OF GOD
GARDEN OF GOD
I'M GOING TO BE GROWING
IN THE GARDEN OF GOD.

*The chorus exits and the Gardener goes back to her station. Herb and Rose are up.*

**ROSE**

"Grow with the flow" – I like that...and that's what I intend to do.

**HERB**

...and you don't need a consultant to grow in that garden. All you have to do is choose to plant yourself there.

**GARDENER**

Both Isaiah and Ezekiel spoke about the garden of God. Later, in the Garden of Gethsemane, Jesus made His choice - He prayed that God's will be done. And, as a result, a few days later, the tomb in another garden was empty!

**ROSE & HERB**

Hallelujah!!

**GARDENER**

And happily for all of us - we each have a choice... and a time to make it.

*She leaves her station and comes forward to the edge of the stage.*

**GARDENER** *(sings)*

TO EVERY THING, THERE IS A SEASON;
FOR EVERY PURPOSE, THERE IS A TIME:

A TIME TO PLANT, A TIME FOR GROWING
A TIME TO REAP, WHAT YOU'VE BEEN SOWING

FOR EVERY LIFE, THERE IS A REASON;
TO EVERY PERSON, A CHOICE SUBLIME:

A CHOICE FOR HOPE, A CHOICE FOR JESUS
IT'S TIME FOR HOPE, IT'S TIME FOR JESUS

We've made that choice... and we're so very glad we did. Won't you... won't you... Come to the garden?

*After a slight pause, the chorus re-enters and takes their places. In the song that follows, each soloist sings a chorus as a curtain call.*

**CHORUS**

JESUS IS MY GARDEN
WHERE I WANT TO GROW
SO I CAN SHARE THE LOVE AND CARE
THAT I HAVE COME TO TREASURE SO

**GARDENER**

MY GARDEN HAS SUCH WONDROUS THINGS
A WELL WHERE LIVING WATER SPRINGS
AND FRANKINCENSE AND MYRRH THAT BRINGS
GLORY TO THE KING OF KINGS

**THE SEEDS**

JESUS IS MY GARDEN
WHERE I WANT TO GROW
SO I CAN SHARE THE LOVE AND CARE
THAT I HAVE COME TO TREASURE SO

**GARDENER**

MY GARDEN HAS A MUSTARD SEED
THAT GREW WITH ALL DELIBERATE SPEED
A PLACE WHERE BIRDS NOW NEST AND FEED
THAT GROWN UP, FAITHFUL MUSTARD SEED

**COL. O'WHEAT**

JESUS IS MY GARDEN
WHERE I WANT TO GROW
SO I CAN SHARE THE LOVE AND CARE
THAT I HAVE COME TO TREASURE SO

**IVY**

CEDARS, HYSSOP, ROSE OF SHARON
ALMOND BUDS ON ROD OF AARON
FIG TREES THAT ARE NEVER BARREN
AMARANTH IS GROWING THEREIN

**ROSE & HERB**

JESUS IS MY GARDEN
WHERE I WANT TO GROW
SO I CAN SHARE THE LOVE AND CARE
THAT I HAVE COME TO TREASURE SO

**GARDENER**

MY GARDEN GROWS ON HOLY GROUND
WHERE TREES THAT CLAP THEIR HANDS ABOUND
WHERE THORNS THAT GROW IN CROWNS ARE FOUND
WHERE PALM LEAVES ALL "HOSANNA" SOUND!

**THE FIG TREE**

JESUS IS MY GARDEN
WHERE I WANT TO GROW
SO I CAN SHARE THE LOVE AND CARE
THAT I HAVE COME TO TREASURE SO

**GARDENER**

MY GARDEN IS A SAVIOR WHO'S
A TREE OF LIFE FOR ME TO CHOOSE
AN OFFER THAT I WON'T REFUSE
A HARVEST THAT IS ALL.... GOOD NEWS!

**ALL**

JESUS IS MY GARDEN
WHERE I WANT TO GROW
SO I CAN SHARE THE LOVE AND CARE
THAT I HAVE COME TO TREASURE SO

*As each solist sings a chorus, the Gardener hands them a rose. After the song and applause, the cast sings a reprise of COME TO THE GARDEN.*

# The Garden: Overture

Clark Tyler
*Arranged by Andrew Bell*

36
F
C♯dim7
F
Dm
C7
Vln.
Pno.
44
F
C
C
F
F
B♭
C
F
F
Swing
q=136
F
Pno.
50
F
C
Pno.
56
F
C
F
3
Pno.
61
F
C
G
C
C
Am
Pno.
66
Dm
G7
G7
C
C
F
Pno.

71
C6
G7
Dm
Em7
Dm
G7
G7
C
Pno.
77
C
G
C
q=90
rit.
Pno.
83
Pno.
90
Pno.
97
Swing feel
C
F
rit.
Pno.
102
F
C7
F
Dm
Pno.
106
F
3
C
C
Pno.

Straight Country Rhythm
110 F rit.
F C
Pno.
115 C7 F B♭ F C
Pno.
120 F B♭ F G7 C
rit.
Pno.
125 F B♭ F G7 C7 F F C
Pno.
130 C F F B♭ C F
rit.
Pno.

# Life Began In A Garden

Clark Tyler
*Arranged by Andrew Bell*

21
C7 F A7 Dm C7
Voice
gar-den puts on quite a show; but a gar-den is al-so a les son in how to take root and
Pno.
26
F C F Gm9/F F
Voice
how to bear fruit and most of all how to grow. Life be-gan in a gar-den.
F
Pno.

# Come To The Garden

Clark Tyler

31
A7
Dm7
C
Voice
life and re - birth and for all of your sins there's a par don. By His grace you'll be -
Pno.
38
F
C♯dim7
F
Dm
C7
Voice
come an e - ter - nal green thumb, when you come. won't you come to the gar - den.
Pno.

# I'm A Seed

Clark Tyler
Arranged by Andrew Bell

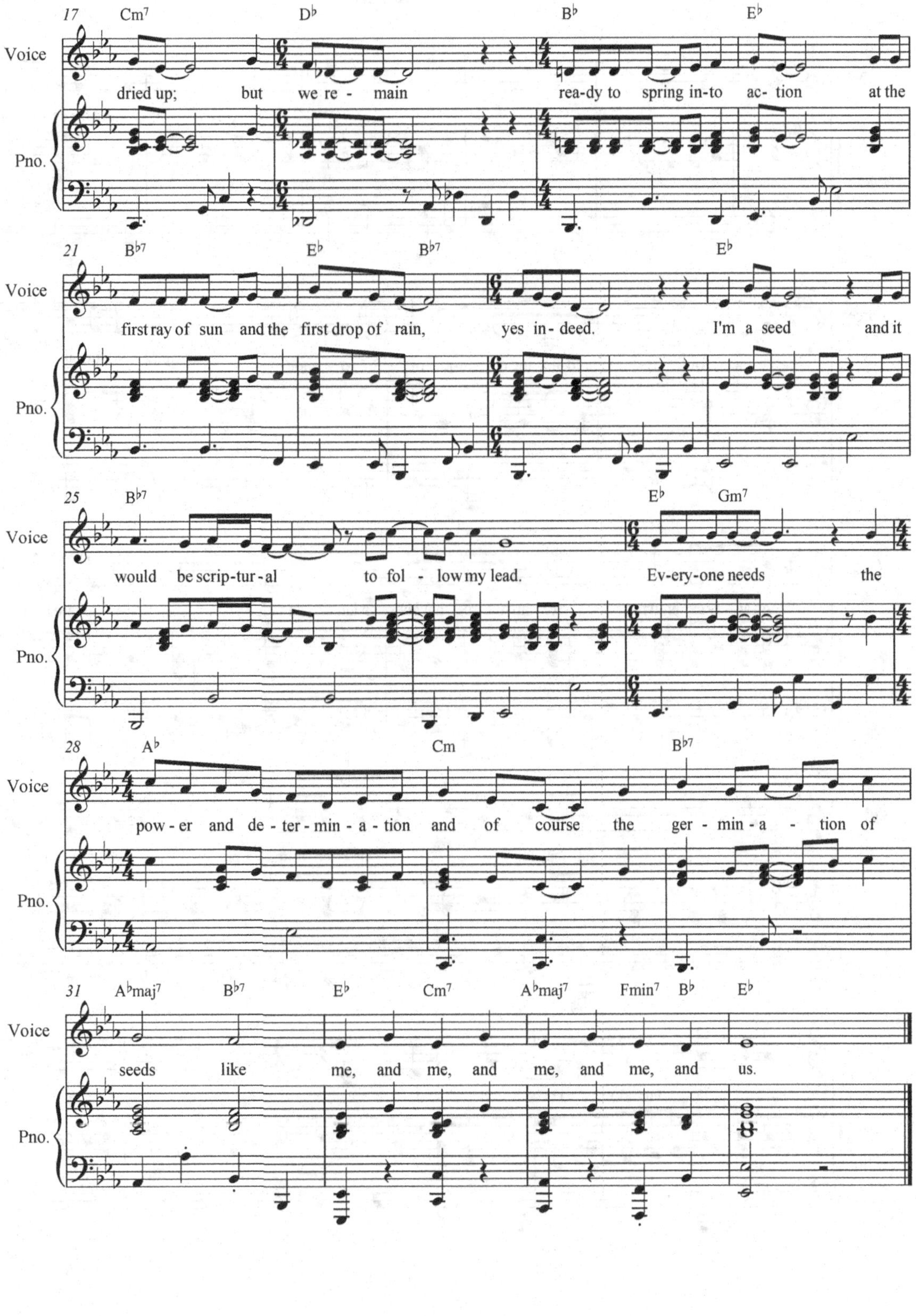
17 Cm7 D♭ B♭ E♭
Voice
dried up; but we re - main rea-dy to spring in-to ac- tion at the
Pno.
21 B♭7 E♭ B♭7 E♭
first ray of sun and the first drop of rain, yes in-deed. I'm a seed and it
25 B♭7 E♭ Gm7
would be scrip-tur-al to fol - low my lead. Ev-ery-one needs the
28 A♭ Cm B♭7
pow - er and de - ter - min - a - tion and of course the ger - min - a - tion of
31 A♭maj7 B♭7 E♭ Cm7 A♭maj7 Fmin7 B♭ E♭
seeds like me, and me, and me, and me, and us.

# Cedars Of Lebanon

Clark Tyler
*Arranged by Andrew Bell*

Instrumental:
21 A D D A
Pno.
26 D D G D A7 D
31 G D E
35 A D D
Voice
But if you're a read-er of se-cond Chron you
40 G D
know what the lea-der of Bab-y - lon did to the Ce-dar of Le-ba - non,
44 A D7 A D E♭ D
and to the tem-ple of Sol - o - mon. Tim - ber!

# The Story Of Wheat

Clark Tyler
*Arranged by Andrew Bell*

# What Is It?

Clark Tyler
*Arranged by Andrew Bell*

Voice
Pno.
22
C G7 C G7 C
lea- ven.
But, you should be care-ful to plan a
You won't find mir-a - cu-lous Man-na
28
G7 C F
me - nu that takes all your Man-na If you store it in your ca - ban-a it - 'll
grow-ing in Maine or Mon - ta - na. They get no-thing like this from Nir - va - na. It's un-
32
Dm G C C
rot and have worms by man - ya- na. Man - na, our dai-ly de-liv-ery from
ique as a leek or ba - na - na.
37
Em G
hea- ven. It's Man - na; not bad if you add a pinch or a tad of pep-per and salt,

3
2.
43 G
C G7 C
3. G
Voice
on-ions and gar-lic and lea-ven.
shal-lots and cap-ers and
Pno.
48
Voice
mus-tard and ba-sil and lem-on and hon-ey, ta-bas-co and cream cheese and lea-ven.
Pno.

# The Fig Tree

Clark Tyler
*Arranged by Andrew Bell*

1.2.
3. Final Verse:
26 G7 G7 C Am7
Voice
Now a That's the par - a - ble of the fig tree Je - sus told in Luke Thir - teen;
Pno.
32 Dm G7 C
Voice
Now you can see what's taught by that tree a-bout fig pro duc tiv - i - ty and that's the
Pno.
36 Am7 Dm7 C C
Voice
key; fig pro-duc-tiv - i - ty. fig pro-duc-tiv - i - ty.
Pno.

Verse 3: Then the master complained to the gardener;
"I have waited three long years;
and a fig can't be found
go ahead, cut it down
it is only using up ground.
I need the ground; this tree is fireplace bound."

Verse 4: But the gardener replied to the master:
"Why not give it one more chance?
I'll give it more care, fertilizer to spare;
then it better have figs to bear!"

# Garden Of God

(Recit. Intro)

Clark Tyler
Arranged by Andrew Bell

Voice
Piano
Pno.
C7
Dm
Page sev-en-ty three of my gar-den-ing guide tells me all that I need
6
C F Em G7
to get a flow-er or fruit From each sprout or shoot or to grow a tree from a seed.
10
C F G7 C
It says you need sun and just e-nough rain, and lots of lov-ing care.
15
C7
Now that sounds fa- mil - iar, I've read that some where;
19
Dm C F Em
growth is a fac - tor of sun, rain and care; three ba-sic tools and three ba-sic rules you've

23 G7 C F C
Voice
got to have sun - light, wa-ter and care; where have I read that; sun-light and rain, and
Pno.
26 C7 F
*To Chorus
Voice
lots of lo - ving care.
Spoken: Of course. It's the gardener's gospel that growers count on.
Pno.

# Garden Of God

Clark Tyler
Arranged by Andrew Bell

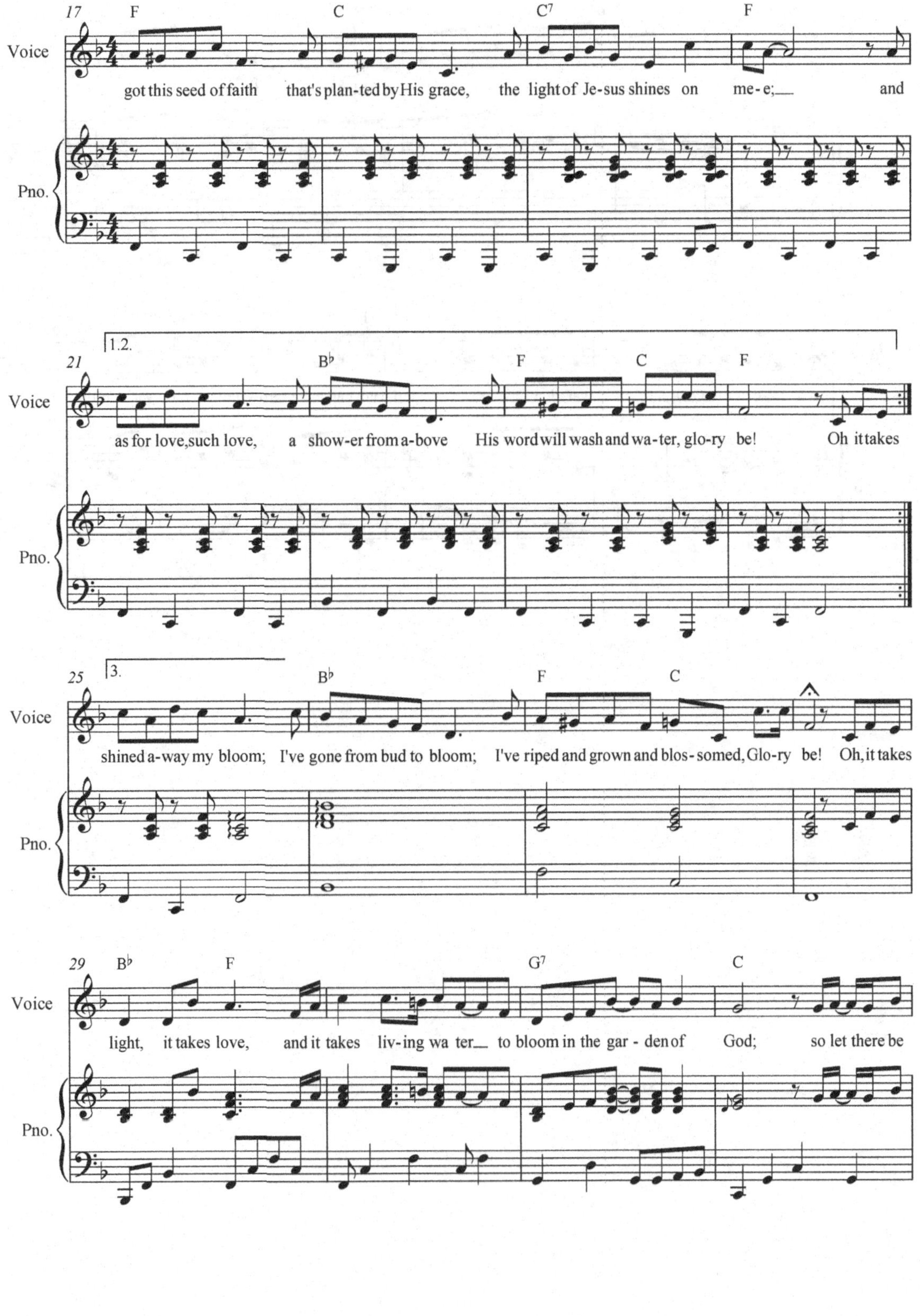
17
F C C7 F
Voice
got this seed of faith that's plan-ted by His grace, the light of Je-sus shines on me-e; and
Pno.
1.2.
21
B♭ F C F
as for love, such love, a show-er from a-bove His word will wash and wa-ter, glo-ry be! Oh it takes
3.
25
B♭ F C
shined a-way my bloom; I've gone from bud to bloom; I've riped and grown and blos-somed, Glo-ry be! Oh, it takes
29
B♭ F G7 C
light, it takes love, and it takes liv-ing wa ter to bloom in the gar-den of God; so let there be

33
F Bb F G7 C7 F
Voice
light, love and a well of liv ing wa-ter and I'll go with the flow in the gar-den of God;
Pno.
37
F C C F F Bb C F
Voice
gar-den of God; gar-den of God; I'm go-ing to be grow-ing in the gar-den of God.
Pno.
Ped.

# There Is A Time

Clark Tyler
*Arranged by Andrew Bell*

18 Am7
Dm7
G7
C
Voice
Pno.
Je - sus, it's time for hope, it's time for Je - sus.

# Jesus Is My Garden

(ABABA C ABABA)

Clark Tyler
*Arranged by Andrew Bell*

20 C6 G7 Dm Em7 Dm G7
Voice
where I want to grow so I can share the love and care that I have come to
Pno.
25 G7 C C Am Dm9 G7 G7
treasure so. Ce-dars, hyss-op, Rose of Shar-on; al-mond buds on
29 C C Am Dm G7 G7
rod of Aar-on; fig trees that are nev-er bar-ren; Am-ar-anth is
33 G7 C C F C6 G7
Je-sus is my gar - den where I want to grow
38 Dm Em7 Dm G7 G7 C
I can share the love and care that I have come to trea-sure so. My

42 C Am9/C Dm G7
Voice
gar-den grows on ho-ly ground where trees that clap their hands a-round; where
gar-den is a sav-ior who's a tree of life for me to choose; an
Pno.
46 C Am9 Dm G7 C
Voice
thorns that grow in crowns are found; where palm trees leaves all "Ho-sanna" sound.
of-fer that I won't re-fuse; a har-vest that is all good news.
Pno.
50 C F C6 G7 Dm
Voice
Je-sus is my gar-den, where I want to grow so I can share the
Pno.
55 Em7 Dm G7 G7 C
Voice
love and care that I have come to trea-sure so.
Pno.
58 C G7 C
Voice
Je-sus is my gar- - - - den.
Pno.

## Chapter 6 - DIGGING THROUGH THE BIBLE

I have always been intrigued with the intellectual tug of war between biblical scholars/believers on one hand and historians/skeptics on the other. Their bone of contention is always the historicity of the Bible...or, stated another way: "Are the stories and characters in scripture real or are they merely literary examples of a spiritual lesson? With depressing regularity, these arguments surface about once a year, or more, and always seem to take on the tone of an argument between two children over whose father is stronger. It's almost like a re-run of the legal wrangling in the famous Scopes Trial of the 1920's which centered on the faith vs. common sense approach to evolution and creation.

Given all this and the fact that hardened positions seem to get more entrenched without really resolving anything, it was with great delight that I discovered the "tie breaker" ... the one scientific discipline that bridged the gap and tilted the scales in favor of faith: ARCHEOLOGY.

Since the establishment of the State of Israel in 1947, hardly a week goes by without some new "dig" or substantial "find" showing just how accurate the Bible really is. Back in 1988, in preparation for a trip to Israel with our church group, I read James Michener's "The Source." That is one of those books that almost demands to be read again and again, since it uncovers and examines almost all of human history in the middle east through the mechanics of an archeologist analyzing the various layers of a "tell" (an archeological dig).

The sequence of my fascination with the subject of archeology was capped by the two-week tour of Israel. In Jericho, for instance, we stood looking down at a below-ground excavation of a Canaanite tower that has been dated to the seventh millennium B.C. That's 9,000 years old! In Jerusalem, we visited the Shrine of the Book, which houses the Isaiah leather scroll discovered at Qumran as part of the famous Dead Sea Scrolls. Learning that this copy of the prophet's book predates by over a thousand years the earliest known manuscript... or that in the messianic chapter 53 only a single inconsequential word varied... is, by any measure an awesome revelation. Seeing the small stone house in Capernaum, where the Apostle Peter is said to have lived, or the 2,000 year old fishing boat dredged up from the mud at the bottom of the Sea of Galilee, or the well worn Ascent Steps on the south side of Temple Mount (where Jesus taught) – these things tend to make the Bible come visually alive and hardly subject to any intellectual question.

As I pondered all these marvelous sights and did further reading from archeological books and essays, I naturally tried to figure out a way of having my Sunday School class experience the same sort of wonder and discovery that had so broadened my understanding of scripture. The answer came from a reference to a turn of the century archeologist named William Ramsay. In a chapter entitled "The Stones Cry Out," in his superb book (Why I Believe), author and teacher D. James Kennedy references these archaeologist/skeptics who changed their thinking:

> "One of the most notable of these was Sir William Ramsay. He was an atheist, the son of atheists; he was wealthy and a PhD from Oxford. He gave his whole life over to archeology and determined that he would disprove the Bible. He set out for the Holy Land and decided to disprove the Book of Acts. After twenty-five or more years (he had released book after book during this time), he was incredibly impressed by the accuracy of Luke in his writings and finally declared that Luke was exact, down to the most minute details. In his attempts to disprove the Bible, Sir William Ramsay uncovered hundreds of things which confirmed the historicity of the Book of Acts. Finally, in one of his books he shocked the whole critical world by declaring himself to be a Christian. The world's greatest authority on the Book of Acts and the travels of the Apostle Paul was converted by his digging, as have been numerous other archeologists over the centuries."

If ever an author was presented with a precise scenario for a play, this was it. Starting with Kennedy's chapter title, "The Stones Cry Out," which comes from Luke's quote of Jesus in chapter 19, verse 40 of his gospel, I could see in my mind's eye my kids holding prop artifacts and singing a song with this title. When a co-worker came around to my office, one day, peddling magazine subscriptions for his son's school, I saw another flashing light – there, among the weird and obtuse magazine titles was something called "Biblical Archeology Review." I signed up and began receiving wondrous contributions to my exploding musical drama. As my library became engulfed in books and pamphlets about archaeology, my wife began to suspect that I was going to disappear into the middle east on some obscure "dig," looking for the Ark (either one) or Jacob's ladder or David's harp. She was almost relieved when I retreated to my typewriter and piano.

As I worked, I began to see a "tell" on stage – out of which would come some artifacts which, if put together, would tell our archeological hero some important truths of the Bible... truths which would convince the most recalcitrant skeptic of God's plan for us all. I knew that two of my biblical favorites, Jacob and Joshua, were prime candidates for this across-the-millenium witnessing. I had recently read two of Frederick B. Meyer's wonderful biblical biographies (he wrote some 11 of them around the turn of the century). To these I added Nehemiah, having heard a series of marvelous teachings by Pastor Jack Hayford on his daily radio program. Not trusting my memory of these teachings (and having missed one or two), I ordered the 8 tape series, and thus had to chance to go back over the story of the cupbearer to King Artaxerxes, who traveled back to the ruins of Jerusalem from captivity in Persia and rebuilt the city's wall.

My incentive, or rather pressure, to put all these pieces together dramatically, was the fact that I had to teach my class on a weekly basis as I wrote. One night as I was telling the children the Nehemiah story, I suddenly realized that most, if not all, of these kids did not know where in the Bible to find Nehemiah... nor anyone else, for that matter. To me, this was a major gap in their understanding of scripture. If they had a way of knowing not only all the books of the Bible, but to what category they belonged and where to find each, then they might become more eager (or at least more enlightend) "hearers of the word." We devised a game to solve this problem: the name of each book of the Bible was lettered on a 3 X 5 card; then we constructed two "gates" - one labeled OLD TESTAMENT and the other NEW TESTAMENT; behind these gates were large signs that said: PENTATEUCH/TORAH, HISTORIES, POETIC BOOKS, PROPHETS (major), PROPHETS (minor); GOSPELS, EPISTLES and ETCETERA. The game was to pull one of the 66 3 X 5 cards out of a box, then race through the appropriate gate and deposit the card in the right bin in front of one of the signs. Of course, just to be slightly mischievous, I added some names that were clearly **not** books of the Bible (names like Charlie, Harry, Drusilla, Haggis or Hermione etc.). The child who picked up such a card was to drop it and pick another.

Yes, it took some practice. However, the class was helped by a new song for this play called "Digging Through the Bible Book by Book." This had a simple chorus repeated after a series of rhyming stanzas that simply listed all the book of the Bible in order. As the kids practiced the song, they began to master the books and the various sections of the Bible. Problem solved.

"Digging through the Bible book by book;
Starting with the Torah, or a Pentateuch;
Learning where to look
For Habakkuk;
Digging through the Bible book by book."

This particular song revealed two things about the whole series of musical plays: First, that my debt to Danny Kaye and Gilbert & Sullivan was immense; and second, that the revue-style format meant that certain songs and/or scenes could be easily lifted out for a special presentation apart from doing the whole play. This "Book By Book" number was often used by our church on Honor the Graduates Sunday - possibly because we staged it with the chorus wearing mortarboards (showing how smart they were!). The song could also be presented as a series of solos with separate children doing the Torah, the Histories, the Prophets, the Gospels etc.

Then there was Erin.

Erin was the young adopted daughter of one of our church's assisting ministers. I'm not sure whether she was autistic, or had some developmental problem, but she was barely able to speak; had very little change of expression; and, as a result could not, or would not, participate with the other children in her Sunday School class. My Pastor's wife, who taught that class, asked me to see what I could do about Erin. I watched her during one of the classes and noticed that the only time she seemed to respond, or have any reaction at all, was when the class would either listen to music or sing a song. As I thought about Erin, I wondered how I might somehow include her in our developing musical play.

It was my original intent to have all of the biblical characters that appeared out of the "tell" be puppets, triggered by a kind of dream sequence by the character of the archeologist.

Each would either have a song of their own, or would act out a skit while the main characters and/or the chorus would sing the song. In the case of the Nehemiah scene, I had two puppets – one for King Artaxerxes and one for Nehemiah. The Nehemiah puppet was supposed to stack up those play cardboard bricks that many pre-schools use, while the kids sang a simple chorus. This was supposed to symbolize the rebuilding of Jerusalem's wall.

> Nehemiah, Nehemiah
> Stacking his stones up higher and higher;
> Restoring the wall, full height, full length;
> Reminding us all
> The joy of the Lord is our strength.

Then it occurred to me that instead of a puppet Nehemiah, Erin could do the brick stacking while the kids sang that chorus...especially if there was a precise musical cue for the brick stacking to begin. So back I went to the sporting goods store and had them (a different clerk, thank heaven!) Make up a "Nehemiah" T-shirt.

Instead of complete costumes, I decided to put the chorus in different hats each time they came on for the next scene. For the Nehemiah scene, it was yellow plastic hard hats. So Erin got a yellow hard hat, a Nehemiah T-shirt and a set of those red and white cardboard bricks. She loved it! I explained all this to her parents and went to her home one night with all this paraphrenalia and a tape of the chorus. I told her that all this was *hers* alone. It didn't take long for Erin to figure it all out. The T-shirt went on, as did the hard hat, and she became a cardboard brick stacker of the first degree. She played that song incessantly. I am sure that Erin practiced more than anyone else in the play, delightedly stacking up her bricks while listening to that chorus repeat over and over.

When this play was presented, Erin knew her cues. When she saw the kids come on with their hard hats, and the puppet Artaxerxes pop up from the "tell," Erin came on strong. With the help of a friend she stacked the bricks during each chorus. No explanation of her role or condition was necessary. It was a living fulfillment of Nehemiah 8:10 because "the joy of the Lord was (her) strength!"

Erin and her family moved away some time later, but I am sure that wherever Erin is she still responds to the name Nehemiah. She probably thinks that every construction worker she sees in a yellow hard hat is possible competition for her role in "STONES!" And I'll bet that she can still sing that song.

"STONES" was more of a book musical in that it told a complete story and had a certain degree of character development. The main character was an archeologist who, in the course of the play is transformed from a biblical skeptic and scoffer into a believer. He becomes convinced by the results of his own discipline – digging up truths. Led by an angelic guide, Gloria Livingstone, he discovers the real meaning of Jesus' resurrection when he digs up a portion of the stone that was rolled away from the Garden Tomb.

Since a part of the archeologist's character was almost cartoon-like (his name was Sir Archie O'Logical), I had to be very careful on how his own personal revelation was depicted. The fine line between "fun" and "message" was critical. Thus this key scene was crafted as a series of interlocking song fragments, dialogue, solos and chorus number that showed this progression in a credible way. The proof that this transformation worked lay in the fact that when this play was performed, Sir Archie's "seeing the light" was always a cause for spontaneous applause.

The main song of this scene was "Risen Indeed," and included a chorus with those words (sung by the younger children) and a number of stanzas sung by Gloria telling of the specifics of that scene in the garden on Resurrection Day. Our church always included this song, performed just this way, during our Easter service. Every time I hear it, I can shut my eyes and see the tears of joy in the eyes of the nursing home residents who saw this play... and heard the song:

"Here was the stone that was rolled away
From a tomb in a garden that fine spring day;
And here was the angel heard to say:
'He is not here, He is risen.'"

Risen indeed, risen indeed,
Christ, the Lord, is risen indeed
Risen indeed.

## Synopsis of Scenes

Prologue The Lecture on Biblical Archeology

Scene 1 The Testimony - We meet Sir Archie O'Logical and hear about his new book and his testimony - "The Stones Cry Out."

Scene 2 The Reception . In a flashback, the Creative Historical Order Revising Understanding of Scripture (C.H.O.R.U.S.) Is bidding bon voyage to Sir Archie, who is off on his latest trip to the Holy Land. We meet his new guide, Gloria Livingstone - "Sir Archie."

Scene 3 The Tell . Gloria shows us the tell and we meet Sir Archie's unseen assistant, Doug Upp. - "Dig."

Scene 4 Jacob's Pillar . A stone is uncovered, dating to the time of the patriarchs. Gloria introduces the story of Jacob. - "Up!"

Scene 5 Joshua's Altar . An ancient signpost for Shechem leads to a presentation of Joshua's farewell address and the commitment - "We Will Serve the Lord"

Scene 6 Nehemiah's Wall. A building plan and a fragment of a hinge embedded in a block enables Gloria to give a modernized version of the restoration after the Babylonian captivity. "Nehemiah"

Scene 7 The Bible. Sir Archie and Gloria discuss in song two differing views of the Bible. "Book By Book."

Scene 8 The Garden Tomb . A Piece of a large round stone is excavated: a well cover? A millstone?. No, it's the stone that wasn't there. "Risen Indeed."

Scene 9 The Revelation. The stones have indeed been "crying out" to Sir Archie, and Gloria leads him to faith. He rushes home, yelling to Doug something about the Book of Acts.

Scene 10 The Act. We meet Manny Arcald ("where the few are chosen") who books "acts." He presents the Quarry Sisters (Rocksanne, Iona and Ruby, who tell how to be a living stone. "Be a Rock, Be a Pillar, Be a Gem."

Scene 11 The Witness. Back at the beginning, Sir Archie finishes his testimony, as Gloria leads the C.H.O.R.U.S. to faith. "In The Beginning." Sir Archie explains his new traveling mission based on Mark 16 and Matthew 28 . "The Stones Cry Out."

# "STONES"

## Lesson Plan

Since the principal characters in this play are to be played by junior and senior high schoolers, the preparatory teaching can be a little more technical and a little more sophisticated. While the action of the play is a living testimony, the basis is archeology - Biblical archeology. For the younger children involved, reliance upon three books is recommended: two books in the Eyewitness series ("Archeology" by Jane McIntosh, Alfred A. Knopf, 1994 and "Bible Lands" by Jonathan N. Tubb, also Knopf, 1991) and the already mentioned "Why I Believe" by D. James Kennedy - particularly the chapter entitled "The Stones Cry Out." Older students can handle many of the articles published in Hershel Shanks" wonderful periodical, Biblical Archeological Review. There is a 2 volume compendium of major articles from that magazine (Biblical Archeological Society, Washington DC, 1990).

I. **Archeology** - the impact of technology (carbon dating, remote sensing by satellites, computers, chemical analysis etc.). Great Biblical discoveries: The Rosetta Stone, the Dead Sea Scrolls, the Amarna letters and more. For an extended listing of these and others, see Hayford's Bible Handbook, Jack Hayford, editor, Thomas Nelson, 1995. Chapter 55 of this work is an excellent presentation. Josh McDowell's book in outline form, "Evidence That Demands a Verdict" also goes into this subject in depth.

II. **Archeology vs. History** - To understand archeology's developing role, especially as it relates to the historicity of the Bible, it is necessary to understand what history is. History, as we know and study it, is the written record of empires, kingdoms and the conflicts and confluences that produced substantial change. Scholars may have a more precise definition, but most students understand that the history we study is generally the record of literate societies led and guided by significant rulers, events and peoples. Of course, such written records are subject to all the biases and predispositions of the "recorder." That section of the Bible, known as "the Histories" - those twelve books that follow the Torah (or the five books of Moses), are, in the worldly view, something quite different from books such as Caesar's Gallic Wars, Thucydides, Prescott, Holinshead and all the rest. From this perspective the Hebrews were a very insignificant people... nomads, slaves, captives or groups of citizens led by a succession of minor leaders – set apart only by their belief in one God and characterized by their law embodying his commandments. Aside from the glory period of David and Solomon, historically there is very little that drew the notice of traditional chroniclers of the day. That is why there is very little mention of Israel outside of the Bible. However, the science of archeology offers a very different approach. There is no bias or "spin" in a shovel. When something is uncovered, analyzed and deciphered, it tells a story without an opinion. Artifacts unearthed tell the story of everyday life, of everyday people, of customs, events and people who might not have made history's "cut."

III. **Proof** - Amazingly, there has never been a discovery or find, or dig, that has disproved anything in the Bible. What has happened is that finds have confirmed what the Bible has said. The last hundred years has seen a quantum leap in the technology propelling archeology In the last ten years, two important artifacts have been uncovered that presented incontrovertible proof of two major persons mentioned only in the Bible. One is King David, and the other is the high priest of Jesus time - Caiaphus. The story of Sir William Ramsay, an archeologist at the turn of the 19th century, and how he used his discipline to try and disprove the Bible - and in the process becoming a believer - is the basis of this play.

IV. **The Focus** - To dramatize the lead character's transformation from scoffer and skeptic to true believer, the stories of Jacob, Joshua, Nehemiah and Peter have been chosen. Pastor Jack Hayford has an excellent 8-tape series on Nehemiah; Jacob, Joshua, and Peter are the subjects of that very special series of Biblical biographies written by Frederick B. Meyer and available at most Christian bookstores. The teaching should focus on these four men and those moments in their lives which are most instructive for the potential believer: Jacob's encounter with God and the "ladder" episode; Joshua's final sermon to the elders of Israel at Shechem; Nehemiah's rebuilding of the wall of Jerusalem; and Peter at the empty tomb. Again, Pastor Hayford's 2-tape teaching, "Peter - the Processing of a Pillar" is most instructive.

The teacher should go over the two one page speeches by The Host at the beginning of the play to make sure that students understand the basic underpinnings of this story. Some noteworthy exercises to be undertaken involve studying the order of the books of the Bible ("Digging Through the Bible Book by Book"), and exploring the fact that much of archeology is picking through rubble and trash over time - for instance, what sort of detective work would reveal answers from such remnants. If someone were to poke through your trash, what would be revealed about you, how you lived, what you did and when you did it?

## Format

This is a full length musical play about an archeologist, an angel and a "tell." It is formatted in the testimony of a well-known skeptic and critic of the Bible... and how he came to know the Lord. There was such a person (Sir William Ramsay) around the turn of the century. He wrote many books critical of the historicity of the Bible. When he turned his attention to the Book of Acts, the inevitable happened and he became a believer and a leading proponent of the application of archeology to the accuracy of the Bible. While this play isn't specifically about Sir William Ramsay, it is intended to show how the science of archeology can play a role in personal revelation of the truth of God's word. Using the framework of a believer's testimony and the setting of a Holy Land "tell" (or dig), a number of Bible stories and lessons are presented which help convince our hero that our God reigns and Jesus is Lord.

The principals in this play are designed for the 12 to 16 year old range, while the chorus can be composed of children in the grade one to six category. There are four main characters with song and dialogue requirements. Most of the other characters are puppets (which emerge in a dream sequence from the tell). Thus, the puppet stage is decorated as a "tell," and from it emerge not only the artifacts uncovered by the archeologist, but also a number of Biblical characters to illustrate the various messages. The chorus functions as an audience, as the archeologist's sponsoring society, as the Hebrew elders in the Joshua scene and a vocal chorus for the other songs. The Biblical scenes are staged with a combination of verse narration, puppets, chorus and solo songs. By this means, the stories of Jacob, Joshua, Nehemiah and Peter are shown.

In a brief introduction, the Host presents some background on Biblical archeology by way of introducing the testimony of the main character. The rest of the play is a flashback to illustrate his testimony.

## Puppets & Costumes

Jacob
two angels
Joshua
King Artaxerxes (with crown)
The Quarry Sisters:
- Rocksanne
- Iona
- Ruby

(These should be decorated with Blocks, columns and an ephod breastplate)

Pith helmet
Dress hats for the "Society"
Kaffiehs for the elders
Hard hats
Israeli tourist hats
White mortarboards
Purple choir robes
Sound effects: party crowd noise, electronic noises
Bowler hat for Manny

## List of Props

| | | |
|---|---|---|
| archeologist's trowel | mid-sized spade | Israel backdrop for tell |
| director's chair | maps & charts | collection of artifacts |
| oil cruse | Jacob's stone | white rope ladder |
| signpost/milestone | family Bible | set of cardboard bricks |
| stone blueprint | teacups & saucers | banner for C.H.O.R.U.S. |
| Circular stone section | telephone | Rolodex file |
| sign: "Tell - A Vision" | wings pin | small folding table |
| fake "rubble" | | |

In the opening number, each chorus member should have a chunk of flat Styrofoam cut and painted to look like an artifact. These can also be colored pictures of artifacts blown up and pasted on cardboard. At the end of the opening number, the chorus members place these around the "tell" as they exit.

The tell is the puppet stage - with a backdrop at the back to look like a typical Israel desert scene. The front of the tell should have a piece of painted muslin to look like a typical archeological mound. The tell should be about ten feet wide as it is the dominant set on the stage. The puppet stage must accommodate three puppeteers on stools within. Behind the puppet stage, an area large enough for the microphones for the puppet "voices" should be set aside.

Costume note: Since the chorus will have five changes of hats (plus a choir robe) according to the appropriate scene, there will need to be a special area set aside near stage left to stack the different hats in the proper sequence. Some of the changes needed will be quick so a separate assistant is a good idea for this function. As an added "visual," the piano player should also have a set of these hats as a "scene indicator."

## Character Descriptions

SIR ARCHIE O'LOGICAL - There are really two Sir Archies; one is the skeptical Biblical critic and archeologist, who is a slightly pandering hustler... slick, smooth, but engaging. The other is the open and receptive one who comes to faith as a result of what he finds and what Gloria tells him. The patter type solo in the song, "Sir Archie" defines the former and his patter in "Book By Book," is the link between the latter and the saved Sir Archie. Sir Archie is not a cartoon character, but must be played with a combination of both fun and credibility. His openness is what Gloria plays to.

GLORIA LIVINGSTONE - There is a brashness along with a confident demeanor about Gloria. Her barbs are not mean put-downs, but poignant and on the mark. She is modern, but has a true love and feeling for scripture... and above all, has that ethereal quality of an angel. Her firm exposition of faith to Sir Archie after the Garden Tomb scene should be a natural extension of her character - not a sudden shift. Her two solos - "Nehemiah" and "He is Risen," suggest the dimensions of her character – fun and sensitive.

DOUG UPP - He is the long-suffering side kick; the Peter Falk type who knows his role, feels slightly unappreciated, but is confident of his contribution. He, too, can guide Sir Archie and channel his acceptance of what Gloria points out to him. He is not the mindless go-along, but rather the informed and open helper. Being only heard and never seen, means that his character will have to be totally defined through his voice and inflections.

THE CHAIRWOMAN - She is the quintessential committee woman. She has the usual self-importance and singsong voice. She dotes on Sir Archie and is "thrilled" to present and sponsor him. There is something comic and yet logical about her not missing a beat in being part of Archie's faith mission at the play's conclusion.

MANNY ARCALD - A Damon Runyon character - the typical NY theatrical agent who can "always come up with something," no matter how silly or inappropriate. In old movies, his type would chomp on a cigar, wear a bowler hat and be coatless with elastics on his upper sleeves. Dumb jokes come naturally to him. The resulting drum "rim shot" is part of his presentation.

JOSHUA - At this point, Joshua is 110 years old and is giving his final speech to the elders. He is the slightly stern, father figure who knows his charges will eventually stray - but he is going to do his utmost to set them on the right path. He is indeed a general and leader, but in this scene is the prophet and the exhorting servant of the Lord.

NEHEMIAH - This part can either be a puppet or, as in the original production, played by a silent actor who will quietly stack up the cardboard blocks during the chorus of the song, "Nehemiah."

THE QUARRY SISTERS - Their song, "Be a Rock, Be a Pillar, Be a Gem" is a jive type song in the Andrews Sisters mode of harmony. Their USO style means that they are totally unaware of how ridiculous they look, sound and act. They think they are a hit and that's all that matters. Reflected by their costumes, each has a distinct personality and they are competitive. Rocksanne is the preachy, serious one... slightly bored, but confident of her "message;" Iona is the Jewish mama type... the older sister; Ruby is the flaky one.... slightly stuck up and proud. As they do "their bits," they are clearly trying to top each other. However, their material is about the Apostle Peter and his admonition to be a "living stone," so it should not be too un-reverential (fun, but not mocking). Their costumes reflect their lyrics - Rocksanne has a vest that is embossed with piles of stones, like a wall; Iona has a column on her front, topped with an ionic capital; Ruby has on a Levite priest's ephod with a setting of the 12 gemstones. These three are a product of Manny's silly stable of "acts," but their message is important - certainly, they think it is important. That is why they reappear at the end as part of the evangelical team that will "go forth."

THE HOST - He is the "authority".... the MC type in the Walter Cronkhite mold, who can give the necessary insightful background to the subject matter. He reveals in advance Sir Archie's transformation from scoffer to believer, and sets the tone for the application of technology to the science of archeology. He is that combination of the professor and the newsman. He knows the value of scripture in the process of Sir Archie's discovery of faith.

Program/Poster design

A spirited rehearsal

# “STONES”

## Cast:

| | |
|---|---|
| THE HOST | The Archeological “authority” and M.C. |
| SIR ARCHIE O’LOGICAL | Noted author, scientist and skeptic. |
| CHAIRWOMAN | Of the C.H.O.R.U.S. |
| GLORIA LIVINGSTONE | Angelic guide to Holy Land sites |
| DOUG UPP | Heard, but not seen, archeological assistant |
| NEHEMIAH | Silent rebuilder of Jerusalem’s wall |
| MANNY ARCALD | Outlandish theatrical booking agent |

Puppets:

| | |
|---|---|
| JACOB | A prince with God |
| ANGELS | On Jacob’s ladder |
| JOSHUA | A servant of God |
| KING ARTAXERXES | Nehemiah’s sponsor |
| THE QUARRY SISTERS | Rocksanne, Iona & Ruby |

## Musical Numbers:

| | |
|---|---|
| OVERTURE | The orchestra |
| THE STONES CRY OUT | The chorus |
| SIR ARCHIE | Chairwoman, Sir Archie, Gloria & chorus |
| DIG | Doug Upp |
| UP! | The angels |
| WE WILL SERVE THE LORD | Joshua & chorus |
| NEHEMIAH | Gloria & chorus |
| BOOK BY BOOK | Sir Archie, Gloria, Doug & chorus |
| RISEN INDEED | Gloria & chorus |
| BE A ROCK, BE A PILLAR, BE A GEM | The Quarry Sisters |
| IN THE BEGINNING | Chairwoman & chorus |
| THE STONES CRY OUT (reprise) | All |

**PROLOGUE:**

*The stage is simply set, as if for a lecture. A lectern is at the center. Just to the right, masked by a curtain, is the puppet stage which, when revealed, is decorated to resemble an archeological dig or "tell." Appropriate ruins and fragments are scattered about. The backdrop behind the stage is of the Israeli desert. The Host enters and goes to the lectern. He picks up a mason's trowel.*

**HOST**

This... is a key – the key to some of the most important discoveries that have been made in the last 25 years. Actually, this is a tool – an archeologist's trowel. But recent events have made it the key to many people's understanding of the Bible.

But this key can open more than just another tomb... or uncover another artifact. It can also unlock the power of God's Word by opening minds and hearts.

That is the starting point of tonight's drama.

Consider that in recent year, the archeologist's trowel has excavated evidence of such Biblical personages as King David, Pontius Pilate and Caiaphas – people who played a major role in the Bible, but who were unmentioned by history.

While the historian's pen conveys a very human point of view, the archeologist's trowel has no opinion, no bias, no"spin."

It can uncover what history - and time - may cover up.

Archeology, as a science, tells it like it really was – all from the remnants and rubbish that history might well overlook.

Thanks to such finds as the Rosetta Stone, the Amarna Letters and the Dead Sea Scrolls, archeology has become the most "revelationary" of sciences... enlightening not just the scholar, but the scoffer as well!

Yet, even though this simple trowel is the basic tool of the trade, some very impressive high technology has made archeology even more exciting and productive in the last decade.

- radiocarbon dating
- chemical and DNA analysis
- infra-red radar and space satellites
- and, of course, computers

How wonderful that such technology - focused on dead civilizations, on precise dates and on crumbling ruins - should now be applied to God's Word... that which embodies life, timelessness and restoration!

In Luke's gospel, the Lord Jesus prophesied that if believers hesitated to carry forth the good news of God's kingdom, then would "the stones cry out." In the growing field of Biblical Archeology, this is exactly what is happening . A very important lesson to us all!

Thus, we are at that point where science becomes revelation - especially to those who are prepared to receive.

*The Host, as he finishes his speech, now moves to the right side. The curtains open revealing the chorus, each member of which is holding a painted "artifact."*

**CHORUS**

OH THE STONES CRY OUT
THE STONES CRY OUT
REVEALING THE TRUTH THEY HAVE STORED
AND EACH STONE IS FOUND
TO WITNESS ABOUT
THE EVERLASTING WORD OF THE LORD

OH THE STONES
OH THE STONES;
TELL OF SERVANTS AND KINGS,
AND MANGERS AND THRONES;
TEMPLES AND TABLETS
AND TOMBS
WITH THEIR TREASURES... OF BONES.

OH THE STONES CRY OUT
THE STONES CRY OUT
FROM RUINS AS YET UNEXPLORED
AND EACH STONE GIVES ME
A REASON TO SHOUT:
OH HALLELUJAH, PRAISE TO THE LORD
HALLELUJAH, PRAISE TO THE LORD!

*The chorus now circles to stage right, depositing their "artifacts" at the base of the tell. They then exit back left, as the Host once more comes to the lectern.*

**HOST**

Our honored guest today, has just written a new book, the title of which you just heard – "The Stones Cry out - Hallelujah!" This is a radical departure from the focus of his earlier works. He is here to give witness on just how that change took place.

There is great irony when an explorer sets out to find one thing, and ends up discovering something really quite different. For instance, in 1513 Ponce De Leon set out to find the fabled Fountain of Youth... what he actually discovered was Florida... which is today the pre-eminent home of senior citizens!

Now it is always exciting to hear the testimony of a new believer. When that person is someone who is well known, and whose loudly professed doubts are even more well known... that is even more exciting.

Our guest today is the noted author, scientist and former Biblical skeptic, Sir Archie O'Logical.

To say he has come a long way is an understatement. He has just returned from a new and most fruitful excavation in the Holy Land... but it is spiritual journey he will tell us about.

How fitting it is that an archeologist and geologist should come upon and recognize the Rock of his salvation! God truly has a sense of humor.

I present to you, Sir Archie O'Logical.. Who will give you both the chapter and verse of his remarkable testimony. Sir Archie...

## SCENE 1 - The Testimony

*The Host backs off, clapping, as Sir Archie O'Logical enters from the right. He is well-groomed and slightly scholarly looking. He is humble, but confident.. And with a slight puckish quality. He speaks with thought and credibility - in marked contrast to how he will appear in the flashback to come. He comes to the lectern, stops , looks around and then, as if pleased that he now knows how to begin, starts his testimony.*

**ARCHIE**

In every kind of "ology"
(Except of course, theology),
I was well-versed... and quite knowledge-y.

Whether technical or scientific,
At Aramaic... hieroglyphic...
I was just terrific.

And each dubious commission
And sponsored expedition
In addition, if you please,
Meant big fees – with ease!

But the stones I found throughout God's word
Were a quarry of salvation;
Awaiting only such as I

To make my declaration;
And learn, discern,
And take a turn
Towards spiritual excavation.

Stones...
In every book and story
Stones
Reflecting God's own glory:

> The five smooth stones for David's sling;
> The 12 gemstones the priests would bring;
> The hailstones which on Pharaoh rained;
> The millstone which had Samson chained;
> The stone that opened Lazarus' tomb;
> The brimstone which spelled Sodom's doom;
> Elijah's stones where fire would perch;
> The living stones to build His church...

But revelation has to me now shown
That once-rejected builder's stone –
The foundation, key and corner stone
Sent for me by grace's throne.

> Jesus
> My Lord, my savior, my Messiah,
> Whom I met
> Through Jacob, Joshua and Nehemiah;
> Like Peter at the empty tomb
> I, too, have joy where once was gloom.
>
> For it was just a few weeks back
> That I was off on another track;
> But before I wrote one mocking sentence
> I found redemption and repentance!
>
> > There, in the ruins
> > I could see
> > One of those ruins
> > Was me!

*As Archie says these last lines, the chorus begins to re-enter from the left. This time they have on formal hats, as if at a party. As Archie concludes his last couplet, a sound effect of party noises comes up as the chorus gets into position.*

**ARCHIE**

Return with me, I'll show you why
The stones and I can testify.

*Archie moves slightly to the right, but stays in view.*

## SCENE 2 - The Reception

*The scene has now shifted as a flashback to an author's reception. The chorus has re-entered, having put on various hats to denote a crowd of do-gooding characters. The effect may be that of kids dressed up as their parents, but that is fine. Some may hold teacups or small plates. These are all members of Sir Archie's sponsoring organization: The Creative Historical Order Revising Understanding of Scripture (C.H.O.R.U.S.). Two members hold up a banner with this acronym. As the chorus exited the last scene, the lectern was removed. As Sir Archie resumes his testimony the chorus freezes in place until he speaks his last two lines and the Chairwoman enters.*

**ARCHIE**

And this is where it all began...
The first step for me in God's own plan

*Archie now exits, and when he does on comes the Chairwoman speaking "welcome" as she does so. This unfreezes the chorus who begin to chat amongst themselves, giving the Chairwoman increasing attention.*

**CHAIRWOMAN**

Welcome... welcome... to our regular meeting of the Creative Historical Order Revising Understanding of Scripture.

Today, we are here to salute our founder - and our friend – Sir Archie O'Logical

*Polite applause from the chorus.*

**CHAIRWOMAN**

...author of those best sellers: "Artifacts and Fiction," "Tombsday or Doomsday?" and "Theology in Ruins!" He is writing a new book called: "Trouble in the Rubble - or Bursting the Biblical Bubble."

Sir Archie is about to go off on his seventh trip to the Holy Land, where he will open a new and exciting "tell" – I think we should name it, the "Tattle Tell."

Time to welcome our guest of honor!

*As introduction, the music begins a light march style vamp, which is Sir Archie's signature theme. The chorus turns right towards where Sir Archie will enter - anticipating. The Chairwoman leads the singing and after the second chorus, Sir Archie enters .... rather, he breezes in – very different from what we saw in the opening scene. He is wearing a pith helmet and desert gear and is very much the slick hustler. The Chairwoman, in the course of her song, presents him with a gold colored archeologist's trowel, which he proceeds to brandish like a swagger stick. He is definitely pandering to his adoring audience.*

**CHAIRWOMAN**

WE NOW PRESENT THE EXPERTISE
OF SIR ARCHIE O'LOGICAL;
PROFESSOR OF ALL MIDDLE EAST-
ERN STUDIES CHRONOLOGICAL.

COMBINING WHAT'S HISTORICAL
WITH ALL THAT'S GEOLOGICAL
AND POKING HOLES IN ANYTHING
THAT SEEMS TO BE... THEO-LOGICAL.

**CHORUS**

A BRILLIANT MIND, A STONY HEART
WE THINK YOU'LL FIND IS QUITE A PART
OF STARCHY, SIR ARCHIE O'LOGICAL!

**CHAIRWOMAN**

HE'S OFF AGAIN TO EXCAVATE
WITH HIS METHODS ANALYTICAL
BY SPELUNKING AND DEBUNKING
AND BY WRITING BOOKS CRITICAL...

OF EVERYTHING THAT'S BIBLICAL
PROPHETIC AND LEVITICAL
IT ALL HAS BEEN QUITE LUCRATIVE
AND EVER SO... POLITICAL!

**CHORUS**

A BRILLIANT MIND, A STONY HEART
WE THINK YOU'LL FIND IS QUITE A PART
OF STARCHY, SIR ARCHIE O'LOGICAL!

**ARCHIE** *(as he enters from right)*
IN EVERY TELL AND WADI
FROM SYRIA TO SAUDI
I'M A VERY BUSY BODY
JUST DIGGING UP THE TRUTH!

AND I CAN TELL WHO'S WHO IN
EACH TOMB AND EVERY RUIN
I CAN FIND A CLEVER CLUE IN
EACH BROKEN POT AND TOOTH!

**CHORUS**
HE'S DIGGING UP THE TRUTH
IN EACH BROKEN POT AND TOOTH.

*Now the music picks up the tempo as Archie recites the following patter*

**ARCHIE**
I love to stick my pick and shovel
Into some old Hittite hovel

Or open up some ancient man's crypt
And read his mail... though it's in sanskrit

The Bible, as I loudly doubt it
Helps sell the books I write about it.

The hokus pokus in my theories
Would make a marvelous min-series!

**CHORUS**
A BRILLIANT MIND, A STONY HEART
WE THINK YOU'LL FIND IS QUITE A PART
OF STARCHY, SIR ARCHIE O'LOGICAL.

*As the music continues underneath, one of the crowd hands a note to the Chairwoman. She looks at it.*

**CHAIRWOMAN**
Sir Archie... your usual guide has had some sort of problem. The Antiquities Commission has sent a last-minute replacement - a Miss Gloria Livingstone... and this must be she!

*The Chairwoman points to the side as Gloria enters. She is bright, modern, confident... and skeptical of this crowd. She knows what* ***her*** *agenda is! She is dressed as a guide with a large pin on her blouse in the form of double wings.*

**GLORIA**

It must!... I'm all set... what's happening?

**CHORUS**

HE'S DIGGING UP THE TRUTH
WITH EACH BROKEN POT AND TOOTH.

**GLORIA** *(aside to the audience)*

AND I WILL GUIDE THIS SLEUTH
TO THE WAY, THE LIFE, THE TRUTH!

*Gloria now turns towards the chorus and "conducts" them – as a way of indicating that she will be in charge of Sir Archie's trip and spiritual progress!*

**CHORUS**

A BRILLIANT MIND, AN OPEN HEART
I THINK YOU'LL FIND WILL BE A PART
OF STARCHY, SIR ARCHIE
(FROM CORINTH TO KARACHI)
IT'S SIR ARCHIE, SIR ARCHIE...O'LOGICAL

**CHAIRWOMAN** *(handing Archie the trowel)*

...and ***this*** is from all of us! - to help you dig up the truth.

**ARCHIE**

Thank you...thank you all for your kind words. AND your most generous support. Miss Livingstone, you're an angel to be available on such short notice!!

**GLORIA**

No problem. In a way, I am heaven sent. I know my Bible... and I know a lot about you and your work, Sir Archie.

**ARCHIE**

Fine...fine. I have a feeling this is going to be a most fruitful trip.

**GLORIA**

You are so right! Well, I must be off...I'll take care of the paperwork and meet you at the new dig

**ARCHIE**

Fine...fine. My assistant should already be there...getting started.

**GLORIA**

What's his name?

**ARCHIE**

Doug...Mr. Doug Upp.

*As Gloria starts to exit, she stops by one of the chorus members who is holding a sign with a series of hieroglyphic markings on it. She turns to Sir Archie...*

**GLORIA**

By the way...what does ***that*** mean?

**ARCHIE**

It's hieroglyphics... it says: "Go, Sir Archie." Very sweet!

*Archie patronizingly pats the sign holder as Gloria exits right. Archie , the Chairwoman and the chorus exit left.*

## SCENE 3 - The Tell

*As Sir Archie exits right, he uncovers the screen from the tell, revealing it along with the associated stones, rubble and ruin-type setting. Now Gloria enters from the opposite side, goes over to the tell, looks at it, seems satisfied. She goes to a music stand at her side of the stage, which is screened by a panel emblazoned with an artifact (right), then turns towards the audience to recite...*

**GLORIA**

This is the tell
Where our tale will be told;
It's a tell that is well
Over 4 millennia old:
    And what's a tell?
    Well, a tell is a mound
    Found on Holy Land ground,
    Where historical/Biblical riches abound;
        Layer on layer
        This tell will tell all
        Yielding up faith
        As part of the haul!

But for this bulge to divulge
Its tales and its tracks;
You have to dig down through stacks and stacks
Of ruins and doin's and artifacts;
Through strata and data, with spade and pick ax.

And once at the bottom
Of this Biblical well;
You work your way up,
That's the way with a tell.

And that's just as well,
For if his faith's gonna jell,
It'll all be because
Of the tales of this tell...

It'll all be because
Of the tales of this tell. *(She peers into the tell)*

Doug... are you down there? Doug????

*Doug is only heard, not seen. As he speaks, a plodding, digging musical beat begins...*

**DOUG**

That's me – Doug... as in the past tense of "dig."

*As Doug sings, we see a shovel flash from time to time above the edge of the tell, flipping material out near Gloria, who watches carefully.*

**DOUG**

OH, YOU DON'T HAVE TO BE
A P.H.D.
WITH A HARVARD DEGREE
IN ARCHEOLOGY

TO GET TO B.C.
ANTIQUITY
YOU JUST NEED ME... TO DIG
AND DIG... AND DIG

NO PHYSICS, NO LATIN, NO TRIG
JUST ME... TO DIG.

NO MECHANIZED MOLE
WILL FIND YOU A SCROLL
PUT ME IN A HOLE
AND I'LL DIG

NO HIGH-TECH OR ROBOTIC RIG
JUST ME.... TO DIG
AND DIG!..AND DIG!

*At the end of Doug's song, Gloria goes to her stage right position and places her large Bible on it with a flourish. As she does so, Sir Archie enters carrying charts under his arm and a case which he sets down on a small table to the left of the tell. From the tell, every now and then, we still see flashes of Doug's shovel and some material being flipped.*

## SCENE 4 -Jacob's Pillar

**ARCHIE** *(as he unpacks & sets up)*
Now, let's see... I've got my guidebook, charts, operating manual, technical references, policies & procedures, historical tracts, genealogies, "how to" books... and my copy of "Who Was Who in Ancient Palestine."

**GLORIA** *(holds up her Bible)*
Me too... and mine's all in one volume!

*Gloria's remark is lost on him and he continues. He peers into the tell*

**ARCHIE**
How are you coming, Doug?

**DOUG**
O.K., Professor. Indications are that we are now at the Middle Bronze Age level.

**ARCHIE** (*looks at books)*
That's about 2,000 to 1,700 B.C.

**GLORIA**
The age of the Patriarchs – Jacob!

**DOUG**
...I see the usual stuff here - parts of idols, fossils, tool heads... coin with Abimilech's face on it..... Hey! This is interesting... a small jug of some sort... all in one piece..

*Doug's hand appear at the edge of the tell passing up the "small jug." Archie takes it and examines it.*

**ARCHIE**
An oil cruse! Very interesting....

**GLORIA** *(reading)*

Genesis 28, verse 18... "and Jacob rose up early in the morning, and he took the stone that he had put for his pillows, and set it up for a pillar; and poured oil upon the top of it."

**DOUG**

Some strange looking stones here, Professor. One looks kind of like the one she's talking about - although I'd hate to use it for a "pillow." ...stain on one side could be oil...

**ARCHIE**

The Stone of Scone! What a find that would be!

**GLORIA**

What?!

**ARCHIE**

Don't you see – the stone underneath the British coronation throne... it's said to be "Jacob's Stone" - the covenant stone you just read about! If what Doug see is the real Jacob's Stone, my new book will be a guaranteed best seller!

**GLORIA**

Let's not miss the point of ***this*** best seller!: "And Jacob went out from Beersheba, and went towards Haran. And he lighted upon a certain place, and tarried there all night, because the sun was set; and he took of the stones of that place, and put them for his pillow, and lay down in that place to sleep."

**ARCHIE** *(yawns and sits down)*

I know how he felt.

*As Archie sits down in his chair and begins to doze, the musical theme from the song, "The Stones Cry Out" establishes a change in the scene. This sequence recurs each time a Biblical scene or character (puppet) appears out of the tell. Gloria sees all this and interacts with the action, even though Archie is "asleep." The lights dim and a light focuses on the top edge of the tell. The music trails off and Gloria assumes the role of narrator to the story that will be acted out by the puppet Jacob emerging from the tell. Gloria watches the puppet Jacob as he lies down on his flat stone...*

**GLORIA**

Consider young Jacob, asleep on that stone;
Fleeing, depressed, hungry, alone;

Having schemed to take birthright, and blessing as well
Cast off from home, he lands at Beth-el;

In fear of his brother and what lies ahead;
He feels only sadness, discomfort and dread;

Adrift and at loss, or so it now seems;
He's come to that place
Where God... will enter his dreams!

God saw something in Jacob, from the very beginning
That could overcome and outweigh
The conniving and sinning...

For Jacob was mean, rebellious, deceptive...
But... he feared God, had faith
And a spirit receptive.

So...
God showed him a ladder
(For his spiritual inspection)
"From where you are, Jacob,
UP is the only direction;
UP, Jacob...
Is your mid-course correction."

*During this last stanza of Gloria's recitation, Jacob is tossing and turning, as if tormented. At the same time, a sparkling white rope ladder appears over the top of the tell's backdrop and is slowly lowered until it comes to rest at Jacob's feet. As the musical introduction begins, two puppet "Angels" appear. As they sing, Jacob sways to the music and gives a little jump at each mention of the word: "UP"*

**ANGELS**

UP
IS THE PLACE WHERE YOU SHOULD BE
UP
IS THE VIEW THAT YOU SHOULD SEE;
AND UP
IS THE WAY OF REACHING HE
WHOSE TRUTH WILL SET YOU FREE.

UP
IS THE COURSE THAT YOU SHOULD SET;
UP
SHOULD BE WHAT YOU NEVER LET;
IF UP IS YOUR GOAL, YOU SURE CAN BET
YOUR NEEDS WILL ALL BE MET.

WHAT EVER YOU'RE UP AGAINST
LOOK AT THE UP-SIDE;
BE UP BEAT, UPLIFTED AND UP-RIGHT;
AND MOVE TO
THE RUNNETH OVER CUP-SIDE.

UP
IS A TRIP THAT YOU SHOULD TAKE
UP
IS THE CHOICE TO VOICE AND MAKE;
SO UP, RISE AND CLIMB, FOR HEAVEN'S SAKE
IT'S TIME THAT YOU WAKE...
UP!

ARISE, SHINE AND SPARKLE
AND ACT PATRIARCHAL, TOO
AFTER ALL, MY FRIEND
IT'S UP
TO YOU!

*The angels drop down out of sight. Archie wakes up and looks around.*

**GLORIA**

Angels are messengers, Sir Archie... and the message to Jacob was: it's wrong to scheme and cheat – and, in Jacob's case, it wasn't even necessary. C'mon..

**ARCHIE**

But that stone... it could be worth a lot!

**GLORIA**

It's not the stone... but the covenant it signified that has value. Don't you see? God saw beyond Jacob's failings, and recognized someone who has a teachable heart. That ladder represented the WAY - prayers go UP and the answers come DOWN. God told Jacob to look up... and to move up... and to stay on the "up and up."... and here's how Jacob responded: "If then God will be with me, and will keep me in this way that I go, and will give me bread to eat, and raiment to put on, so that I come again to my father's house in peace; then shall the Lord be my God; and this stone, which I have set for a pillar, shall be God's house; and all that thou shalt give me, I will surely give the tenth unto thee..."

*The puppet Jacob drops down into the tell; the ladder also drops down as the lights come up.*

**ARCHIE**

A tenth!

**GLORIA**

There's a lesson there, Sir Archie. If there was hope for Jacob, there's hope for all us schemers and connivers! Jeremiah 31 says: "Sing with gladness for Jacob... for God has redeemed him."

**ARCHIE** *(pauses)*

Doug.... leave that stone there. Gloria's right.... besides, this oil cruse will tell the story.

**GLORIA**

Too bad it's empty, Sir Archie. Imagine all the attention you'd get saying you had discovered oil in Israel!

**ARCHIE**

Let's move on, Doug.

**DOUG**

You mean "UP," Professor!

*At the mention of the word: UP, the music from that song begins and Archie gives a little inadvertent jump, the way Jacob did. Now, from the tell, comes some sound effects of electronic noise, squeals, buzzes, bleeps etc.*

## SCENE 5 - Joshua's Altar

**DOUG**

Metal detector is going wild, Professor!... got a whole layer here of spears, arrowheads, bashed-in helmets – usual battlefield stuff...

**ARCHIE**

The battles of Joshua!... about 1260 B.C.... that would be about right

*As Archie is checking his charts and maps, Doug's hand passes up a flat stone artifact with some strange writing on it.*

**DOUG**

...and this... looks like a signpost of some sort.

**GLORIA**

A milestone... to... Shechem!

**ARCHIE**

How would you know that? *(He examines the stone)*

Yes... yes... by golly, you're right! This clearly identifies Shechem.. but there was no battle ***there!***

**GLORIA**

The name, Shechem, in Hebrew means: "a place of diligence, a place of faithfulness."

**ARCHIE** *(looking at books)*

A lot happened at Shechem...

*From the tell comes a sound effect of a lot of metal clanking and banging.*

**DOUG**

No wonder they called it, The Bronze Age!"

**GLORIA** *(reads)*

..."and Joshua gathered all the tribes of Israel to Shechem, and called for the elders of Israel and for their judges and for their officers; and they presented themselves before God." That must have been quite a sight!

**ARCHIE**

Shechem is quite a sight. It lies in a small strip of lush green land about 500 yards wide. On one side, the terraced slope of Mount Gerazim; on the other, the rocky hillside of Mount Ebal. It made an incredible natural amphitheater. One man, standing at the base, could be heard by thousands on the hillsides - no sound system needed!

**GLORIA**

Imagine, such a spot - all the tribes of Israel gathered to hear Joshua's last speech... a sacred spot....and a sacred pledge.

*As before, the musical theme of "The Stones Cry Out" is played as the lights dim. The chorus re-enters and takes their place. They are dressed as Hebrew elders with desert headgear. Sir Archie is paying a little more attention than before. Gloria assumes her narrator role. The light focuses on the top edge of the front of the tell.*

**GLORIA**

To the valley of Shechem
They came, as before,
When the blessings and curses
Of Deuteronomy's verses,
Echoed across the valley floor...

Shechem:
Where Abraham and Jacob erected their stones;
Where refuge was granted in one of six zones;
Where rest would be given to Joseph's bones;
There,
In the valley of Shechem

To the valley of Shechem
They came, as a stream
Of elders and scribes,
From each of twelve tribes
Lining the slopes.. Of Ebal and Gerazim.

Shechem:
Where just as Moses had once foreseen,
The covenant people would in triumph convene,
And recite all the law with "Amens" in between;
There,
In the valley of Shechem.

Now,
Imagine that moment, that special day
When Joshua (aging), but with fire still raging,
Would speak for the Lord...
And would say:

*As Gloria recites this last stanza, the puppet Joshua emerges from the tell; looks around, as if checking on his audience, and then speaks:*

**JOSHUA**

Whom will ye serve? –
The covenant-keeping, miracle-making Lord?
Who guided your feet, your bow and your sword?
Who delivered you cities you did not build?
And vineyards which you never tilled?
All the land of His promise – now fulfilled...

Choose you this day, whom ye will serve;
Choose you this day, whom ye will serve.... *(Sings)*

EVERY DAY, EVERY HOUR
WE FACE MANY CHOICES;
TRIALS, TEMPTATIONS, COMPETING VOICES;
WHAT TO SAY, HOW TO ACT, WHAT TO DO?
GOD PUTS IT UP TO YOU...

Well?... well?

**CHORUS**

AS FOR ME AND MY HOUSE
WE WILL SERVE THE LORD,
OBSERVE HIS WORD,
AND SERVE THE LORD;
THOUGH AT TIME, WE SURELY DON'T
DESERVE THE LORD
WE WILL SERVE THE LORD
AS FOR ME AND MY HOUSE
WE WILL SERVE THE LORD
WE WILL SERVE THE LORD!

**JOSHUA**

NOW, FROM EGYPT TO MOAB
ACROSS JORDAN'S RIVER,
GOD WOULD PROVIDE AND THEN DELIVER;
WITH HIS GRACE, WITH HIS LOVE, MERCY TOO;
WHEN GOD CHOSE, HE CHOSE YOU...
well?... well?...

**CHORUS**

AS FOR ME AND MY HOUSE
WE WILL SERVE THE LORD
OBSERVE HIS WORD,
AND SERVE THE LORD;
THOUGH AT TIMES, WE SURELY MUST
UN-NERVE THE LORD,
WE WILL SERVE THE LORD
AS FOR ME AND MY HOUSE
WE WILL SERVE THE LORD
WE WILL SERVE THE LORD!

**JOSHUA**

LED BY GOD AND HIS SPIRIT,
HIS LAW, HIS PROVISION;
OR ON YOUR OWN, IT'S YOUR DECISION;
BUT YOUR CHANCES ARE FEW, NONE AND SLIM;
TURN FROM, OR TURN TO ...HIM...

Well?... well?...

**CHORUS**

AS FOR ME AND MY HOUSE
WE WILL SERVE THE LORD
OBSERVE HIS WORD,
AND SERVE THE LORD;
THOUGH AT TIMES, WE SURELY DON'T
DESERVE THE LORD,
WE WILL SERVE THE LORD
  AS FOR ME AND MY HOUSE
  WE WILL SERVE THE LORD
  WE WILL SERVE THE LORD!

**GLORIA** *(reads)*

..."and Joshua wrote these words in the book of the law of God, and took a great stone, and set it up there under an oak, that was by the sanctuary of the Lord. And Joshua said unto all the people:

**JOSHUA**

Behold, this stone shall be for a witness unto us; for it hath heard all the words of the Lord which he spake unto us; it shall be therefore a witness unto you, lest ye deny your God.

**CHORUS**

AS FOR ME AND MY HOUSE
WE WILL SERVE THE LORD
OBSERVE HIS WORD,
AND SERVE THE LORD;
THOUGH AT TIMES, WE SURELY MUST
UN-NERVE THE LORD
WE WILL SERVE THE LORD.
  AS FOR ME AND MY HOUSE
  WE WILL SERVE THE LORD
  WE WILL SERVE THE LORD!

**GLORIA**

and Joshua was right to be concerned. He died soon after this... and it wasn't long before the Hebrews lost sight of their commitment. The whole Book of Judges tells of their ups and (mostly) their downs.

**ARCHIE**

But Joshua's stone at Shechem stayed... as a witness.. Throughout the ages. It's still there today.

**GLORIA**

Stones can be a powerful witness, Sir Archie.

**ARCHIE**

I can see how the geologists might miss that... but not us archeologists!

**DOUG** *(sings)*

OH, YOU DON'T HAVE TO BE
A P.H.D.
WITH A HARVARD DEGREE
IN ARCHEOLOGY...

*The music repeats the phrasing of "As For Me and My House, we Will Serve the Lord" to end the scene.*

## SCENE 6 - Nehemiah's Wall

**DOUG**

Hey... look at this, Professor! Fancy coin... but I don't recognize the face on it..

*The hand appears at the edge of the tell, holding a large coin. Archie takes it and examines it.*

**ARCHIE**

Artaxerxes!

**DOUG**

Gesundheit!

**ARCHIE**

No, Doug... this is nothing to sneeze at. This is the royal seal of King Artaxerxes... the Persian monarch who took over what had been Babylon in...ahhh... let's see... (*Searches book)*

**GLORIA**

465 B.C. - the time of Nehemiah... and it was in Shushan.

**DOUG**

Gesundheit!. Hey, are you guys allergic to something up there? Hey, here's something else.... interesting....

**ARCHIE**

What is it, Doug?

**DOUG**

Well, if I didn't know better, I'd swear it was a blueprint – well, actually in stone it's more of a greyprint... with lines and measurements and stuff.... here..

*The hand appears again, this time with a rectangular gray stone "with lines and stuff." Archie takes it, begins to read as Gloria comes over to look at it.*

**ARCHIE**

...and a lot of different words listed down one side.... Hebrew I should think.

**GLORIA** *(reads over his shoulder)*

"valley," "sheep," "fountain," "fish," "refuse," "water"....

**DOUG**

A shopping list??

**ARCHIE**

No...no! Those are the names of the gates in the wall around the old city of Jerusalem.

**DOUG**

Gates! That explains this stone here with the bolts and bars in it – like a hinge of some kind. ...but it looks charred.

**GLORIA** (*back at her Bible...reads)*

Nehemiah, chapter one, verse three... "and concerning Jerusalem, they said unto me, the remnant that are left of the captivity there in the province are in great affliction and reproach: the wall of Jerusalem also is broken down, and the gates thereof are burned with fire."

**ARCHIE**

Nehemiah... I always skip over that book. Seems like mostly just a list of family names like Azbuk, Halohesh and Hashub.

**DOUG**

Bless you..

**ARCHIE**

.... and place names like Adonikam, Ziklag and Michmash...

**GLORIA**

Oh, it's much more than that! It's a wonderful story of exhortation, and of restoration... and of one man's incredible commitment. After all, Nehemiah was a high official in Artaxerxes' court... and he left all that to travel back over 1,000 difficult miles to return and rebuild Jerusalem... after it had lain in ruins for over 100 years.

**ARCHIE**

Well.... the wall, anyway...

**GLORIA**

More than the wall. He restored his people's faith and their commitment to God. His name means "comfort of God"... and he was like a picture of the Holy Spirit.

**DOUG**

Gloria, I'm embarrassed to say that I wouldn't know Nehemiah from Oscar Meyer. Tell us more.

**GLORIA**

Well, it ***is*** a meaty story. Here's a condensed version... just for you *(looks at Sir Archie)*

**DOUG**

And who was the king?... Art somebody??

**GLORIA**

Artaxerxes.

*Archie sneezes.*

*Now the music begins with a modern swing beat as the lights go down and focus on the top of the tell, indicating puppet activity. Nehemiah can either be a child with a Nehemiah T-shirt & hard hat, or a puppet. In either case, as the chorus is sung, Nehemiah stacks up the cardboard brick blocks as the chorus is sung. Every time the name Artaxerxes is mentioned a "King" puppet comes up briefly, then drops down again. The chorus comes on now, all wearing yellow hard hats and each carrying one of the cardboard bricks. Archie is paying close attention to all this.*

**GLORIA** *(sings)*

AND IT CAME TO PASS
IN BABYLON
DURING THE REIGN OF KING ARTAXERXES
THAT HIS CUPBEARER NAMED, NEHEMIAH, CLAIMED
THEN AND THERE AS PART OF HIS PERKS, HE'S
JUST GOT TO RESPOND TO THE HEBREW DESPOND
OVER THE WALL ALL DOWN IN HIS HOMETOWN, ZION;
SO THE KING SAYS: "GO, BUT YOU SHOULD KNOW,
THAT I'LL BE KEEPING AN EYE ON"...

**CHORUS**

NEHEMIAH, NEHEMIAH
STACKING THOSE STONES UP
HIGHER AND HIGHER;
RESTORING THE WALL, FULL HEIGHT, FULL LENGTH;
REMINDING US ALL...
THE JOY OF THE LORD, IS OUR STRENGTH!
NEHEMIAH!

**GLORIA**

AND SO OFF HE GOES
TO JERUSALEM
WITH THE SUPPORT OF KING ARTAXERXES;
NEHEMIAH WILL FIND, MORALE HAS DECLINED
AND BEFORE THE START OF HIS WORK, SEES...
A CHANCE TO CEMENT, MORE THAN WALLS THAT ARE SPENT
SO TO HIS CHUMS BECOMES AN EXHORTER;
WITH THE BLOCKS ON BLOCKS, JERUSALEM ROCKS
AS GOD IS USED FOR THE MORTAR...

**CHORUS**

NEHEMIAH, NEHEMIAH
STACKING THOSE STONES UP
HIGHER AND HIGHER;
RESTORING THE WALL FULL HEIGHT, FULL LENGTH;
REMINDING US ALL...
HE JOY OF THE LORD IS OUR STRENGTH
. NEHEMIAH!

**GLORIA**

NEHEMIAH WORKS
WITH ALL HIS TEAMS
CHARGING THE WORKS TO KING ARTAXERXES;
AND THEY WORK TIL THEY'RE PRONE, KEEPING NOSE TO THE STONE
"SEE THAT NO ONE DEPARTS OR SHIRKS, PLEASE"
WITH THE WALLS ON THE RISE, AND DOORS CUT TO SIZE
THE CITY IS SURE SECURE FOR THE DURATION'
NEHEMIAH UP TOP, WON'T EVEN STOP
TO ADMIRE THE RESTORATION...

**CHORUS**

NEHEMIAH, NEHEMIAH
STACKING THOSE STONES UP
HIGHER AND HIGHER;
RESTORING THE WALL, FULL HEIGHT, FULL LENGTH;
REMINDING US ALL....
THE JOY OF THE LORD IS OUR STRENGTH!
NEHEMIAH!

**GLORIA**

NOW, NOT EVERYONE
WANTS THIS JOB DONE
IN SPITE OF DECREES FROM KING ARTAXERXES;
AND SO TWO LOCAL CHIEFS, COME DISPENSING SOME GRIEF;
NEHEMIAH, HE'S SMART AND HE IRKS THESE
LOCAL ARMED TOUGHS, CALLING THEIR BLUFFS
WON'T TAKE A BREAK OR MAKE AN APPOINTMENT;
AND SO THESE TWO GUYS WILL NOT BE FLIES
IN OUR MAN'S ANOINTMENT...

**CHORUS**

NEHEMIAH, NEHEMIAH
STACKING THOSE STONES UP
HIGHER AND HIGHER;
RESTORING THE WALL, FULL HEIGHT, FULL LENGTH;
REMINDING US ALL:
THE JOY OF THE LORD IS OUR STRENGTH!
NEHEMIAH!

*The chorus exits to the left as the music continues underneath. Gloria continues in recitation*

**GLORIA**

And the joy of the Lord was most evident
That day at the wall where everyone went
To hear Ezra read the Law to them all
As they dedicated themselves... and their wall

With prayer and praise
To their sovereign Lord
They celebrated all
That had been restored:

Their hope, their pride
Their city, their nation,
Their spirit, their faith...
Their dedication.

All, by God's spirit working through one man
An incredible plan; and incredible man...

*The musical beat, as before, with Archie, Gloria and Doug singing the chorus*

**ARCHIE, GLORIA, DOUG**

NEHEMIAH, NEHEMIAH
CALLING THEM ALL UP
HIGHER AND HIGHER
RESTORING THEM ALL, FULL HEIGHT, FULL LENGTH
AND SOUNDING THE CALL....
THE JOY OF THE LORD IS OUR STRENGTH
THE JOY OF THE LORD IS OUR STRENGTH!
NEHEMIAH*!*

## SCENE 7 - The Bible

**DOUG**

I guess my problem is, I never know where to look in the Bible to find Nehemiah.

**ARCHIE**

Right between Ezra and Esther – the last of the twelve books of history... and just before the books of poetry or wisdom.

**GLORIA**

That's pretty good, Sir Archie!

**DOUG**

How do you keep them all straight, Professor? I can dig them all up... but I don't know where they are!

**ARCHIE**

Well, take a little break, Doug... and I'll tell the secret.

**GLORIA**

...and this from the author of "Bursting the Biblical Bubble in the Rubble" – or whatever that is!

**ARCHIE**

Doug, here's a road map so you can really dig through the Bible. Remember this, and you can not only find Nehemiah – you can find Habakkuk!

**GLORIA**

That's pronounced: Ha-BACK-kuk!

**ARCHIE**

Trust me... my way rhymes better!

*Sir Archie leaves his book and chart table and comes forward to center stage. The chorus re-enters dressed as scholars with white mortarboards.*

**CHORUS**

DIGGING THROUGH THE BIBLE BOOK BY BOOK
STARTING WITH THE TORAH, OR A PENTETEUCH;
LEARNING WHERE TO LOOK...
FOR HABAKKUK
DIGGING THROUGH THE BIBLE
BOOK BY BOOK.

**DOUG**

DIGGING THROUGH THE BIBLE BOOK BY BOOK

**ARCHIE**

GENESIS, THEN EXODUS,
LEVITICUS COMPOSES,
WITH NUMBERS, DEUTERONOMY -
THE PENTETEUCH BY MOSES.

JOSHUA, JUDGES, BOOK OF RUTH,
THE HISTORIES, THEN TWO OF
SAMUEL, KINGS AND CHRONICLES
AND EVERYTHING THEY KNEW OF.

EZRA, NEHEMIAH, THEN
THE STORY OF QUEEN ESTHER;
NOW HERE'S ANOTHER CHORUS, THEN
I'LL TELL YOU WHAT THE REST ARE...

**CHORUS**
DIGGING THROUGH THE BIBLE BOOK BY BOOK
STARTING WITH THE TORAH, OR A PENTETEUCH;
LEARNING WHERE TO LOOK
FOR HABAKKUK:
DIGGING THROUGH THE BIBLE
BOOK BY BOOK!

**DOUG**
DIGGING THROUGH THE BIBLE BOOK BY BOOK

**ARCHIE**
POETIC BOOKS ARE FIVE, THERE'S JOB,
AND PSALMS, THE SHORT AND LONG OF;
THEN PROVERBS AND ECCLESIASTES,
SOLOMON, THE SONG OF.

PROPHETS NEXT, ISAIAH,
JEREMIAH, LAMENTATIONS;
FOLLOWED BY EZEKIEL
AND DANIEL'S REVELATIONS.

Ready for a dozen minor prophets??

**ARCHIE**
HOSEA, JOEL AND AMOS,
OBADIAH, JONAH, MICAH,
NAHUM, THEN THERE'S HABAKKUK
(THAT'S THE ONE I LIKE-A!)

ZEPHANIAH, HAGGAI, ZECHARIAH,
(NO ONE FINER)
FINALLY, THERE'S MALACHI -
THE LAST OF PROPHETS, MINOR!

**CHORUS**
DIGGING THROUGH THE BIBLE BOOK BY BOOK
STARTING WITH THE TORAH, OR A PENTETEUCH;
LEARNING WHERE TO LOOK
FOR HABAKKUK;
DIGGING THROUGH THE BIBLE
BOOK BY BOOK.

**DOUG**
DIGGING THROUGH THE BIBLE BOOK BY BOOK.

**ARCHIE**

THIRTY-NINE OLD TESTAMENT
THE BOOKS THAT I JUST LISTED;
TWENTY-SEVEN IN THE NEW,
SO KEEP THEM ALL UN-TWISTED!

MATTHEW, MARK AND LUKE AND JOHN,
THE ACTS, THEN THE COLOSSAL
TWENTY-ONE EPISTLES
WRITTEN MOSTLY BY APOSTLES.

And Paul was the first string letter-man.

TO ROMANS AND CORINTHIANS,
GALATIANS AND EPHESIANS,
PHILIPPIANS, COLOSSIANS, THESS-
ALONIANS (ALL GRECIANS)

TO TIMOTHY AND TITUS;
TO PHILEMON AND THE HEBREWS,
BY JAMES AND PETER, JOHN AND JUDE
TO SPREAD THE GOSPEL'S KEY NEWS.

**GLORIA**

AND WHAT BEGAN WITH GENESIS
THE STORY OF CREATION,
ENDS IN TRIUMPH AND IN HOPE -
THE BOOK OF REVELATION.

**CHORUS**

DIGGING THROUGH THE BIBLE BOOK BY BOOK;
STARTING WITH THE TORAH, OR A PENTETEUCH;
LEARNING WHERE TO LOOK
FOR HABAKKUK;
DIGGING THROUGH THE BIBLE
BOOK BY BOOK

**DOUG**

DIGGING THROUGH THE BIBLE BOOK BY BOOK

**GLORIA**
BUT WHAT ABOUT THE COVENANTS,
THE MIRACLES UNENDING;
ALL THE PROMISES OF GOD,
THE MESSAGES HE'S SENDING?

AND MESSIAH, SENT FOR US,
ATONEMENT AND REDEMPTION,
GRACE AND MERCY, PEACE AND LOVE;
YOU ALSO DIDN'T MENTION.

OF COURSE, IT'S NICE TO KNOW THE NAMES
THE ORDER OF THE SECTIONS;
BUT WHAT GOOD IS A MAP TO YOU,
IF YOU DON'T HAVE DIRECTIONS?

*Gloria, as she has done in the past, now turns and directs the chorus, which now sings a changed verse, a la Gloria...*

**CHORUS**
DIGGING THROUGH THE BIBLE BOOK BY BOOK
SEEING HOW THE GOSPEL FULFILLS THE PENTETEUCH;
SEEING JESUS EVERYWHERE YOU LOOK;
AS YOU READ THE BIBLE
BOOK BY BOOK!

**ARCHIE & DOUG**
AS WE READ THE BIBLE... BOOK BY BOOK!!

## SCENE 8 - The Tomb:

*The chorus now removes their mortarboards, and passes them to the rear. They are now wearing purple choir robes.*

**ARCHIE**
What's this, Doug?

*Archie is examining a large crescent section of stone that has been passed up.*

**DOUG**
I was hoping you'd know, Professor. Looks like a piece of a big wheel – had to have been about six or eight feet in diameter.

**ARCHIE**

Too big for a wheel. Could be a millstone... or maybe even the cover for a well. By my calculation, it must have weighed several tons!

**DOUG**

Put that on your well, Professor, and you'll die of thirst!

**ARCHIE**

Even for a millstone, it would have been too big and too heavy to move - even for oxen.

**GLORIA**

Man was not meant to move a stone like that – only an angel.

**ARCHIE**

An angel!

**GLORIA**

The most important stone in the whole Bible was like that. It sealed a tomb... and it was important because it wasn't there when it was supposed to be.

**ARCHIE** *(examines the piece)*

Let's see... thermo-luminescense dating can tell us exactly when this stone was....

**GLORIA**

It was 30 A.D. - just after Passover. A beautiful spring day... in a garden.

*Archie is clearly impressed by Gloria's certainty. He looks at the stone fragment, then pays close attention to what she sings.*

.

**GLORIA** *(sings)*

HERE WAS THE STONE THAT WAS ROLLED AWAY
FROM A TOMB IN A GARDEN THAT FINE SPRING DAY;
AND HERE WAS THE ANGEL HEARD TO SAY:
"HE IS NOT HERE, HE IS RISEN."

**CHORUS**

RISEN INDEED, RISEN INDEED
CHRIST THE LORD
IS RISEN INDEED...
RISEN INDEED

**GLORIA**

HERE WAS THE CLOTH THAT ENCIRCLED HIS HEAD
AND HERE WERE THE WORDS THAT THE ANGEL SAID:
"WHY SEEK YE THE LIVING AMONG THE DEAD?"
HE IS NOT HERE, HE IS RISEN.

**CHORUS**

RISEN INDEED, RISEN INDEED
CHRIST THE LORD
IS RISEN INDEED...
RISEN INDEED

**GLORIA**

HERE WERE THE WOMEN WHO SAW HOW HE DIED;
AND HERE WAS THE DAY THAT WAS PROPHESIED;
HERE IS LIFE, HERE IS TRUTH, NO ONE CAN HIDE;
HE IS NOT HERE, HE IS RISEN.

**CHORUS**

RISEN INDEED, RISEN INDEED
CHRIST THE LORD
IS RISEN INDEED...
RISEN INDEED.

RISEN INDEED, RISEN INDEED
CHRIST THE LORD
IS RISEN INDEED...
RISEN INDEED.
RISEN INDEED!

## SCENE 9 - the Revelation:

**GLORIA**

Don't you see, Sir Archie? The stones are indeed crying out to you. God wants you to know their true meaning. They're not just artifacts to be excavated, sold and then tucked away in some museum. These stones come from the ROCK - THE Rock, which Psalm 89 says is "the rock of your salvation."

Jacob's stone signified God's covenant - his promise that he will never forsake us.

Joshua's stone was for a witness of his word - and a reminder that our words aren't anywhere near as solid!

Nehemiah's stones showed restoration, re-birth and redemption.

The stone rolled away from the tomb was a memorial – not to death, but to life – everlasting life through the sacrifice of the Lord Jesus.

Your work, far from disproving the Bible, confirms its very message - its reality and its meaning to all of us.

The point is, that each stone, each "find," tells us something, not just about Jacob, Joshua or Nehemiah - but something about God.

First of all, he's a living God - and he's provided Jesus to live in each of us... if we will let Him.

Look at that moon up there, Sir Archie - shining so bright it can even be seen in the daytime. Now consider this: *(Sings)*

SCIENTISTS SAY
THE MOON IS A ROCK;
LIFELESS, WITH NO LIGHT OF ITS OWN;
BUT THE MOON LIGHTS THE NIGHT,
WONDERFULLY SO
REFLECTING THE LIGHT THAT THE SUN HAS SHONE.

ALL OF US HERE
ARE JUST LIKE THE MOON;
WE CANNOT SHINE ON OUR OWN;
BUT WE ALL CAN REFLECT
THE LIGHT OF GOD'S SON
AND SHINE WITH THE LOVE HE HAS SHOWN.

**CHORUS**

RISEN INDEED, RISEN INDEED
CHRIST THE LORD
IS RISEN INDEED...
RISEN INDEED

RISEN INDEED, RISEN INDEED
CHRIST THE LORD
IS RISEN INDEED...
RISEN INDEED

RISEN INDEED!

**ARCHIE**

I see it now. I see it!

**GLORIA**

Doug, you're awfully quiet down there!

**DOUG**

I can even see it from down here, Professor. Hallelujah!

**GLORIA**

In a way, Sir Archie, we are all stones - sculpted and fashioned by God... just as Jacob was. God chose him, loved him and perfected him. And Simon Peter, the one who said that we are living stones, here to build his church... Jesus chose him, called him a rock, and over time fashioned him into a pillar. That wonderful story is all there in the Book of Acts - the power that spread the gospel and changed the world. That's what you should be digging into!

**ARCHIE**

The Book of Acts! The Book of Acts!

**DOUG**

What, Professor?

**ARCHIE**

The Book of Acts, Doug! You wrap up here. I'm going back to my sponsors with the good news - and a great idea. The Book of Acts...of course!

*Sir Archie gathers up his things and races off right, followed by Gloria. Chorus also exits left*

**DOUG**

Acts....acts.... Oh well. I'll dig something up; I always do!

## SCENE 10 - The Act:

*The light goes off on the top of the tell. From the left side of the tell, there enters a Damon Runyon type character... Manny Arcald, the theatrical agent. He puts a telephone and a rollodex down on the small desk Archie has vacated; flips down his nameplate and moves it forward. He sits down as the telephone rings. He answers it. After each dumb joke line of Manny's, there is a drum rim shot.*

**MANNY**

Yeah??? This is Manny...
Acts??? of course I book acts.
Look, pal... this is Manny Arcald - "where the few are chosen!"
I book only the best acts...
Biblical acts are my specialty.
Just you leave it to old Manny, Doug...
Now , let's see (do I book acts!).... (*Takes card out*)

How about a drill team? Moses and the Ten Commanders – with their do's and don'ts... Great for legal conventions... or Bar Mitzvah's ... and speaking of the law... what about some dancers? I got 613 dancers - The Torah Doras!!
No?.... huh? Hey, what about animal acts?? I got some great ones!
Like Balaam and his Talking Donkey... nope, no good -
they're off on a political gig for the Democrats... Here's one–
Samson! This guy wrestles a lion! No...no...no.. The lion doesn't get hurt..
He's got this ***claws*** in his contract. (That's a little lion joke, Doug)
Or what about a trained whale? Comes out with this guy, Jonah... what an entrance!!!
Musical acts??? Sure, sure... now, let's see... Here's Miriam and her Tambourine..
Too quiet, huh? Hey, what about Gideon??? He works with 300 trumpeters! Too loud??
What kind of gig is this for, anyway? What's the theme?
Archeology? Stones??? What about a rock group??
Here's a hot one - Beelzebub and the Accusations?? Nope, they're permanently assigned to MTV
Let's see.... archeology...stones.... BINGO!! This is perfect! The Quarry Sisters!!!
Just you leave it to old Manny, Doug.
No.. Of course they're refined... very refined.. They're a work of art!

*Manny hangs up the phone and goes off with the desk. At this, the lights come up on the tell and flash as three puppets come up in a row with their backs to the audience. Manny comes back on to do their introduction.*

**QUARRY SISTERS**

WHEN IT COMES TO STONES...
HOLD THE PHONES;
THERE'S A LESSON TO BE LEARNED;
FROM THE BOOK OF ACTS
WE'VE DUG UP THE FACTS
LEAVING NOT A STONE UN-TURNED!
SO HERE'S SOME SCRIPTURAL GOALS FOR YOU
THREE GREAT SUPPORTING ROLES FOR YOU;
TAKE IT FROM US, THEN ON YOUR OWN...
YOU, TOO, CAN BE....
A LIVING STONE!

*A boogie woogie beat starts as Manny gives his introduction*

**MANNY**

Presenting.... the Quarry Sisters!
Rocksanne.....Iona.... and Ruby!

*As Manny calls each name, that puppet turns around to face the audience. Rocksanne wears a costume that suggests a masonry wall; Iona has on what appears to be a Grecian column with a ionic capital; Ruby is wearing a priest's ephod with the 12 sparkling gemstones. Their song is 1940's style, in the manner of the Andrews Sisters. Manny exits behind the tell.*

**QUARRYS**

BE A ROCK
BE A PILLAR
BE A GEM..
BE LIKE PETER, NEHEMIAH
JACOB, JOSHUA AND THEM;
TAKE YOUR PLACE, BY HIS GRACE
IN THE NEW JERUSALEM

BE A ROCK; BE A PILLAR; BE A GEM!

*As each sister solos, she speaks a brief introductory couplet; then pauses while the beat begins. In a spoken jive style, she then recites against the beat as the other two sisters turn to watch.*

**ROCKSANNE**

Now, what does it mean to be a rock?
Like Peter, the rock... the builder of the flock...

Now a rock is a block
In a firm foundation;
And the rock puts a lock
On your salvation.

The rock is where
You're rooted and grounded;
And on a rock...
Your house should be founded

Put your stock in the rock, Doc
Answer the knock
And be a rock... around the clock!

**QUARRYS**

TAKE YOUR PLACE
BY HIS GRACE
IN THE NEW JERUSALEM..
AS A ROCK, AS A PILLAR, AS A GEM.

**IONA**

Now, Peter was a pillar of the early church
To find a better pillar,
You'd have far and wide to search

So, what's a pillar??

> Around the temple
> Around the court
> A pillar is the
> Visible means of support;
>
> Over time it'll hold up;
> Won't crumble or fold up;
> A real long-laster...
> In marble, cedar or alabaster;
>
> A pillar does more than its share
> Making columns everywhere;
> Solid and groovy –
> That's a pillar;
> Like an epic movie:
> A Cecil B De Mille-er
>
> So
> Don't be a space filler
> Plan to be
> A pillar with a capital "P"

**QUARRYS**

> TAKE YOUR PLACE
> BY HIS GRACE
> IN THE NEW JERUSALEM
> AS A ROCK, AS A PILLAR, AS A GEM.

**RUBY**

A pillar, a rock; it's great to be either of them;
But the top of the line - the creme de la creme
Is a gem....

> I'm a gem who aims
> To shine like the twelve
> That scripture names...
> So here are my claims:

I'm valuable and precious
What more can I say?
I'm a prize...
Any size; any day.

Always true, never foolish;
And proud to be jewel-ish;
I'm polished, not clever...
But I'll last forever;

There's twelve of us
In each Testament;
In any setting, thus
We're a great invest-a-ment.

Be like me... and them... Be a gem!

**ALL**

AS A ROCK, AS A PILLAR, AS A GEM
YOU'LL RATE
A POSSIBLE APOSTLE, YOU CAN EMULATE

BE A ROCK, BE A PILLAR, BE A GEM
BE LIKE PETER, NEHEMIAH,
JACOB, JOSHUA AND THEM
TAKE YOUR PLACE
BY HIS GRACE
IN THE NEW JERUSALEM

AS A ROCK, AS A PILLAR, AS A...
VALUABLE AND PRECIOUS...
GEM!

## SCENE 11 - The Witness:

*The scene now shifts back to the way it was in Scene 1 at the Testimony. Sir Archie is back at the lectern at center stage. The stage is empty, except for the tell, which is dark.*

**ARCHIE**

And that is how it all happened. But the best part is what happens next... sales from my testimony book, "The Stones Cry Out - Hallelujah," have been so spectacular that's it's financed my next trip - with a lot of help from my dear friends - who have also changed...

*At this, Gloria enters with the Chairwoman, leading the chorus who now have on Israeli tourist hats. The lights come up on the tell.*

**CHAIRWOMAN**

That's right... we no longer are the Creative Historical Order Revising Understanding of Scripture...

**GLORIA**

They're now "Christians Having Only Recently Understood Scripture." *(Points to banner)*

**ARCHIE**

I thought of taking tours to see the stones that God showed me... but then Gloria had me read the Book of Acts and Mark 16...

**GLORIA** *(reads)*

... "and ye shall be witnesses unto me both in Jerusalem and unto the uttermost parts of the earth." And : "Go ye into all the world and preach the gospel to every creature."

**ARCHIE**

So I'm off with my friends to preach the gospel in the "uttermost" - to make disciples, just as the Lord Jesus has commanded us. And I'm taking the stones with me - in a model of the tell.... to give everyone a glimpse of the same vision I had.

**GLORIA**

And we have a name for this exhibit that we know will attract crowds. *(To the tell)* Doug??

*A sign is poked up from the tell. It says: TELL – A VISION!*

**CHAIRWOMAN**

And we're all with you, Sir Archie... not going to be left out this time! After all, we are your C.H.O.R.U.S.

**ARCHIE**

Everything all packed in there, Doug?

**DOUG**

With loving care, Professor.

*From inside the tell, up come the three Quarry Sisters.*

**QUARRYS**

Let's get this show on the road!

**GLORIA**

And this is just the beginning. Right, Sir Archie?

**ARCHIE**

The beginning is the most important part - especially since the beginning never ends. John's gospel put it best. Chorus??

**CHORUS**

IN THE BEGINNING WAS THE WORD
AND THE WORD WAS WITH GOD
AND THE WORD WAS GOD
FULL OF GRACE AND TRUTH

AND WE BEHOLD HIS GLORY
AND WE BEHOLD HIS GLORY
AND WE BEHOLD HIS GLORY
FULL OF GRACE AND TRUTH

IN THE BEGINNING THERE WAS LIFE
AND THE LIFE WAS THE LIGHT
AND THE TRUE LIGHT CAME
FULL OF GRACE AND TRUTH

AND WE BEHOLD HIS GLORY
AND WE BEHOLD HIS GLORY
AND WE BEHOLD HIS GLORY
FULL OF GRACE AND TRUTH

IN THE BEGINNING WAS THE WORD
AND THE WORD WAS MADE FLESH
MADE TO DWELL IN US
FULL OF GRACE AND TRUTH

AND WE BEHOLD HIS GLORY
AND WE BEHOLD HIS GLORY
AND WE BEHOLD HIS GLORY
FULL OF GRACE AND TRUTH.

*As a curtain call, all sing a reprise of the opening title song , "The Stones Cry Out," as first the puppet characters emerge from the tell: Jacob, the two angels, Joshua, Nehemiah, Artaxerxes and the Quarry Sisters. The Manny and Doug, followed by the Chairwoman, Sir Archie and Gloria. The Host returns to call each by name.*

**ALL**

OH THE STONES CRY OUT
THE STONES CRY OUT
FROM RUINS AS YET UNEXPLORED;
AND EACH STONE GIVES ME
A REASON TO SHOUT:
OH, HALLELUJAH, PRAISE TO THE LORD!

HALLELUJAH, PRAISE TO THE LORD!

*Curtain*

# Stones - Overture

Clark Tyler
*Arranged by Andrew Bell*

33 E♭ B♭7 E♭
Pno.
3
39 E♭ A♭ B♭ E♭ A♭
45 B♭ E♭ B♭
51 E♭ B♭ E♭ Fm B♭ E♭
rit.
57 B♭ B♭7 E♭sus E♭ B♭ B♭7 E♭ Cm7 B♭sus
rit.
63 B♭7 E♭ B♭ E♭
accel.

68
B♭ B♭7 E♭ E♭ E♭7 A♭ E♭ B♭7 E♭
Pno.
rit.
74
B♭ B♭7 E♭sus E♭ B♭ B♭7 E♭ Cm7
Pno.
79
B♭sus Fm B♭7 E♭
Pno.
rit.

# The Stones Cry Out

Clark Tyler
*Arranged by Andrew Bell*

Voice
Piano
Pno.
C F C
Oh the stones cry out, the stones cry out.
C F G C Am F G C
Re-veal ing the truth they have stored. And each stone is found to wit- ness a-
Am F G C C
bout the ev-er last-ing word of The Lord. Oh the stones,
C F G7 C
oh the stones tell of ser- vants and kings, and man- gers and thrones;

Voice
Pno.
21 Dm G C Dm7 G
tem- ples_ and tab- lets and tombs with_ their trea- sures of bones. Oh the
25 C F C F G
stones cry out, the stones cry out. From ru-ins as yet un-ex-
30 C Am Dm G C Am
plored and each stone gives me a rea son to shout: Oh
34 F G C Am F G C
Hall-e - lu-jah praise to The Lord. Oh Hall-e - lu-jah praise to The Lord.

# Sir Archie

Clark Tyler
*Arranged by Andrew Bell*

22
B7 E B E B
Voice
A brill-iant mind, a sto-ny heart we think you'll find is quite a part of star-chy Sir Ar-
Pno.
28
E E B E
Voice
chie O' log - i - cal.
Pno.
34
A E B7
Voice
In ev-ery tell and wa-di from Sy-ri-a to Sau-di I'm a ve-ry bus-y bo-dy just
Pno.
41
E A E B
Voice
dig-ging up the truth! And I can tell who's who in each tomb and ev-ery ru-in; I can find a cle-ver
Pno.

48
E
Tutti cantano:
B
E
Voice
clue in each bro-ken pot and tooth. He's dig-ging up the truth in each bro-ken pot and tooth.
Pno.
55
E
B
Voice
(Patter:) I love to stick my pick and sho - vel in - to some old Hit-tite ho - vel.
Pno.
61
E
B7
E
B7
Voice
(Repeat patter ad lib over chords:)
Lyrics: Or open up some ancient man's crypt and read his mail...though it's in sanscrit.
The Bible as I loudly doubt it helps sell the books I write about it.
The hocus pocus in my theories would make a marvelous mini-series.
Pno.
68
E
B7
B7/D♯
E
B7
Voice
A brill-iant mind, a
Pno.

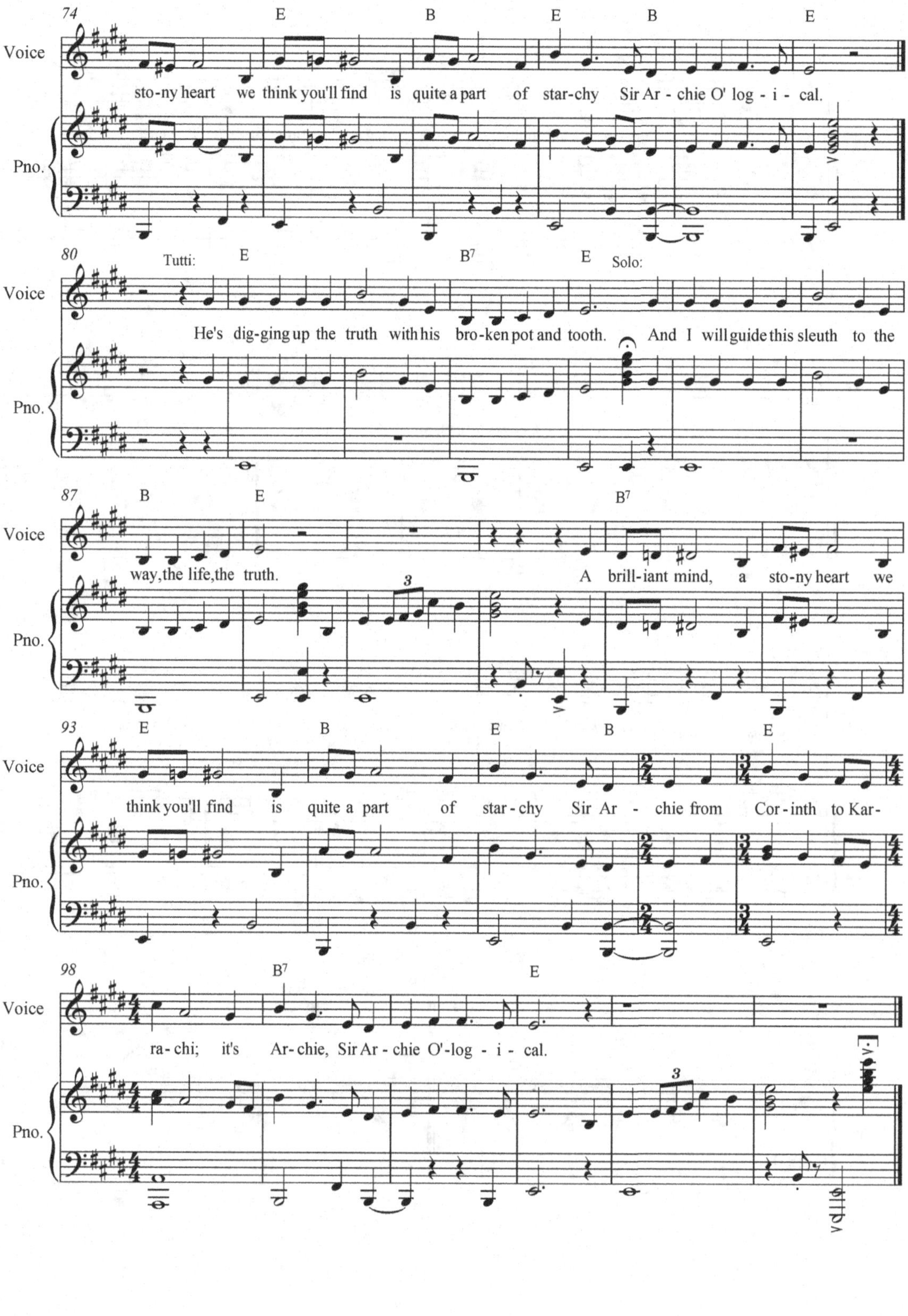
74
E B E B E
Voice
sto-ny heart we think you'll find is quite a part of star-chy Sir Ar - chie O' log - i - cal.
Pno.
80
Tutti: E B7 E Solo:
Voice
He's dig-ging up the truth with his bro-ken pot and tooth. And I will guide this sleuth to the
Pno.
87
B E B7
Voice
way, the life, the truth. A brill-iant mind, a sto-ny heart we
3
Pno.
93
E B E B E
Voice
think you'll find is quite a part of star - chy Sir Ar - chie from Cor - inth to Kar-
Pno.
98
B7 E
Voice
ra - chi; it's Ar - chie, Sir Ar - chie O'-log - i - cal.
3
Pno.

# Dig

Clark Tyler
*Arranged by Andrew Bell*

21
G
C
F
C
Voice
me in a hole and I'll dig. No high - tech or rob - o - tic rig, just
Pno.
25
G
C
Voice
me to dig, and dig, and dig!
Pno.

# Up

ClarkTyler
*Arranged by Andrew Bell*

25 C6 G7
Voice
Up is a trip that you should take. Up is the choice to voice and make; So
Pno.
29 C F Dm7 G G7 C C7 F
Voice
up, rise and climb for hea-ven's sake it's time that you wake up! A - rise, shine,and spar - kle and
Pno.
34 C D Gm
Voice
act pa - tri - arch - al, too. Af - ter all, my friend it's
Pno.
37 C F
Voice
up to you! Get up!
Pno.
3
3

# We Will Serve The Lord

by Clark Tyler
*Arranged by Andrew Bell*

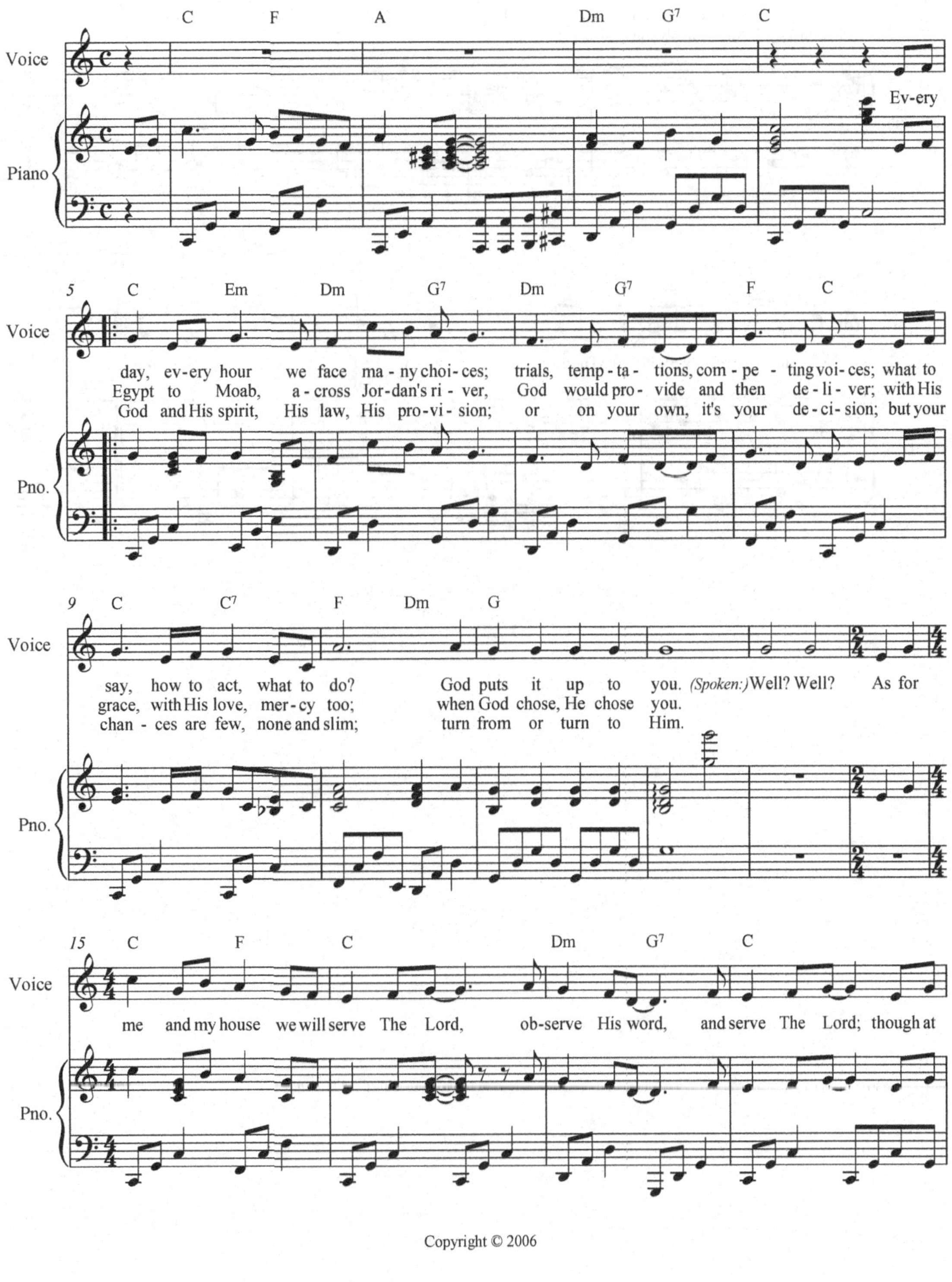

*Repeat Chorus after Joshua speaks. Repeat instrumental music to end of scene.*

# Nehemiah

Clark Tyler
*Arranged by Andrew Bell*

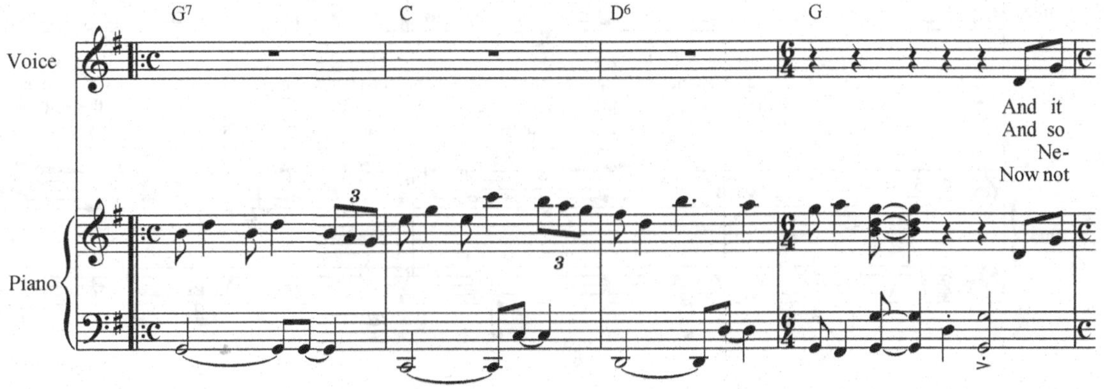
G7
C
D6
G
Voice
And it
And so
Ne-
Now not
3
3
Piano

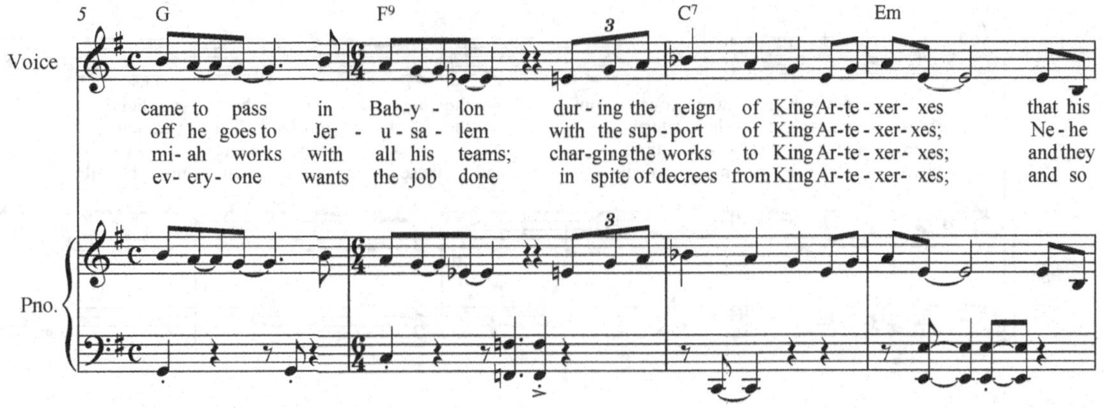
5
G
F9
C7
Em
Voice
came to pass in Bab-y - lon dur - ing the reign of King Ar-te - xer- xes that his
off he goes to Jer - u - sa - lem with the sup - port of King Ar-te - xer- xes; Ne - he
mi- ah works with all his teams; char-ging the works to King Ar-te - xer- xes; and they
ev- ery- one wants the job done in spite of decrees from King Ar-te - xer- xes; and so
3
3
Pno.

9
G
C7
G
Voice
cup-bear - er named Ne - he - mi - ah claimed then and there as part of his perks;
mi - ah will find, mor-ale had de - clined and be - fore the start of his work
work 'til they're prone, keep-ing nose to the stone; "see that no one de - parts or shirks
two lo - cal chiefs come dis - pen-sing some grief; Ne - he - mi - ah, he's smart and he irks
Pno.

12 D7 G Cm7
Voice
he's just got to res - pond to the He-brew des pond; o - ver the
sees... a chance to ce - ment more than just walls that are spent so to his
please." with the walls on the rise, and the doors cut to size the city is
these lo - cal armed toughs, cal - ling thier bluffs won't take a
Pno.
15 C7 D7♭9 G C7 G
Voice
wall all down in his home-town Zi- on; so the king says go but you should know that
chums be-cmes an ex - hor - ter; with the blocks on blocks Je-ru - sa-lem rocks; as
sure secure for the dur - a - tion; Ne-he - mi - ah up top, won't e - ven stop to
break or make an ap - point- ment; and so these two guys will not be flies
Pno.
19 D7 G C
Voice
I'll be keep-ing an eye on (Chorus:) Ne-he - mi - ah, Ne - he-mi- ah;
God is used for the mor - tar...
ad-mire the res-to-ra - tion.
in our man's a - noint - ment.
Pno.

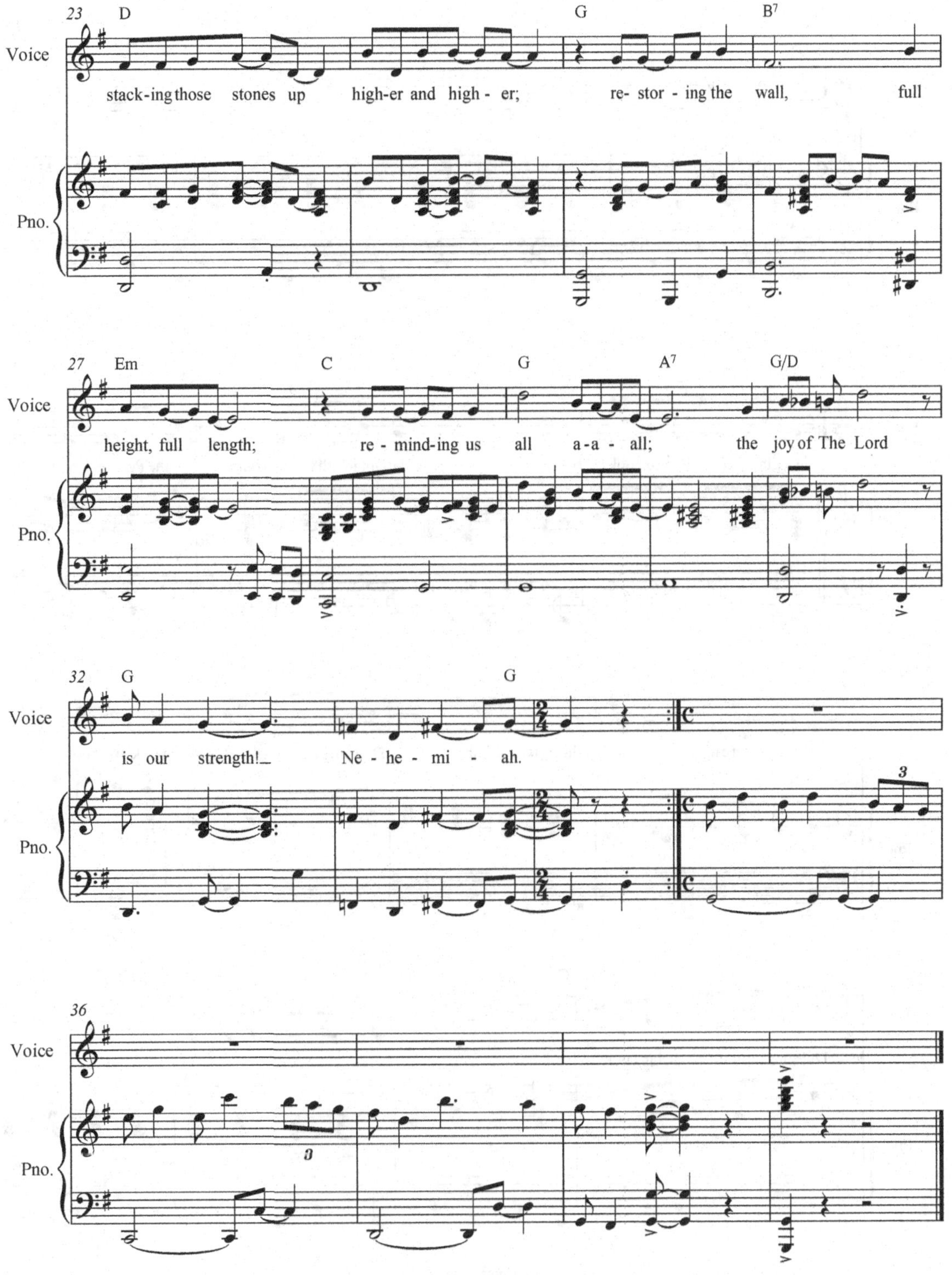
23 D G B7
Voice
stack-ing those stones up high-er and high - er; re- stor - ing the wall, full
Pno.
27 Em C G A7 G/D
Voice
height, full length; re - mind-ing us all a - a - all; the joy of The Lord
Pno.
32 G G
Voice
is our strength! Ne - he - mi - ah.
Pno.
36
Voice
Pno.

*For ending repeat verse progression with arpeggiated chords, then repeat chorus slower building faster to end with Archie, Gloria, and Doug singing.

# Book By Book

Clark Tyler
*Arranged by Andrew Bell*

17 G7 C Am Dm
Voice
Pno.
21 E C
Voice
Pno.
25 B G C E7
Voice
Pno.
30 Am (Ending)
Lento ed espressivo
C C G
Voice
Dig-ing through the Bib - le book by
Pno.
poco
Ped.
Ped.

*Patter One:*

Genesis, then Exodus; Leviticus composes,
With Numbers, Deuteronomy, The Penteteuch by Moses.

Joshua, Judges, Book of Ruth, The histories, then two of Samuel,
Kings and Chronicles, and everything they knew of.

Ezra, Nehemiah, then the story of Queen Esther;
Now here's another chorus and I'll tell you what the rest are.

**Repeat Chorus**

*Patter Two:*

Poetic Books are five, there's Job, and Psalms, the short and long of;
Then Proverbs and Ecclesiastes, Solomon, The Song of...

Prophets next Isaiah, Jeremiah, Lamentations;
Followed by Ezekiel and Daniel's Revalations.

*Spoken:* "Ready for a dozen minor prophets?

Hosea, Joel, and Amos; Obadiah, Jonah, Micah;
Nahum, then there's Habakkuk, (That's the one I like-a!)

Zephaniah, Haggai, Zechariah, (No one finer)
Finally there's Malachi - The last of prophets minor!

**Repeat Chorus**

*Patter Three:*

Thirty-Nine Old Testament, the books that I just listed;
Twenty-seven in the New, so keep them all un-twisted!

Matthew, Mark, and Luke and John; the Acts, then the Colossal
Twenty-one Espistles written mostly by apostles.

*Spoken:* "And Paul was the first string letter-man.

To Romans and Corinthians, Galatians and Ephesians;
Philippians, Colossians, Thessalonians (all Grecians).

To Timothy and Titus; to Philemon and the Hebrews;
By James and Peter, John and Jude to spread the Gospel's key news.

And what began with Genesis, the story of Creation?
Ends in triumph and in hope - The Book of Revelation.

**Repeat Chorus**

*Patter Four:*

But what about the covenants, the miracles unending;
All the promises of God, the messages He's sending?

And Messiah, sent for us atonement and redemption,
Grace and mercy; peace and love; you also didn't mention.

Of course it's nice to know the names, the order of the sections;
But what good is a map to you if you don't directions?

**Repeat Final Chorus**

# Risen Indeed

Clark Tyler
*Arranged by Andrew Bell*

Voice
Kbd.
G7 C G7 C 1.2. Cm
Chri - st The Lord is ris - en in- deed. Ris-en in- deed.
Cm Fm B♭ E♭
Here was the cloth that en - cir-cled His head, and here were the words that the an - gels said "Why
Here were the wo-men who saw how He died, and here was the day that was pro - phe-sied;
Cm Fm G7 Cm C7
seek ye the liv-ing a - mong the dead?" He is not here, He is ris - en.
Here is life.Here is truth. No one can hide.
3. D G B7 Em D
Sci - en-tists say the moon is a rock;

29 G7 Am D7 G G7 C A7
Voice
life-less, with no life of its own; but the moon lights the night, won-der-fully so; re-
Kbd.
33 D C/D D7 G G B7 Em D
flec - ting the light that the sun has shown. Now all of us here are just like the moon; we
37 G7 Am D7 G G7 C A7 D
can - not shine on our own; but we all can re-flect the light of God's son and shine in the love that
42 C/D D7 G C C7 F C
He has shown. Ris - en in-deed, Ris - en in-deed;
45 G7 C G7 C
Chri - st The Lord is ris - en in-deed. Ris-en in-deed. Ris-en in-deed.

# Be A Rock

Clark Tyler
*Arranged by Andrew Bell*

30
C (no chord)
Voice
...Iona...
...and Ruby!
Pno.
36
Be a
41 C
C7
rock, be a pil- lar, be a gem;
Be like
45 F
C
G7
Pe- ter, Ne- he- mi- ah, Ja- cob, Josh- u - a and them;
Take your
49 C
C7
F
Dm
place, by His grace in the new Je- ru- sa - lem.
Be a rock,

53 G
C
Voice
— be a pil- lar,_ be a gem!
Patter: Now
Pno.
58 C5
(Recite patter ad lib over chords)
Voice
what does it mean to be a rock?
Lyrics: Like Peter the rock. The builder of the flock.
Pno.
Patter 1: Now a rock is a block in a firm foundation; and the rock puts a lock on your salvation.
Patter 2: Around the temple, around the court; a pillar is the visible means of support.
Patter 3: I'm a gem who aims to shine like the twelve that scripture names; so here are my claims:
63
Pno.
C
The rock is where you're rooted and grounded; and on a rock your house should be founded.
Over time it'll hold up; won't crumble or fold up; a real long-laster in marble, cedar, or alabaster.
I'm valuble and precious what more can I say? I'm a prize...any size, any day.
68
Pno.
F
C
Put your stock in the rock, Doc. Answer the knock and be a rock...around the clock!
A pillar does more than it's share; making columns everywhere. Solid and groovy that's a pillar; like an epic movie: A Cecil B. De Miller
73 Always true, never foolish; and proud to be jewelish. I'm polished, not clever, but I'll last forever. There's 12 of us in each Testament;
Pno.
G
F
C

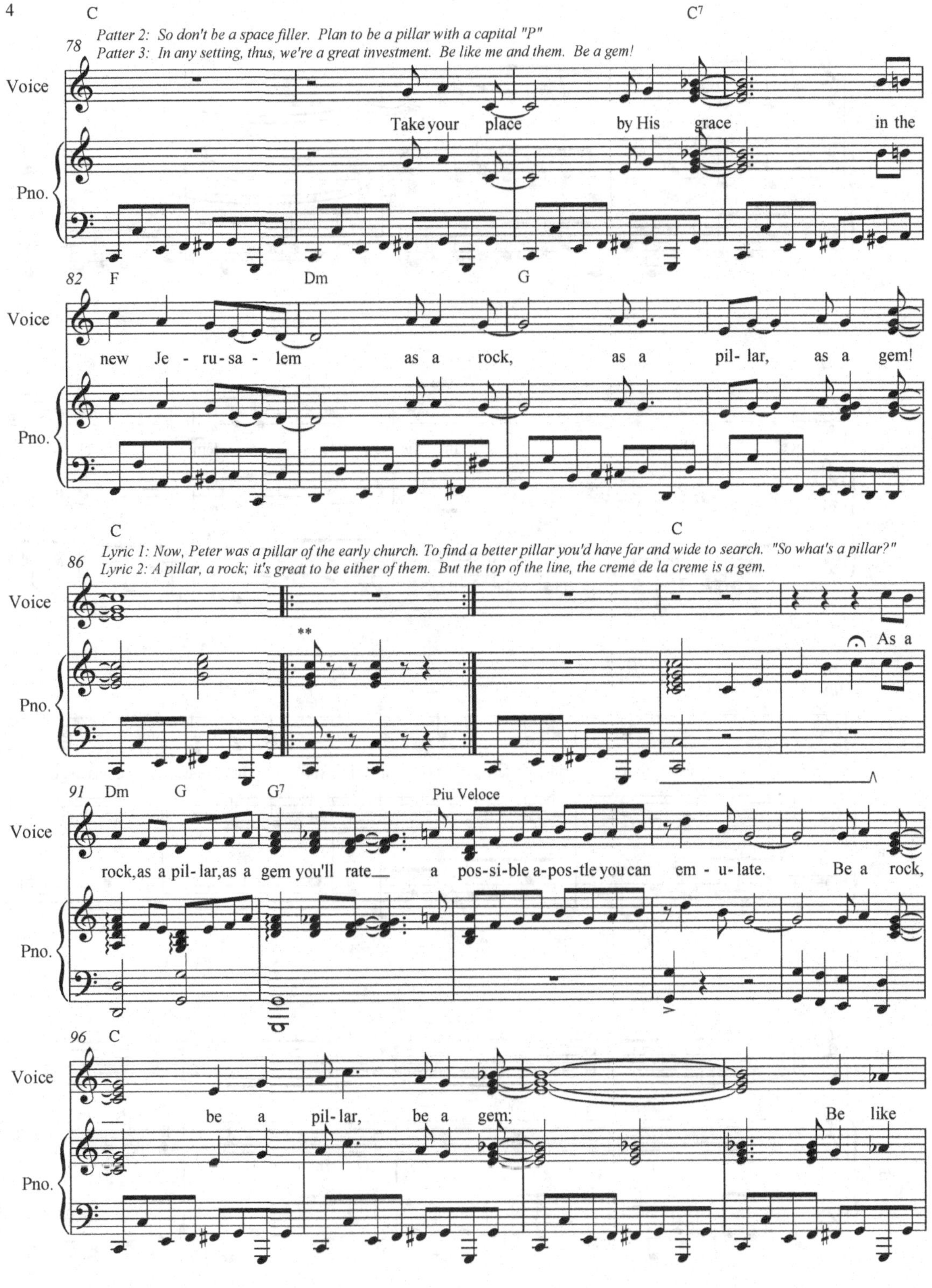


**(Starting here: repeat stop chords and recite lyrics 1 and 2 then repeat previous chords with patter #2 and #3 then proceed to next section.)*

100 F C G7
Voice
Pe-ter,Ne-he-mi-ah, Ja-cob,Josh-u-a and them; Take your
Pno.
104 C C7 F Dm
Voice
place by His grace In the new Je-ru-sa-lem as a rock,
Pno.
108 G
Voice
as a pil-lar, as a val-u-ble and pre-cious gem!
Pno.
112 C Cm Gm/D C
Voice
Pno.

# In The Beginning

Clark Tyler
*Arranged by Andrew Bell*

Voice
Piano
Bm7 Asus A A7 D D
In the beg-
In the beg-
In the beg-
6 A7 D A A7 D D D7
in-ning was the word; and the word was with God; and the word was
in-ning there was life; and the life was the light; and the true light
in-ning was the word; and the word was made flesh; made to dwell in
Pno.
11 G D A7 D A A7 Dsus D
God; full of grace and truth. And we be-hold His glo - ry; and
came;
us;

16
A A7 D Bm7 Asus
Voice
we be-hold His glo - ry; and we be-hold His glo - ry; full of
Pno.
1.2. 3.
20
A7 D molto rall. A7 D
Voice
grace and truth. grace and truth.
molto rall.
Pno.

# Chapter 7 - A CELEBRATION OF PURIM

This is one of those stories where you need to hear the punch line first.

Rose was a resident of one of the nursing/retirement homes we regularly went to. She was in her mid 90's; spry, active, interested, Jewish. I had seen her on at least three other occasions when she came to the little chapel room to see our musical presentations. On this day, there she was, near the front, attentive to every word in our newest play called "Song of Purim." At the end of the performance, as the kids were mingling with the residents, Rose came up to me with tears in her eyes. She took both my hands in her's and said: "I have never, in all my years, heard Christians express sensitivity or understanding of things Jewish. This was wonderful." She hugged me.. Then **I** had tears in my eyes.

Several weeks later, I got a message that told me Rose had died. Had we planted a seed in that dear woman that day? I believe so. My sadness at her passing was considerably tempered by the joy of that seed having indeed been planted. I will never forget Rose, and I always use her example to tell the children how important their "seed planting" is.

The unlikely vehicle for this spiritual germination, "Song of Purim," came about when I was asked by a group of Jewish believers if I would look at a little Purim play they had and perhaps add some songs to "spruce it up." I read the play and realized it was well beyond my ability to "fix." It was a little silly and very in-bred in terms of Jewish jokes and traditions. I couldn't imagine our kids ever understanding what it was all about. However, this group of Jewish believers was under a severe time constraint and needed help.

My familiarity with Jewish holidays stemmed from my very first job - as a lowly listings clerk in the publicity department of the American Broadcasting Company in New York. When I was hired, my new boss said to me: "Tyler..you are going to be the only goy (gentile) in this office; so I want to give you some valuable advice." I looked expectantly at him and waited for the words of wisdom. "Think Jewish," he intoned. I found out later exactly what this meant – that on every Jewish holiday, I alone was the designated coverer of the office!

As a believer, I had long been interested in the background and scriptural basis for the ten or so Jewish holy days and feasts, especially in their relevance for Christians. Partially this was because my first Pastor was Jewish and often preached on the subject. Also I had gotten a series of 6 videotapes from Living Way Ministries (Pastor Jack Hayford), called The Jewish Roots of Christianity. These wonderful teachings had further sparked my interest in teaching our Sunday School children on the subject. Our church had a tradition of having a Seder dinner at the time of Passover, linking the traditional Hebrew celebration with the obvious Christian implications, and I had given an annual teaching to the children on exactly what this was all about.

As a result, I had two very important books, which I now turned to: one was a children's book called "Jewish Days and Holidays," which had all the stories, foods and various traditions in the Jewish celebrations; the other was more for Christians and was titled, "The Feasts of the Lord." This latter book was a highly detailed exposition of not only the scriptural basis for these feasts, but dwelt extensively on the linkage between the Old Testament basis and the New Testament fulfillment of the prophetic implications. It also explained the incredibly complex arrangement of the Hebrew calendar to determine just when these days would fall each year.

With these two books in hand and a careful rereading of the Book of Esther, I decided that while I was unable to "fix" the Purim skit the group had, I might be able to come up with a replacement that was more in keeping with what was appropriate for our church and our kids. I was also thinking about the nursing home audiences that we would more than likely be appearing before. I wrote one song ("Turn to the Book of Esther") and put together an outline of what I thought could be done. The group who contacted me was thrilled and encouraged me to go ahead. I decided that I did not have time to involve all the smaller children in our Sunday School, so I conceptualized the play with two major ingredients: one was to have the story told and sung by four narrators who would be girls from our teenage youth group; the second, was to have the story illustrated, not by puppets, but by a series of icons ( or representative items) that would illustrate both the characters and the main elements in the Purim/Esther story. There were about 40 of these that would have to be integrated with the songs and narration - requiring two icon manipulators with great powers of concentration and dexterity. For this role I selected two young men who had been in several of our musical productions in the past.

The logic in using icons rather than human type figures (puppets or otherwise) recognizes the stipulation in Hebrew law that in artwork, there should be no recognizable human form representing God or holy things (given the stricture against "graven images"). While not technically covered by this, here was a chance to underline sensitivity of "things Jewish." It also produced an unusual visual effect, as well as some humor, in the elements so represented. Thus, while the characters were portrayed by items such as a tiara & veil (Esther), a three cornered black hat (Haman), a throne (Xerxes), other things such as a "Do Not Disturb" sign , a hangman's noose, a large set of dice and party decorations illustrated key points in the story.

Since the various messages and lessons in these plays were so important, it was necessary to explore every opportunity to make the presentation more visual. Otherwise, I feared they may become just a collection of words. In this instance, the use of icons sprang from a substantive part of the message, but they added an important visual technique as well as an element of humor.

The icon stage (a black curtained frame of PVC piping) was situated between the two sets of 4 narrators, focusing the audience's attention on the center of the stage. Behind this was a large colored map of ancient Persia, the locale of the story. All this took some considerable logistical planning because with 40 icons (all numbered and pre-positioned behind the curtained framework) the handlers had to have easy access to present the right one at the right time. The constant flashing of these icons added a pacing and a flow that would have been impossible to achieve otherwise. It also kept the narrators on their toes!

As for content, there were three overlapping goals: first, to preserve the lighthearted fun of the traditional Jewish observance of Purim; second to focus on the seriousness of the "holocaust" plot against the Hebrews in ancient Persia; and third to integrate the relevance of the story for Christians. Many biblical scholars are fond of pointing out that the Book of Esther is the only book of the Bible that does not specifically mention God. Some Christians have taken this as a reason to not pay a whole lot of attention to the story of Esther. I have always believed that every part of the Bible is critical to our faith, and if God's word tells us that we should keep these feasts in perpetuity as a memorial, then we should do exactly that. As for God not being named in the story of Esther, I learned that in the original Hebrew scroll (or Magillah), the name of God appears as an acrostic at five key points in the story - thus disguised, because as captives of the Persians, the Hebrews were forbidden to openly worship or even acknowledge God.

Given the tendency throughout the world to have to combat anti-semitism from time to time, plus the not-so-proud history of this attitude during the Crusades, the Inquisition, World War II and the more modern Middle East, I felt that this aspect needed emphasis. Here again, the treatment of this story tried to combine the aura of seriousness with a sense of fun and humor. As proof that this may have worked, I had the reaction of Rose.

In the traditional Jewish celebration of the feast of Purim, a Hebrew chorus is sung which closes with the words: "ki immanuel." This comes from Isaiah 8:10 and makes the point that all plots against God's people will come to nothing because *God is with us*. Those last four words are the translation of "immanuel." Of course, the prophet Isaiah also identified Immanuel as the coming Messiah of Israel, saying further that he would be born of a virgin and reign upon David's throne.

I decided that the closing chorus in this Purim play would concentrate on precisely that duality - the admonition that "God is with us" and the identity of the Messiah - Jesus. That is exactly what makes the Purim story so relevant for Christians. And that is why I remember Rose with such joy - I believe she recognized precisely that.

# SONG OF PURIM

## Lesson Plan

Of all the Jewish Holy Days, Purim is undoubtedly the least understood. The traditional celebration is both boisterous and reverential. There is great joy in the deliverance of the Jews from this ancient holocaust, but there is an undertone that these types of attacks are unfortunately recurring throughout history. For this reason alone, there is a special meaning for Christians. Much harm has been done by Christians against, Jews throughout history: the Crusades, the Inquisition; the Nazi-inspired holocaust, the Middle East wars are the obvious ones. The pogroms of Czarist Russia, the polemics of Martin Luther's later ministry, the so-called "replacement theology ,"U.S. anti-semitism as depicted in the movie "Gentleman's Agreement," and the rantings of the Ku Klux Klan are less well known, but none-the-less real to the Jewish people. Since this play is designed to be presented by high school children, they are certainly capable of grappling with all of this. A visit to the Washington DC Holocaust museum drove home the point as nothing else could. Since there is a growing movement in the Christian church to reach out to and include Jewish believers, it is even more important for Christians to be sensitive to these things and to understand the basis for what are called, The Feasts of the Lord.

The "Feasts of the Lord" is also the title of an excellent book on the subject. This work is written by Kevin Howard and Marvin Rosenthal (Zion's Hope, Inc., 1997). Much of this play is based on the Purim chapter from this book, especially that part that relates to the implication for Christians.

Another important work on the subject is "Abandoned" by Stan Telchin (Chosen Books, 1997). This thoughtful work lays out a detailed plan for relating to Jewish believers in the church.

It is important to note that unlike Hanukkah (which is also a happy Holy Day), Purim's celebration is dictated by the canon of the Hebrew Bible - the Book of Esther. God wants the Jews to memorialize their victory over evil - a near miss which Esther, Queen of the Persian court, achieved with her cousin Mordecai, with great faith and courage. That is the lesson.

Since the foundation of this play is the Book of Esther, any teaching should concentrate on this and the points listed above.

## SONG OF PURIM

### Cast:

*There is no cast, in the usual dramatic sense. Instead, this play is written for four "presenters" who give the background of The Feast of Lots, taking different parts from time to time and reciting the story of Esther. This is done in league with a series of "icons" which not only illustrate the dramatic components, but which also represent the key characters in the story:*

KING AHASUERUS .............................Xerxes to those who can't pronounce this.
QUEEN VASHTI ...................................The "late" queen of Persia
HAMAN.................................................Prime Minister & royal confidante
ESTHER.................................................The new queen
MORDECAI..........................................Esther's cousin
THE CANDIDATES ..............................Miss Shushan, Miss Ur, Miss Chaldea, Miss Babylon, Miss Zion (Esther)

### Musical Numbers:

ADAR .......................................................The eccentricities of the 12th month of the Hebrew calendar.
TURN TO THE BOOK OF ESTHER....What Purim is all about
THE CONTEST ....................................How the new queen of Persia is chosen
HAMAN.................................................The villain of the piece
THREE DAYS ......................................Esther's intercession
GUESS WHO?.......................................A royal invitation to dinner at the palace
IMMANUEL.....................................................The single word that connects the Old and The New Testaments.

### The Format

This play is presented by four narrators, two each positioned on either side of a 6 to 8 foot wide puppet stage. From inside this stage appears 40 different icons which represent key parts and key characters of the story. Two agile puppeteers are needed to handle the sometimes swift sequence of these icons, as they must be in synch with the verse of the narration and the lyrics of the songs.
The narrators all have groggers (noisemakers).

## List of Props (the Icons)

(In order of appearance)

1. Scroll
2. Tiara & veil (Esther)
3. Throne (Xerxes)
4. Black hat (Haman)
5. Beard & yarmulke (Mordecai)
6. "Welcome to Shushan" (sign)
7. "Queen Impeached" (headline)
8. Party favors & balloons
9. "Do Not Disturb" (sign)
10. EXIT (sign)
11. Trumpet
12. *The beauty parade:*
    Miss Shushan
    Miss Ur
    Miss Chaldea
    Miss Babylon
    Miss Zion
13. Star of David
14. Calendar - ADAR
15. Ear & dagger
16. Hangman's noose
    (*Note: 10, 13, 14, 16 & 17*
    *Are used more than once)*
17. MY DIARY (book
18. Two dice (lots)
19. MY DIARY
20. Noose
21. Royal decree
22. Calendar - ADAR
23. Slingshot
24. Dove
25. Ribbon bow
26. Banquet table setting
27. Musical notes
28. Royal invitation
29. Star of David
30. Spider's web
31. Noose
32. EXIT (sign)
33. Noose
34. Royal decree
35. Star of David
36. 1st Place badge
37. Scroll
38. Calendar - ADAR
39. IMMANUEL (sign)
40. Scroll

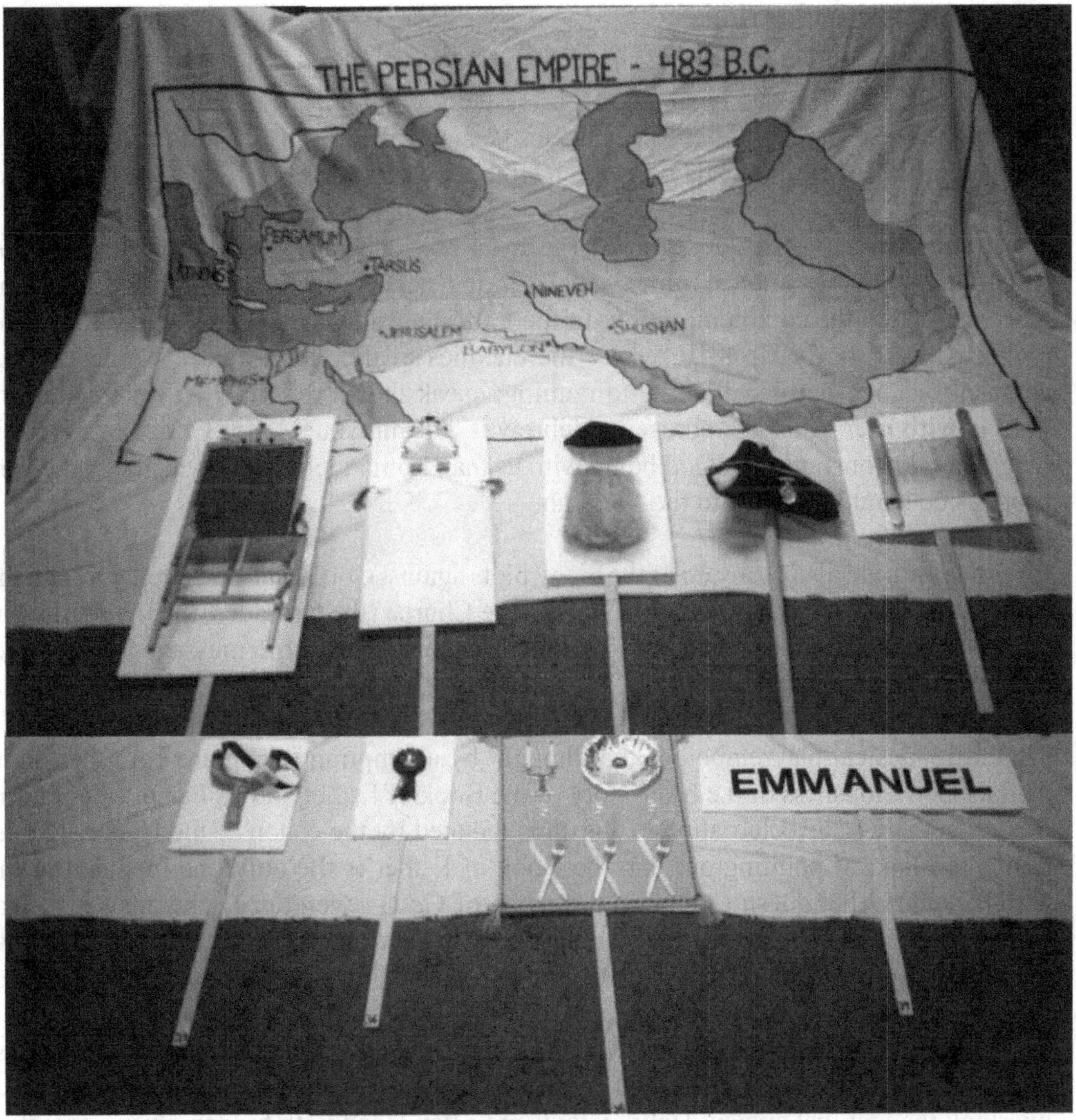


Shown are the icons for the main charatcres (l. to r.): The King, Esther, Mordecai, Haman and the scroll. Underneath are some of the other icons used.

## Director's Introduction

Purim is the most joyous of all the Hebrew Holy days. Purim means "lots," and it is called The Feast of Lots. That's because in the story of Purim (the Book of Esther), the evil Haman chose by lot the day on which all the Jews of Persia were to be exterminated.

The traditional Jewish celebration of Purim is both a happy and boisterous occasion (involving masks, costumes, mime, special foods, noisemakers and comedy skits)...and a deeper side to the commemoration. In the traditional Jewish celebration, there is sung a chorus based on Isaiah 8:10, where the enemies of the Hebrews are warned: "Take counsel together, but it will come to nothing; speak the word, but it will not stand, for **God is with us."** This last phrase in Hebrew is "ki immanuel." For Christians, there is no greater demonstration of God being with us than Immanuel - the very name that Isaiah prophesied would be given to the Messiah.

Christians should also be aware of the many plots against God's chosen people through the ages: many of which unfortunately involved the Church (the Crusades, the Inquisition, as well as various state-sponsored anti-Semitic measures). The Purim message is, therefore, one of deliverance and hope.

This little musical play embodies that thought by attempting to capture both the fun as well as the seriousness of the basic story of the Book of Esther and its Purim celebration. Yet, even though the celebration of Purim is dictated by the canon of the Hebrew Bible, critics are fond of pointing out that the Book of Esther is the only one included in the Old Testament that doesn't mention the name of God – even once. The answer to that comment often centers on the fact that Esther's fast and prayer, and that of the Hebrew community in Shushan were certainly God-centered. They sure weren't praying to any of the Persian gods! Also, the deliverance of the Hebrews from Haman's plot, as well as their military triumph at the end were clearly the result of God's intervention against those who would come against His covenant people. But beyond this, Biblical critics overlook the fact that ancient Hebrew texts are often laced with hidden clues - acrostics - and even codes.

In the case of Esther, the ancient Hebrew text contains five acrostics which highlight and spell out God's Hebrew names. These acrostics occur in the configuration of the handwritten inscribed text, where the first letter of a sentence (larger and in a different color or style) lines up vertically to spell out the shorthand for the name of God at five key points in the story.

Now, for those of you not blessed by being Jewish, there are a few important words that you may not be familiar with - but that you should understand. *MEGILLAH,* for instance... "megillah" means a scroll. In the traditional celebration of Purim a scroll (or megillah) of the handwritten text of the Book of Esther, is brought forth and read; often, this is accompanied by a *SCHPIEL,* or dramatic re-enactment of the story. This can sometimes be boisterous, with costumes, masks and noisemakers (called *GROGGERS),* which are sounded to drown out the name of Haman every time he is mentioned. All this is usually followed by a *SEUDAH* (the festive meal of Purim) which features such things as "kreplach," and of course *HAMANTASHEN.* This is actually a German word, derived from the name of Haman. Hamantashen is a special pastry in the triangular shape of the three-cornered hat always associated with the evil Haman. These pastries are usually filled with a poppy see or prune filling.

The last word you need to know is *ADAR* - the name of the twelfth month of the Hebrew calendar. This is when God's word says we are to celebrate Purim. However, there are a couple of unique things you need to know about "Adar"... and that is where we begin...

*Immediately after the Director's introduction, the music begins. The stage is set with a 6 or 8 foot wide puppet stage in the center. There is a painted backdrop on the rear of the puppet stage which depicts a colored map of ancient Persia and surrounding areas. On either side of the puppet stage are two music stands. The four narrators are in position. The songs, unless otherwise noted are sung by all four narrators; the verse narration should be split up stanza by stanza equally among the narrators, or with one having a particular line. The effect should be to include both sides of the stage, since the icons will appear in the middle. The 35 or so icons should all be numbered and hung on a supporting rack or board inside the puppet stage so the "handlers" can easily access them in the right sequence . The numbers which appear on the right margin of the script refer to the icon that is to appear at that juncture.*

*The narrators sing:*

THE MONTH OF ADAR
THE MONTH OF ADAR
WHERE TWENTY-NINE, OR THIRTY,
OR FIFTY-NINE DAYS ARE;

THE MONTH OF PURIM,
WITH ESTHER, THE STAR;
A TIME TO REJOICE
A TIME TO MAKE NOISE

ON THE FOURTEENTH
AND THE FIFTEENTH
OF ADAR
THE MONTH OF ADAR!

*Now, with lines alternating between the left and right side, the music continues underneath as the following verse narration is given.*

But hey!
How can you say
That one month can have
A fifty-ninth day!

No way.

Is their calendar designed by Rip Van Winkle?
How does a month get that kind of wrinkle?

Each month of the Hebrew calendar
Has twenty-nine days.... or so...

But after twelve months, their solar year still
Has eleven days to go!

What?!

That's right - the Hebrew calendar
Is what as known as "lunar;"

So each date will fluctuate
And we'll celebrate it sooner...
And sooner...

Til Purim's not in the spring at all;
It'll back into the winter, and even the fall;

Now, for this reason, every season
The Hebrews try and keep clear;

They fixed this complication
By adding in a leap year...

Actually, seven of them, my dears,
Every nineteen years;

And so our friend, Adar;
Gets not just an extra day, buy hey,
What is most bizarre –
Each leap year gets an extra month,

Also called “Adar.”

We’re not making this up...
To keep their year at par;

So their calendar might, come out alright
They counted on...

Adar!

*As this last word is said in unison, the music comes up and all four narrators repeat the chorus*

THE MONTH OF ADAR
THE MONTH OF ADAR
WHERE TWENTY-NINE, OR THIRTY,
OR FIFTY-NINE DAYS ARE:

THE MONTH OF PURIM
WITH ESTHER, THE STAR:
A TIME TO REJOICE,
A TIME TO MAKE NOISE

ON THE FOURTEENTH,
AND THE FIFTEENTH
OF ADAR;
THE MONTH OF ADAR!

So, now that you know where you are -
Adar -

It’s time for us to reveal
The basic plots of the Feast of Lots
In our little Purim schpiel.

With a musical assist
We’ll give you the gist;
But first on our list...

We insist...

Turn to the Book of Esther.

*As they say this line in rhythm, the music begins in a klezmer-type tempo. They all sing:*

TURN TO THE BOOK OF ESTHER;
THE STORY OF THE FEAST OF LOTS;
A THRILLAH TOLD IN ROLLED MEGILLAH;
A TRIUMPH OVER EVIL PLOTS.

TURN TO THE BOOK
AND LEARN FROM THE BOOK
OF ESTHER.

PURIM; PURIM:
A STORY FOR TODAY FROM YESTERDAY;
COME CELEBRATE
THE COURAGE OF ESTHER DAY.

TURN TO THE BOOK
AND LEARN FROM THE BOOK
OF ESTHER.

A STORY OF DELIVERANCE, HATE AND HOPE;
A HAT, A THRONE AND A HANGMAN'S ROPE;
A FITTING END FOR A MISANTHROPE

(LOOK THAT UP LATER) AND
TURN TO THE BOOK OF ESTHER.

PURIM, PURIM:
A STORY FOR TODAY FROM YESTERDAY
COME CELEBRATE
THE COURAGE OF ESTHER DAY.

TURN TO THE BOOK
AND LEARN FROM THE BOOK
OF ESTHER.

Now among observant Jews
It's frowned upon to use...
Anthropomorphic images
To illustrate God's word;

So we've amassed, for our Purim cast
Some this 'n that -
A throne, a hat -
To show you what occurred.

Queen Esther you'll see as tiara and veil;
The king, of course, is a throne;
And Haman, the rat, is a three-cornered hat;
Mordecai, by a beard will be shown.

A noose, the lots and scrolls...
Will all have supporting roles.

*They all sing:*

PURIM, PURIM
A STORY FOR TODAY FROM YESTERDAY
A STORY OF HOW GOD HAD BLESSED HER DAY;
COME CELEBRATE
THE COURAGE-OF-ESTHER DAY

TURN TO THE BOOK
AND LEARN FROM THE BOOK
OF ESTHER!

*They return to the verse narration...*

In the capital of ancient Persia
It's 483 B.C.

King Aha...aha...su-er...
Call him Xerxes, and among his quirks, he's
Changing queens as we see.

Why, you may ask,
Would he start such a task?

Well, there's a week long feast at the palace
For princes, nobles and such;

Towards the end of this bash, he...sends for Queen Vashti
King wasn't asking for much;

But she has her pride
And a headache beside.

"Vashti, vamoose, King has no use
For a queen who can't be displayed;"

Thus casting aspersion, King starts Persian version
Of a nationwide beauty parade.

The royal net cast far and wide;
Wannabe interns all applied.

*Special Arabian-type music begins as a series of icons come up from the puppet stage and move slowly from right to left. These depict a collection of contestants - each represented by a veil and a sash. The sashes are labeled: MISS SUSHAN, MISS UR, MISS CHALDEA, MISS BABYLON, and the last is MISS ZION. As each "parades across to the music, one of the narrators holds up a score card with various low numbers on it for each contestant. When MISS ZION crosses, the score card comes up "10."*

Then one prevailed over all the rest -
Esther, old Mordecai's cousin;

Now it was slightly taboo-ish to be caught being Jewish;
So Esther, she don't say nuzzin'

A Jewish star, this Esther gal is
And not the last to play the palace!

So the stage is set, the characters posted
And the month of Adar is the date;

King in his throne room; Queen in her own room
Mordecai hanging out by the gate.

Then enters: "the Hat"
An Amelikite bureaucrat!

*The music starts a vamp as the three-cornered black hat, representing Haman, comes up. The four narrators split up the stanzas of this song: the two on the left do the first two and the two on the right finish up.*

UNDER THE HAT WAS HAMAN
(I HESITATE TO EVEN NAME HIM)
EAGERLY FILLIN' THE, ROLE WITH HIS VILLAINY
HATEFUL, HORRIBLE
HAMAN!

UNDER THE HAT WAS HAMAN
(THE DEVIL WOULDN'T EVEN CLAIM HIM)
SLEAZY AND SINISTER, HE'S THE PRIME MINISTER:
HATEFUL, HORRIBLE
HAMAN.

NOW HE'S PRETTY SEEDY
AND FULL OF PRUNES;
PUFFED UP AND FLAKY AS WELL;
AND THAT'S THE PURIM RECIPE
THE COOKBOOKS TELL;
AND HOW HAMANTASHEN BECAME
THAT SEEDED, PRUNE-FILLED,
PUFFY, FLAKY PASTRY...
THAT BEARS THE NAME...
OF...

HATEFUL, HORRIBLE
HAMAN!

Let's hear it for the prime minister (*Noise*)

HATEFUL, HORRIBLE
HAMAN!

*The narration of the story continues...*

Out at King's gate, old Mordy
Hears a plot to do in the King

The plot is un-hatched, assassins dispatched
And the good noose is in use...full swing!

And with prose quite fiery
This deed makes the King's diary.

Now the hatful of hateful old Haman
Is strutting all over Shushan

Promoting kow-towing and worship-like bowing

The exception is one Jewish man..

It's Mordecai claimin'
That *his* God ain't Haman!

The Hat now hatches a nightmare
The most anti-Semitic of plots;

He trumps up an excuse, to exterminate Jews
On a day that is chosen by lots.

...and he sells this hideous thing
To a compliant, paranoid king.

...and speaking of king, he is sleepless
So his diary is then read aloud;

Hearing Mordecai's deed, the king quickly decreed

That Mordy be publicly "wowed."

...and the one to acclaim him
Is decreed to be – Haman!

So, while Haman is leading old Mordy
Through a ticker-tape hero's parade

He vows to subject, poor Mordecai's neck
To a gallows he's having made.

But before it can claim him
A trap will be sprung – but on Haman!

By now, Haman's "final solution"
Has been published throughout all the land;

And for near and for far, the 13th of Adar
Is date set for last Jewish stand.

And no Jew is schleppin'
A defensive weapon.

So Mordecai gets word to Queen Esther:
"You must intercede with the king,

Or all will be lost, in a grim holocaust

That Haman is aimin' to bring.

Now as if He would test her
God's spirit comes on Esther –

Who has a suspicion
This chance IS her mission.

*As the Esther icon comes up, one of the narrator's sings Esther's song:*

WHAT I NEED IS..
THREE DAYS,
TO FAST AND TO PRAY;
THREE DAYS,
TO SEEK AND TO FIND THE WAY;
TO LISTEN WITH AWE
FOR THE GOD THAT THE LAW PORTRAYS;
I MUST SPEND THREE DAYS.

FOR GOD SPENT THREE DAYS
PREPARING THE EARTH FOR ALL LIVING THINGS;
AND THREE DAYS, IT'S SAID
WILL RAISE UP THE KING OF KINGS

SO I'LL WAIT...
THREE DAYS
IN FASTING AND PRAYER;
THREE DAYS,
TO MEDITATE AND PREPARE;
WITH GOD AS MY GUIDE
I WILL SHUT OUT THE WORLD OUTSIDE...
ABIDING IN PRAISE...
THREE DAYS.

*At the end of the song, the narration continues as before.*

Queen Esther approached the king boldly,
Determined to now intercede;

Heart right, mind made up; empowered and prayed up

She just had one little need....

But she didn't let on
WHO her sights were set on.

Compliant as ever, king beckoned;
(He still in her beauty was basking)

"What's mine is yours, a large chunk of Persia
Can be given you just for the asking."

Shrewd, yet demure, young Esther,
Was a much more modest requester.

"Get the good china, polish the silver;
We're having a three-person party,

"Just me and the king, and one guest who'll bring...

"An appetite for evil that's hearty."

And, as preparations moved right along...
She sang to herself, sweetly,
This song:

*The two narrators on the left, sing Esther's little "party" song:*

GUESS WHO
IS COMING TO DINNER?
GUESS WHO
IS LESS THAN A WINNER?
IT'S WHO
HAS THE MONOGRAM "H" IN FULL VIEW
THAT'S WHO!

GUESS WHO
WILL BE NONE THE WISER?
GUESS WHO
GETS THE CROW APPETIZER?
IT'S WHO...
HAS A THREE-CORNERED HAT, THAT'S A CLUE...
THAT'S WHO.

A ROYAL FEAST
IS THE VENUE
AND SOME SWEET JUST DESSERTS
COMPLETE THE MENU...

GUESS WHO
WILL BE IN THE SOUP NOW?
GUESS WHO
WILL BE IN THE "LOOP" NOW?
IT'S WHO
WE WILL FITTINGLY SERVE TURKEY TO
THAT'S WHO!

*The music ends with the "Haman" signature phrase. The narration continues...*

Haman was thrilled and excited
By the royal invite he got;

In his puffed up condition, he had no suspicion

Of Queen exposing his plot.

Plus, he was totally clueless
That his Queen just might be Jewish.

So picture old Haman all costumed
In medals, gold buttons and braid

With no hint of a de-frock, this proud Persian peacock

Struts into the web Queen Esther has made.

Of course, right on time when he came in
He'll exit the "late" Mr. Haman.

Dispensing with small talk, Queen Esther
Said: "King, what would you do if you knew...

"Of some little creep who'll, kill my family and people...
On a set day, by the way... I'm a Jew."

King: "Just bring me that pest here."
Queen: "I have... it's our guest here."

His appetite gone, old Haman,
Is nervously eyeing the exit;

Being quite well versed in the darkest and worst

As a causer of trouble, he expects it.

And trapped by what just occurs, he
Leans on the Queen for her mercy.

When the king sees Haman, the plotter
Apparently pawing his Queen;

He flies in a fury, condemns in a hurry...

No appeal, no trial, no jury –

Not to worry...
The King says: “I hear by...
The grapevine a gallows is nearby.”

It was, so the king is proclaiming
“Off with his hat and on with the noose!”

And with that valedictory, King then signalled victory

Could come to all Persia’s Jews.

(Actually, he decreed it might be alright
If they took up arms in a defensive fight.)

King then gives his ring to Mordecai
Along with a royal promotion;

Which would clearly state he’s, number one from Euphrates

All the way to the Indian ocean

A Jewish Prime Minister, by King’s assertion
“Mazeltov, Morchecai” was chanted in Persian.

So just like the wars with the Arabs
All weapons against them would fail

Thus protected by YHWH, the Mosaic law way
Would, as it has to this day, prevail.

...and the lesson for anti-Semitic molesters?
Is: Go study this story of Esther’s.”

And so it is written that Purim
(The fourteenth and fifteenth of Adar)

With its joy and its glory’ll, serve as memorial

To Esther, whose name means: “a star.”

Of course Mordecai is honored as well

But the key word that’s heard is.... “Immanuel.”

So behind all traditions and features
Of this happiest of all holy days;

Like groggers to heckle, kreplach, half shekel,
Gifts, and costumes and plays...

Is the phrase...:

“Ki Immanuel,” from Isaiah 8:10
Meaning: “God is with us... again and again.”

And this should send a big message
To the Hamans who always appear;

With plan, plot, or guile, shouting “killer” or “sieg heil”
In uniforms, cassocks or desert headgear...

It is clear...
That protected and redeemed by the blood of the Lamb
Are those that bless the people
Of the God of Abraham.

*At the conclusion of the narration, all four narrators sing the final song:*

NO WEAPON FORMED AGAINST US WILL PROSPER
NO WOE, OR FOE, CAN BEND US OR BREAK US;
IF WE HAVE FAITH AND TRUST IN GOD’S PROMISE,
THAT HE WILL NEVER,
EVER FORSAKE US.

IMMANUEL:
GOD IS WITH US
IMMANUEL:
WE ALL PROCLAIM;
IMMANUEL:
THE HOPE OF GLORY
THE VERY SAME,
IMMANUEL
IMMANUEL! *(repeat)*

# Adar

Clark Tyler
*Arranged by Andrew Bell*

*repeat music with actors speaking over chord progression then sing entire song again to end.

# Turn To The Book Of Esther

Clark Tyler
*Arranged by Andrew Bell*

Voice
Pno.
14 C D Em D Cmaj7 B7
hat a throne and a hang-man's rope, a fit-ting end for a mis-an-thrope. Look that up la-ter and turn to the book of
17 Em Cmaj7 G Em D C
Es-ther. Pu-rim, Pu-rim; a sto-ry from to-day from yes-ter-day, come
20 G Em Em B7 Em
cel-e-brate the cour-age of Es-ther Day; Turn to the book and learn from the book of Es-ther.
Lento
24 Em G Em D C D Em
Pu-rim, Pu-rim; a sto-ry from to-day from yes-ter-day, a sto-ry of how God blessed her day; come

Piu Mosso
27
G
Em
Em
B7
Em
Voice
cel-e-brate the cour-age of Es-ther Day; Turn to the book and learn from the book of Es-ther.
Pno.

# Under The Hat Was Haman

Clark Tyler
*Arranged by Andrew Bell*

G7 G9 C Dm7 G7 C Dm7
Voice
Un-der the hat was Ha - man; I hes-i-tate to ev-en name him. Eag-er-ly fill-ing the
Piano
6 Em Dm7 F♯dim G7 C G7 G9 C
Voice
role with his vill-ain-y; hate-ful, horr - i-ble Ha - man. Un-der the hat was Ha - man; the
Pno.
11 Dm7 G7 C Dm7 Em
Voice
dev-il would-n't ev - en claim him. Sleaz - y and sin - is - ter, he's the prime min-is - ter;
Pno.
15 Dm7 F♯dim G7 C C7 F C
Voice
hate-ful, hor - i-ble Ha - man. Now he's pret-ty seed-y and full of prunes;
Pno.
3

20 Dm C C7 F Em G7
Voice
puffed up and flak ey as well; and that's the Pur-im rec-i-pe the cook-books tell; and
Pno.
24 F Em G Cdim7
Voice
how Ha-man-tash-en be-came that seed-ed, prune-filled, puf-fy, flak-ey pas-ter-y that
Pno.
28 G7 A69 Adim G7 C
Voice
bears the name of hate-ful hor-ri-ble Ha - man.
Pno.

# Three Days

Clark Tyler
*Arranged by Andrew Bell*

16 G7 F/G Am7/G Gadd9/D Em Dm Em
Voice
Kings; So I'll wait three days in fast - ing and prayer; three days to med-i-tate
Pno.
20 Am7/D G C Cmaj7 F
Voice
and pre - pare; with God as my guide I will block out the world out - side;
Pno.
23 Dm Am G7 C
Voice
a - bid - ing in praise three days.
Pno.

# Guess Who?

Clark Tyler
*Arranged by Andrew Bell*

20
B♭m7
G7
Voice
sweet just des- serts com - plete the me - nu.
Pno.
2.
22
C
Cdim7
C
Voice
Pno.
Ped.

# Emmanuel

Clark Tyler
*Arranged by Andrew Bell*

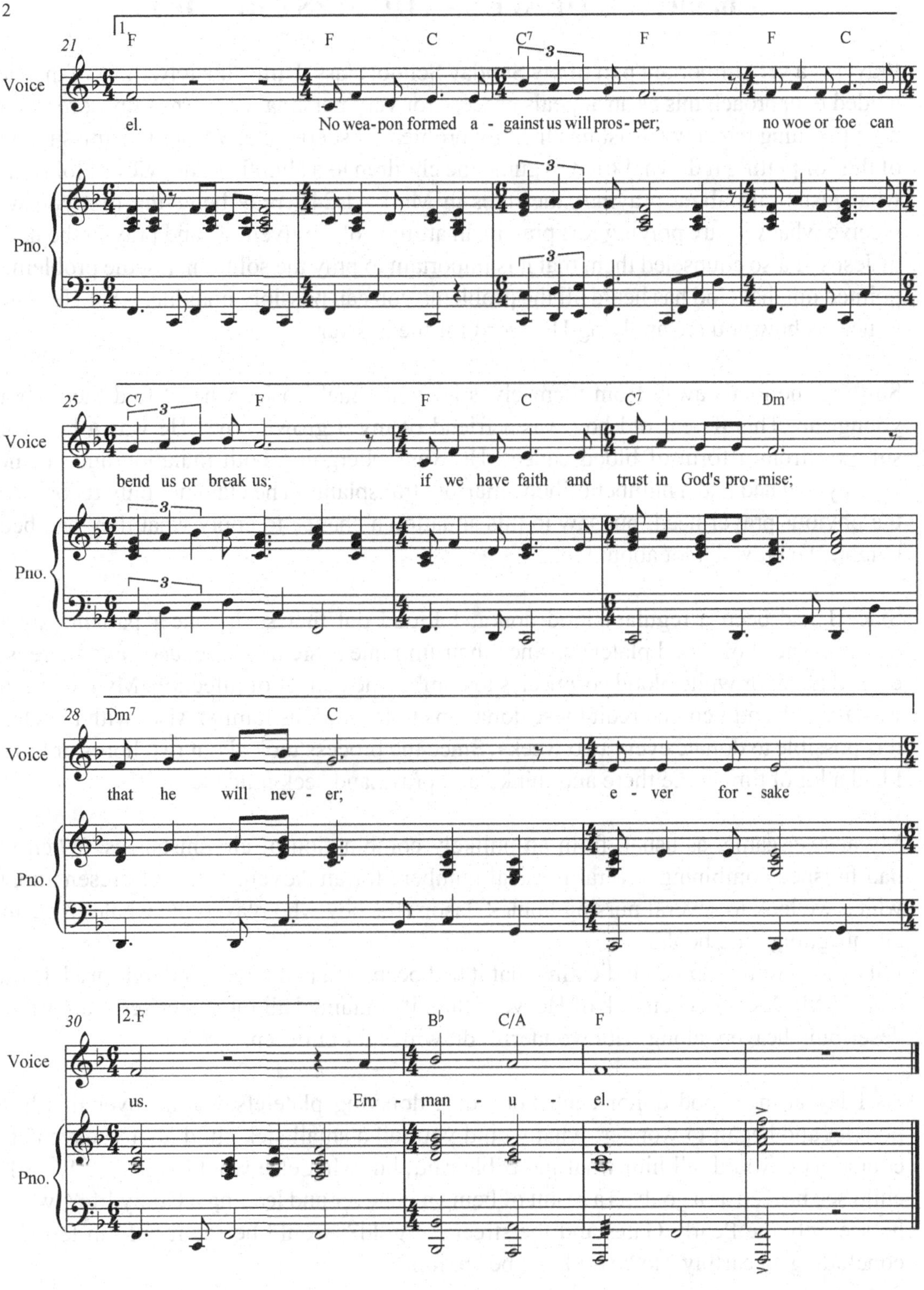
21
Voice
Pno.
F F C C7 F F C
el. No wea-pon formed a - gainst us will pros-per; no woe or foe can
25
C7 F F C C7 Dm
bend us or break us; if we have faith and trust in God's pro-mise;
28
Dm7 C
that he will nev- er; e - ver for - sake
30
2.F B♭ C/A F
us. Em - man - u - el.

## Chapter 8 - HEAVEN - THE FIRST RESORT?

Prayer is a very important part of my Sunday School class. Unfortunately, most of the kids tended to approach this as an appeals process for very personal concerns - my sore throat, my upcoming test, my Christmas list, my problem at school etc. Without dismissing any of this, or putting it down, I tried to guide the children to a slightly wider view. I told them what Jesus said about praying...the rules in Mark 11:24 : pray believing that you will receive what you are praying for; pray in an attitude of forgiveness; and pray in the name of Jesus. I also counseled them that it is important to pray the solution, not the problem. I pointed out that God has heard all the problems you can possibly imagine; what He wants to hear is how you are applying His word for the answer.

Shifting the focus away from themselves became much easier when I told them about young Ian. This 8 year old boy was a friend of my 3 grown boys. He was a boy who suffered from a form of blood cancer. He was undergoing both radiation and chemotherapy and had had a number of bone marrow transplants. The class not only recognized the obvious prayer need, but saw in this situation a chance to apply what they had been taught. We prayed a lot about Ian.

Since I had been a regular blood donor, I found out that such cancer patients are in desperate need of blood platelets, since their immune systems are reduced and there is a critical need for white blood corpuscles to combat the danger of infection. My blood type was a match and I could credit these donations to Ian and his family. Also, with platelets, it is possible to donate every two weeks. Since the process took about two hours or more, I had a lot of time to lie there and think...and pray...and seek guidance.

My answer came, as usual, from an unlikely combination of circumstances. When we had finished combining several musical numbers for an Advent series of presentations, which we took to several nursing homes, Jason (the boy who played the whale) gave me an intriguing little booklet.
It had been well thumbed indicating that it had been read and reread and treasured. It was called "My Jesus Pocketbook of Heaven," and it contained all the major scripture verses describing heaven, along with wonderful drawings for children.

As I lay at the blood donor center one day, donating platelets, I went over this little booklet and began to wonder: what would you tell a small sick child about heaven? Of course, you would tell him what the Bible said, but what else would you say? Would a child see heaven as a goal; as a result of being a believer and leading a Godly life?; would he see only the Pearly Gates and the streets of gold?; would he see it only in terms of concluding an earthly life?; would he be anxious?

I turned to one of my favorite books - D. James Kennedy's "Why I Believe." There were two particular chapters - "Why I Believe in Heaven," and "Why I Believe in Hell" - that gave me a head start on all my questions. Then, just for the heaven of it, I turned to the Internet and typed in the word, "Heaven," to my browser. Once I sorted through the recipes for chocolate cake, various not-too-edifying songs and plays, and ads from a multitude of purveyors of earthly (if not earthy) artifacts, I found an excerpt from a book, "The Narrow Way," by William C. Nichols. The excerpt was entitled, "The Glory of Heaven." It was a home run!

While, clearly, adults and children must necessarily look at the concept of heaven in different ways, there are inevitably some aspects where the two viewpoints come together. This is what I was searching for, because I knew that, yes, the kids must understand it, but they must also be able to witness it to adults because of the audiences we would be performing for if this ever got to be a musical play.

My problem was that I didn't want to force the message into a format that didn't fit - just for the sake of doing a musical. These were the things that began racing around in my mind as I lay on my back with blood flowing out of one arm and back into the other. From the books I found, three purposes emerged as to why its important to think about and consider heaven: first, as a comfort to believers; second, to empower believers to witness to friends, family and neighbors; and third, to remind all that there is a reward for obedience as well as a punishment for disobedience. Now these are not light, fun-filled concepts that lead to happy musical numbers. There was only one thing to do - go back to the Word of God and see what a child might think of when hearing the "heaven" verses.

I opened up Jason's little "heaven" booklet again and read the verses and studied the pictures. There was the answer - on hearing all these descriptions of heaven, a child might well imagine it to be like an endless vacation at a fancy resort hotel. At least, such a setting might well be a suitable showcase for the scriptural truths involved. I could almost hear a child asking a parent: "what is heaven like?; isn't it just full of old people?...but what if my friends don't go there? That would be sad – and there is no sadness there. **That** means it's up to **me** to tell them the way to be sure and get there!"

"Paradise Inn" began to unfold, almost like a rose opening up in time lapse photography. I could see the sequence of the revelation that had to take place in the sick child, as well as the resolve to carry the message to friends. This was the "witnessing" element that was always so important in the development of both the teaching curriculum and the crafting of these plays. Certainly, this was critical when it came to performing before adults... at our church before friends and neighbors and particularly at the nursing homes.

Now, I must admit that the idea of a fancy resort was considerably enhanced by the fact that my wife and I had just returned from a stay at a most sumptuous and grandiose Marriott Hotel in San Jose, Costa Rica. The total service, the wonderful menus, the gift shops, the tropical setting and the friendly staff were all indelibly etched in my mind as I considered the "showcase." As the storyline of this production tumbled through my mind, I began to realize that the message embedded was a little more complex, in terms of presentation, than I thought my younger Sunday School class could handle. Since the Purim play had been performed by members of the high school Youth Group, the junior high class had been pressing for their own chance. Most of the members of this class had been in any number of past productions, so they all knew what to expect in terms of teaching, commitment and performance.

I decided the best course was to simply lay out the idea before them and to see if they wanted to do it. It didn't take long for them to reach a unanimous decision. Their Sunday School class studies were such that the messages in this play would be quite suitable and in keeping with their own reasonably advanced knowledge of scripture. The only problem was that this class were all girls - no young men at all. Since young Jason had been the one who had given me his little "Heaven" pocket book, how could I not use him? Besides, he had become a wonderful performer and really knew scripture. Thus, "Tip" the Bellhop became the connecting link in the various scenes and would be the scene changer and sign bearer - he would also be perfect for the "calls" at the end of the play. As it turned out, this was an inspired choice – Jason would be a star!

With two more platelet donation sessions (and the resulting 4-plus hours to think things through), the story line and the characters came into focus:

> We meet Meera, a very sick little girl, as she asks her mother what heaven is like.
>
> The mother answers by quoting (singing) those wonderful verses from I Corinthians 2:9 ("the eye has not seen, the ear has not heard...."); this introduces a song, "Heaven is being with Jesus."
>
> The mother leaves Meera to ponder all this, and she sleepily imagines a heaven-like resort hotel. Whereupon she is visited by a heavenly "concierge" who will take her on a dream-like visit to exactly such a place. Off they go.
>
> They arrive at Paradise Inn and meet the friendly staff - Dora Passki, the room clerk; Belle Tell the message clerk; Chef Anna Manna, the banquet manager, Grace Charisma, the gift shop manager, another guest, named Bea Liever, and of course "Tip" the bellhop. We are entertained by a Salvation Rock group, "The Grateful Living." Each of these has an instructive scene or number which further educates Meera on what heaven is all about. She even gets to visit the "competition," a place at a much lower level called Motel 666, run by the infamous Lucy Fur.
>
> Meera returns to her sick room and breathlessly tells her mother what she has learned. She is not only healed, but is energized to spread the gospel to her friends so "when the time comes, they'll all be heaven bound."

As in past plays, the songs emerged from the messages in the plot. That way, the musical numbers are not interruptions, but help advance the story and define and develop the characters. With almost a dozen musical numbers, and the use of music to transition from scene to scene, the dream sequence aspect of the story was reinforced. The reality of it all, of course, was revealed in the child's healing at the end. The basic lesson that our salvation is not an end in itself, but is an empowerment to grow and to spread the gospel, was something that this group of junior high kids could credibly minister to adults.

When all this had been crafted and produced, we were scheduled to present it on a Saturday night at our church and then the next day at two nursing homes in the area. I had invited little Ian and his family to come Saturday night. They did, and it turned out that it was his birthday.

I was told that his cancer was in remission.

# PARADISE INN

## Lesson Plan

Heaven, to many children, is simply a reward for being good. Yes, that is simplistic, and not particularly scriptural...but it is understandable. Eternal life can't be easily intellectualized by a 12 year old. Immortality, at that age, seems like a safe bet. The well-known Bible teacher, Marilyn Hickey, always makes the point that heaven is not just the chance to fly around on a little pink cloud and eat chocolates and listen to (or play) harp music. In reality it engages believers in the exacting necessity of spiritual warfare. Somewhere between these two opposing pictures is the depiction of heaven. For kids at the Junior High level, it is important to set aside the "pink cloud" concept and concentrate on what scripture says about heaven. Heaven, described in Biblical terms, can certainly replace fear and anxiety in a seriously ill child...but it can also give children a solid basis for reaching out to friends and relatives in a true evangelistic sense.

I. What does the Bible say about heaven? Read Chapter 2 of Paul's First Letter to the Corinthians. Verse 9 contains the basic message, but the context of the chapter is very important. The words, "God hath revealed" are key. He wants His children to fully understand His plan for them. Now turn to Mark 16:19 and know that the hallmark of heaven is the presence of Jesus. What does that mean for each of us? John 3:16 tells us explicitly who gets to go there. Luke 10:20 talks about whose names are written there. Matthew 8:11 tells us that we also get to sit down with Abraham, Isaac and Jacob. Matthew 25:34 describes heaven as a kingdom. Matthew 6:20 tells us the parable about storing our treasures there. John 14:2 speaks of heaven's beauty and how it has "many mansions." Jesus said he goes to prepare a place for us. Revelation 21:11 talks of sharing the glory of God and verse 4 says there is no death, sadness, crying or pain. Psalm 23:6 speaks of "my home forever." And in II Corinthians 5:1, Paul tells us we will have wonderful new bodies there. All of Revelation, chapter 21 describes heaven as the "New Jerusalem."

II. Now, try and find out what the class knew about heaven before you read all those scriptures. The answers may surprise you - or you may want to ask this question before you tell them what God says. In Genesis, Chapter 1, the first thing God created was Heaven. The last Chapter of Revelation describes Heaven. In between, Heaven is referred to more than anything else in the Bible. It is the major point of salvation, the destination of believers, the Fellowship Hall of the saints. Concentrate now on the key question about heaven: how do you get there? Many people quote John 3:16, but the whole of chapter 3 has the answer. The Pharisee, Nicodemus, asked Jesus just that question. Their conversation and the concluding verses of the chapter are important study points for your class.

III. What would you tell your friends about Heaven? This is a simple evangelical exercise - not a structured dissertation on the gospel, but a straightforward presentation of repentance, obedience and righteousness. Discuss the concept of "commitment" and what it means .

IV. If - repeat IF - a child were to imagine that eternal life in heaven was a vacation at a fancy resort, then how would the basic tenets of the gospel be presented?

- acceptance of the Lordship of Jesus
- repentance
- commitment to work to be in God's perfect will
- following His commandments
- constantly giving thanks and praise
- speaking to God - prayer
- listening to God - reading His word
- reaching out to others, sharing the gospel
- witnessing to those you care about

As you work with the class on this, be sure and avoid lapsing into doctrinal jargon - and replace such words that come back to you from the children with words and concepts (and examples) they can easily relate to.

V. Explore the meaning of the "baggage" scene, the "gifts" scene, and the "testimonies" in the "Jesus Is the Key" song. Do they know anyone who is part of a "whining and bellyaching" ministry? What parts of the gospel are highlighted in "The Grateful Living" number? What is it about Lucy Fur and Motel 666 that is an accurate presentation of the activities of Satan? Has anyone ever been to a hotel that had any of these things?

Note: D. James Kennedy's book, "Why I Believe" and "The Narrow Way" by William C. Nichols have already been mentioned. The selected chapters in these books are perfect reading assignments for children of the Junior High School age.

## The Format

This is a play with nine basic characters. Two double up to portray other characters. The action takes place centered on two main characters: the sick little girl, Meera, and her angelic guide, Purlie Gates. It is the growing awareness in Meera that she has a special earthly role to perform, that is the basis of her healing. Most of the other characters populate her vision of heaven as a first class vacation resort called Paradise Inn. It is in the Inn that most of the action takes place, as the various characters are introduced and explain their roles.

The overall impact should be directed to emphasize the point that heaven is not a goal or an end in itself, but an inducement to the harnessing of spiritual prowess to reach out to others. With such a focus, Meera's healing is not a miracle, so much as a natural conclusion.

Care should be taken to portray Paradise Inn through a series of visual effects and props that will provide a realistic (and humorous) context for this message. It is for this reason that "the flip side" (namely, Motel 666) is depicted in verse, song and the person of the night manager, Lucy Fur, who is played by the actress doing Purlie Gates. Scene changes are signaled by the action of Tip the Bellhop who comes on to change the signage of each interior venue of the Inn. Continuity of these changes is provided by the piano echoing the music of each previous song. Pre-positioning of each succeeding set of characters (and props)is critical to avoid gaps and lapses in the action.

The curtain calls at the end are sequenced by Tip who announces "calls" for each player. When all are assembled, a reprise is given by the cast of "Heaven Is..."

## List of Props

| | | |
|---|---|---|
| wheelchair & plasma bag | nurse's cap & stethoscope | Panel: My Heaven Report |
| halos | Feather quill pen | Hotel summoning bell |
| 5 fans | 6 bellhop red caps | Bellhop jacket |
| suitcase | 6 cutout gold keys | Fruit basket & fruit |
| 2 menus | Order book - waitress | Telephone operator's set |
| coffee mug | Bible panel | Panel: Gifts Catalogue |

**Signs**:

| | | | |
|---|---|---|---|
| ELEVATOR | PARADISE INN | REGISTRATION | |
| CONCIERGE | GIFTS BY GRACE | BANQUET HALL | |
| MOTEL 666 | MESSAGE CENTER | NIGHT MANAGER | |
| Sale - 100% Off | Sinners Welcome! | Bitterness | |
| Guilt | Pride | Anger | |
| Doubt & Fear | Blame | Denial | Self-Pity |
| PROPHESY | ENCOURAGING | TEACHING | |
| LEADERSHIP | SERVING | MERCY | |
| Purlie Gates | Lucy Fur | | |

# PARADISE INN

## Cast:

| | |
|---|---|
| NURSE | Caregiver indicating seriousness of Meera's illness |
| MEERA | A sick child, wondering about heaven |
| MOTHER | Meera's mother |
| PURLIE GATES | Concierge at Paradise Inn |
| DORA PASSKI | The Room Clerk |
| BELLE TELL | Message clerk & switchboard operator |
| GRACE CHARISMA | Gift Shop Manager |
| CHEF ANNA MANNA | The Banquet Manager |
| BEA LEIVER | A New Guest |
| "TIP" | The Bellhop |
| LUCY FUR | Night Manager at Motel 666 |
| THE GRATEFUL LIVING | Salvation Rock Group |

## Musical Numbers:

| | |
|---|---|
| OVERTURE | The Orchestra |
| I CORINTHIANS 2:9 | The Mother |
| HEAVEN IS | The Mother & Meera |
| PARADISE INN | The Staff |
| THE CONCIERGE | Purlie Gates |
| THE BAGGAGE ANTHEM | "Tip" & the Staff |
| JESUS IS THE KEY | Dora Passki, Tip & Staff |
| THE GIFTS | Grace Charisma |
| THE GRATEFUL LIVING | The Staff |
| MOTEL 666 | Lucy Fur |
| BE ANXIOUS FOR NOTHING | Belle Tell & Meera |
| HEAVEN BOUND | Meera & Friends |
| HEAVEN IS | All |

## Director's Introduction

There have been many recorded instances of believers having near-death or "out-of-body" experiences. Almost all of them conclude with the person realizing (or being told) that they have much to do in spreading the gospel before their time to "go home" is upon them. As the Apostle Paul says in his letter to the Ephesians, our mission in God's plan is "for the perfecting of the saints, for the work of ministry, for the edifying of the body of Christ." This should be as true for children as it is for adults - to learn and be able to respond to God's plan... in this life.

The well-known Bible teacher, Marilyn Hickey, has often said that we should not assume that our role in heaven is to sit around on a pink cloud eating chocolates. We will have important work to do in the heavenly kingdom – and we'd better be ready and well prepared to "rise" to the occasion.

Conveying all this to children, and then equipping them to witness this message to others, seems to me to fulfill Paul's admonition. That's what this little play is all about.

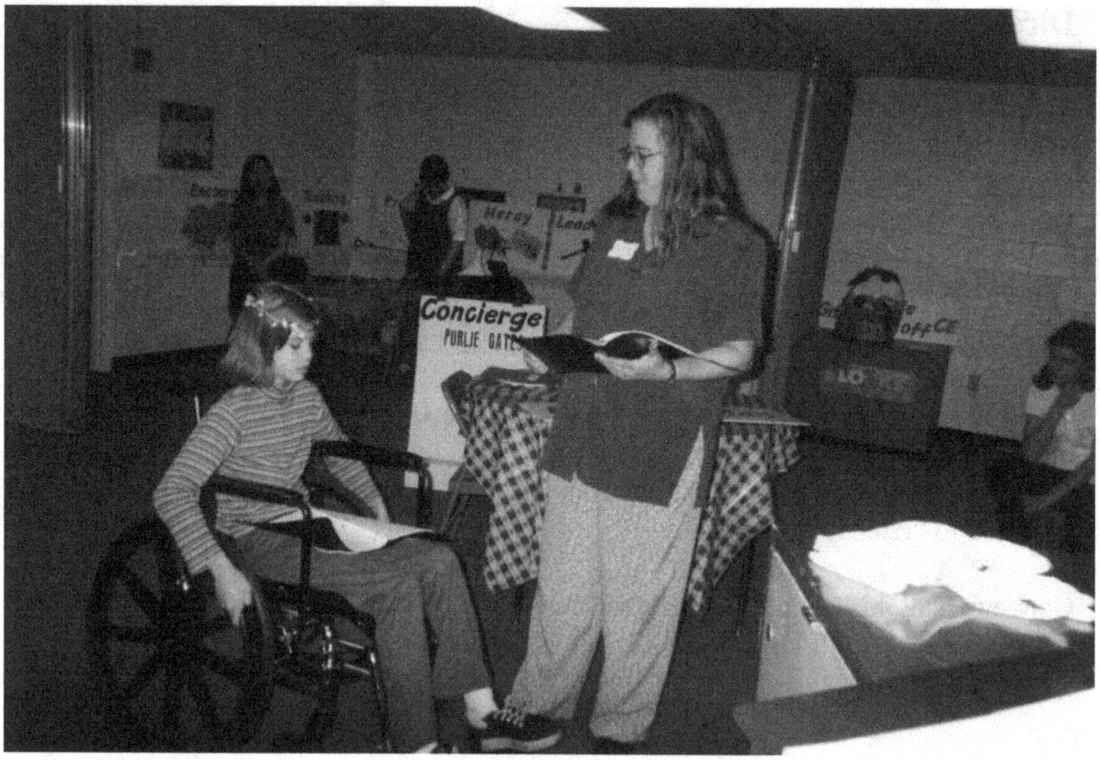


Meera and her mother rehearse

Rehearsing Chef Anna Manna

*During the last 30 seconds of the Overture, Meera and her mother take their place - Meera in a wheelchair at stage left, the Mother in the center, holding a Bible. Behind the Mother is a six foot black draped section. On the right of this is a narrower black draped section with a sign over it saying : "Elevator." The 2 characters are frozen in place. At the end of the Overture, the Nurse hurriedly enters up the center aisle; she goes to Meera, feels her forehead and takes her pulse. She then turns to the Mother...*

**NURSE** *(to Mother)*

She seems comfortable. I think the pain is less.

**MOTHER**

Thanks you.

**NURSE**

I'll be in the next room; call me if you need me.

*The Nurse exits to one side of the elevator, as the Mother steps forward to Meera.*

**MOTHER**

Meera?... how do you feel now?

**MEERA**

It doesn't hurt as much.... *(pauses)*.... Mother?

**MOTHER**

Yes?

**MEERA**

What is heaven like? Are there just a lot of old people there?..... Are there really pearl gates and streets of gold? Will it be fun?

**MOTHER**

Well, Meera, you know what the Bible says about heaven: Matthew spoke of heaven as a kingdom; and Jesus said that there, we can sit down with Abraham, Isaac and Jacob.

**MEERA**

...and I won't hurt anymore...when I go there?

**MOTHER**

Well, Paul said we will have wonderful new bodies. And the Book of Revelation said that there would be no death, crying, sadness or pain. Isaiah also spoke of everlasting joy and gladness.

**MEERA**

It's hard to imaging what it will be like.

**MOTHER**

Well, remember that verse when we read Paul's First letter to the Corinthians:

*after a brief musical introduction, the Mother sings:*

THE EYE HAS NOT SEEN, THE EAR HAS NOT HEARD
AND THE HEART CANNOT POSSIBLY KNOW;
WHAT WONDERFUL THINGS
GOD HAS PREPARED
FOR ALL THOSE WHO LOVE HIM...
AND SO...

WE CAN ONLY IMAGINE AND SPECULATE
ON WHAT AWAITS US
THROUGH HEAVEN'S PEARL GATE...

**MOTHER**

And remember what the best news of all is?...

**MEERA**

What?

**MOTHER** *(sings)*

HEAVEN IS BEING WITH JESUS
HEAVEN IS KNOWING THAT HE
HAS PREPARED ME A PLACE
IN HIS FATHER'S HOUSE
WHERE HE'S LOVINGLY WAITING FOR ME.

THAT'S HEAVEN
THAT'S HEAVEN
AND THAT'S WHERE I WANT TO BE
FOR ALL ETERNITY

HEAVEN IS JOY EVERLASTING
HEAVEN: GOD'S ANSWER TO PRAYER
AND ALL THOSE WHO BELIEVE
HE WILL GLADLY RECEIVE
FOR THEIR NAMES ARE WRITTEN RIGHT THERE

*she turns to Meera and says:*

Now, you try it... *(They both sing:)*

THAT'S HEAVEN
THAT'S HEAVEN
AND THAT'S WHERE I WANT TO BE
FOR ALL ETERNITY

**MOTHER** *(sings)*

HEAVEN: THE REALM OF THE ANGELS
HEAVEN: THE HOUSE OF THE LORD;
WITH THE ELDERS IN PLACE
'ROUND THE THRONE OF GRACE
AND THE SPACE WHERE YOUR TREASURES ARE STORED.

**BOTH**

THAT'S HEAVEN
THAT'S HEAVEN
AND THAT'S WHERE I WANT TO BE
FOR ALL ETERNITY

THAT'S HEAVEN
THAT'S HEAVEN
AND THAT'S WHERE I WANT TO BE
FOR ALL ETERNITY.

**MOTHER**

So you see, Meera, the Bible really tells us a lot about heaven. That's where we get to be with Jesus; that's where the throne of Grace is - God's throne; it's a beautiful place with no sin, sadness or pain; it shines with the light of God's glory. John saw it as a beautiful city- he called it the New Jerusalem... with streets of gold and pearl gates. And all those who have made Jesus Lord of their lives have their names written there - Jesus said He would prepare a place there for each of us...

**MEERA**

...like having a reservation..?

**MOTHER**

Well... sort of... Now you try and get some sleep, and then I'll come back with some heavenly hot chocolate.

*The Mother exits right and Meera seems to ponder what has been said. She pauses, as if gathering her thoughts. She picks up a panel labeled: "My Heaven Report."*

**MEERA**

Okay... Heaven...
Sounds like a vacation;
A vacation that never will end;
Lots to do and to see there
And of course I will be there
With Jesus, my very best friend.

It might be like that place we stayed at
A couple of years ago;
Exciting and fun;
Inviting, well-run,
Where the whole staff put on quite a show!

It's not so hard to imagine;
I'll have a new body to wear;
I can run, jump and climb
And it's light all the time,
(It sound neat, like last year's state fair!)

But... what if my friends all don't go there?
That would be awful... and sad –
But there's no sadness there,
So I'll just have to share
The good news that made me so glad!

I've just got to tell them that heaven
Is where they all have to be
I'll ask God, and pray, to show them the way
To spend their eternity....

I'll bet heaven is lovely and special
Like that big Marriott resort
I can just visualize
When I shut my eyes
What I'll write in my heaven report....

*Abruptly, Purlie Gates enters through the curtains marked "Elevator" When she speaks, Meera opens her eyes and sits up...*

**PURLIE**

...and I'll help you.

**MEERA** *(startled)*

Who are you?

**PURLIE**

I'm Purlie Gates... the Concierge.

**MEERA**

The whaaat?

**PURLIE**

The Concierge. Look, you just imagined that heaven was like a fancy resort hotel... and they all have a concierge. It's a kind of super guide and helper - like at the Marriott. Here's the deal.

**PURLIE** *(sings)*

ETERNALLY AT YOUR SERVICE
IS THE CONCIERGE
WHAT HEAVENLY GUESTS DESERVE IS
A COMPETENT CONCIERGE

WHO COORDINATES
THE JOY THAT AWAITS
ALL OF LIFE'S HEAVEN-BOUND GRADUATES
SO HERE I AM:
MISS PURLIE GATES –
YOUR CONCIERGE!

Now, just come with me and I'll take you on a visit to what you just imagined heaven would be like – it's a place called Paradise Inn.

**MEERA**

But... I'm not well... I can't get up.

**PURLIE**

Sure you can - remember you can have a new body.

**MEERA**

Am I going to heaven?

**PURLIE**

Well.... eventually. But this "new body" is just a loaner. You see, I'm going to help you learn what to tell your friends and family... so they will understand how important heaven is. Here... Put this on

*Purlie hands Meera a gold halo*

It's like a ticket.

**MEERA**

How will we get there??

*Without thinking, Meera put on the halo and starts to stand up.*

**PURLIE**

On the Glory Express, of course. Let's go... and don't worry, I'll have you back in a wink... in time for that hot chocolate!

*Purlie goes over to Meera and takes her by the hand. They start to exit through the Elevator door, Meera looks back at the wheelchair... then shrugs, adjusts her halo and goes off with Purlie. As they exit, "Tip" the Bellhop comes on from the right and hangs up a large sign saying: Paradise Inn on the black screened section in the center. As the rest of the "staff" comes on, the wheelchair is wheeled off left; a Registration Desk appears on the right; a Concierge station is now where the wheelchair was. Two palm trees are hung on either side of the black screened section. On the Registration Desk is a large book, a quill pen and a summoning bell. This "staff" now assembles in a line towards the front of the stage. They sing:*

PARADISE INN
COME TO PARADISE INN
WHERE THE DAYS FULL OF PRAISE
AND FEAST BEGIN;
WHERE THERE'S ROOM FOR YOU
BUT NO ROOM FOR SIN;
SCRIPTURES SAY, THERE'S ONE WAY
TO PARADISE INN

NOW MOST COME BY CHOICE
NO ONE BY CHANCE
(ONE CAME BY FIERY CHARIOT)
AND ONCE THROUGH THESE DOORS
ALL HEAVEN IS YOURS
LET'S SEE THEM SAY THAT
AT THE MARRIOTT...

COME TARRY AT...

PARADISE INN
COME TO PARADISE INN
TO THE PLACE WHERE EACH FACE
WILL WEAR A GRIN;
WHERE YOU MIGHT MEET FRIENDS
OR RUN INTO KIN –
IF YOU SHOWED THEM THE WAY
TO PARADISE, PARADISE INN!

WHEN YOU CHECK OUT ON EARTH
CHECK INTO A BERTH
AT PARADISE, PARADISE INN!

*At the end of the song, the Staff stays in a line, moving back slightly. Purlie enters from the elevator and goes to the Concierge station. She then motions for Meera to follow her. As Meera comes in, she looks all around in wonderment.*

**PURLIE**

Come on in, Meera. I'll introduce you to the whole staff here at Paradise Inn. First, there's our Manager – Rod Aaron.

**DORA**

He's not here, Purlie.

**PURLIE**

Where is he? *(Dora points upward)*
Oh.... of course. Well, if he were here, he'd give his usual welcoming speech... about service and how our guests are the most important people here... and all the facilities here at the Inn. Then, he'd end with his usual line about making you comfortable – *(Clears throat for emphasis)* "Your comfort is why we're here. That's why we like to say.... 'Rod and his staff will comfort you.'"

*The staff all groan in reaction to this pun. Meera is still looking all around*

**MEERA**

This is quite a place.

**PURLIE**

...and quite a staff. Here is our Room Clerk, Dora Passki.

**DORA**

Hi. As soon as you check in, I'll tell you about your key.

**PURLIE**

...and this is Belle Tell, our Message Clerk and switchboard operator. She can help you send those messages you wanted to give to your friends.

*The phone rings and Belle, with her headset, answers*

**BELLE**

Halo!, Paradise Inn... halo...

**MEERA**

What messages?

**PURLIE**

The messages that would get them here when the time comes. Like a "wish you were here" card.

**MEERA**

Oh.

**PURLIE**

...and this is Miss Grace Charisma... who manages our Gift Shop.

**GRACE**

..and the gifts we feature are all free! I was just making our promotional sign.

*Grace holds up a sign which proclaims: SALE - 100% OFF!*

**MEERA**

Wow!

**PURLIE**

Chef Anna Manna is our Banquet Manager. What's on the menu, Chef?

**ANNA**

Well, today we have two separate menus - one for King Solomon's Feast – that's the kosher one... and one for Belshazzar's Feast – that's the non-kosher one.

**MEERA**

And what is it, exactly, that you do, Purlie?

*A simple 4/4 beat starts and Purlie begins to recite against it*

**PURLIE**

Now I can get you tickets for the Angel Choir
Introduce you to your choice of Messianic Prophesier;
Fit you out with wings and halo from our very own supplier;
Let you sightsee New Jerusalem from the wall of Nehemiah...
Or...

How about a concert by King David
Playing psalms upon his lyre?
Or a telescopic view
Of Satan's cookout with hellfire?
Whatever you require – set your expectations higher

Go ahead and splurge - call the Concierge!

*Purlie then repeats her original song, and sings:*

ETERNALLY AT YOUR SERVICE
IS THE CONCIERGE
WHAT HEAVENLY GUESTS DESERVE IS...
A COMPETENT CONCIERGE:

WHO COORDINATES, THE JOY THAT AWAITS
ALL OF LIFE'S HEAVEN-BOUND GRADUATES
SO HERE I AM - MISS PURLIE GATES
YOUR CONCIERGE –
YOUR MOST RESPONSY
NOT TOO FONCY,
CONCI- CONCI-ERGE!!!

**MEERA**

Wow.. I would love to do all those things! It sounds great!

*"Tip" the Bellhop enters and stands as if waiting for his introduction. He is dressed in a gold-trimmed red jacket with epaulets, medals and a red cap.*

**PURLIE**

And this is "Tip" the Bellhop. You won't believe what he does!

*"Tip" salutes as a Guest enters from the right with a small suitcase. She goes to the Registration desk , looks around, then bangs the summoning bell impatiently.*

**GUEST**

Can I get some service???

**PURLIE**

Sure... but first you have to understand the rules.

**GUEST**

Rules??

**PURLIE**

...about your baggage.... (*turns to Meera*)
We all wear many hats here. Listen carefully...

*The Staff then puts on red caps similar to "Tip's" They then line up to sing, anthem style:*

**STAFF**

BAGGAGE, BAGGAGE, BAGGAGE
WE'LL RELIEVE YOU OF YOUR BAGGAGE;
WE'RE HERE TO SET YOU FREE
AND MAKE YOUR BURDEN LIGHT.
BAGGAGE, BAGGAGE, BAGGAGE
GET RELIEF FROM ALL YOUR BAGGAGE;
AND WE DON'T MEAN BAGGAGE
MADE BY SAMSONITE – NOT QUITE..
WE DON'T MEAN BAGGAGE MADE BY SAMSONITE!

**DORA**

BRING YOUR BAGGAGE HERE
WE'LL CHECK IT, THEN WE'LL CHUCK IT;
THE BAGGAGE WE HAVE GOT WOULD STRETCH
FROM NEVADA TO NANTUCKET!

**BELLE**

TO NANTUCKET

**STAFF**

SO IF YOUR BAGGAGE, BAGGAGE
HAS COME TO BE A DRAG;
WE ARE HERE TO HELP YOU, 'CAUSE
YOUR BAGGAGE IS OUR BAG!

YES, WE ARE HERE TO HELP YOU, 'CAUSE
YOUR BAGGAGE IS OUR BAG!

*"Tip" now steps forward to assist the Guest. He puts her suitcase up on a small table & recites:*

**TIP**
Cause we're strict on peace and purity
You first have to pass. SECURITY.

To get a handle on your baggage
(Making sure there is no sin there)
You will have to open up
So we can see what's in there.

**GUEST**
Well, I just have one little "carry-on"...

**TIP**
Judging from the weight of this,
I think you've been "carryin' on" all right!

*"Tip" opens the suitcase and peers in.*

**TIP**
Lady, you are well over the weight limit!

**GUEST**
I beg your pardon!

*"Tip" resumes his recitation and as he does so, he begins to pull signs out of the suitcase, .. Each one labeled with an enumerated "sin."*

**TIP**
Here's a ton of BITTERNESS
You've been carryin' around;
And here's that PRIDE you've tried to hide,
And ANGER by the pound...
GUILT, SELF-PITY, DOUBT & FEAR
The BLAME that you've been shifting...
Here's a pile of DENIAL...
Ma'am, you're into heavy lifting!

I can see there's even more
That you have packed and stowed there;
Time to leave your burden here
And lighten up your load – there!

*"Tip" puts all the sin signs back in the bag and heaves it off stage right. The Staff repeats their Baggage Anthem:*

**STAFF**

SO IF YOUR BAGGAGE, BAGGAGE
HAS COME TO BE A DRAG
WE ARE HERE TO HELP YOU, 'CAUSE,
YOUR BAGGAGE IS OUR BAG!

YES, WE ARE HERE TO HELP YOU, 'CAUSE
`YOUR BAGGAGE IS OUR BAG!

**GUEST**

I feel lighter already. I guess I didn't need any of that "baggage." Now, should I check in?

*The Guest goes over to Dora at the Registration desk..*

**DORA**

Let's see if your name is in the Book.... name?

*The Guest peers over at the Book, trying to see.*

**GUEST**

Bea Liever... there I am!

**PURLIE**

And, Dora... Meera here needs to know about the key.

**DORA**

Actually, there is only one key... and I've got one here for each of you. Here.

*Dora passes out a large gold scroll-type key to each of them. The bottom part of the key is in the shape of a cross. After a musical chord, Dora starts her song. The song is staged with a chorus and three whining "testimonies" with each soloist taking a part. Tip has the "exhortation" line.*

**DORA**

WHEN WE'RE CALLED TO ENTER HIS KINGDOM
WE HAVE THE PROMISE OF GOD
AND WE'RE FOLLOWING IN THE FOOTSTEPS
WHERE ALL OF THE SAINTS HAVE TROD.

AND THE GATES OF HEAVEN SWING OPEN
BECAUSE OF THE CHOICE WE HAVE MADE;
AND BECAUSE OF THE GRACE WE'VE BEEN GIVEN;
AND BECAUSE OF THE PRICE
THAT'S ALREADY BEEN PAID

SO NO MATTER WHAT TROUBLES COME AGAINST ME
I HAVE HOPE 'CAUSE I HAVE THE KEY...

**TIP**
JESUS IS THE KEY!

**STAFF**
JESUS IS THE KEY
JESUS IS THE KEY
FILLING MY CUP OF JOY TO THE BRIM
HELPING ME TRY TO BE MORE LIKE HIM
AND WELCOMING ME TO HIS ETERNITY;
JESUS, JESUS, JESUS... IS THE KEY!

**DORA**
THERE'S OLD SATAN AT MY DOOR AGAIN
CONFIDENT HE CAN "UP" HIS SCORE AGAIN;
DEALING HIS CARDS FROM UNDERNEATH,
PROBABLY LYING THROUGH HIS TEETH

HOW CAN I BEAT THAT OLD ENTRANCER?
IF SIN IS THE QUESTION – WHAT'S THE ANSWER?

**TIP**
JESUS IS THE KEY!

**STAFF**
JESUS IS THE KEY
JESUS IS THE KEY
FILLING MY CUP OF JOY TO THE BRIM
HELPING ME TRY TO BE MORE LIKE HIM
AND WELCOMING ME TO HIS ETERNITY;
JESUS, JESUS, JESUS...IS THE KEY!

**ANNA**

FEELING BAD - ALL SICK AND FEVERISH
MAKING IT HARD TO BE "BELIEVER-ISH"
THOSE ACHES AND PAINS DISCOURAGE ME
I NEED SOME SHOTS - OR SURGERY.

I'M AT THE END OF MY ENDURANCE
NEED A PRESCRIPTION AND INSURANCE

**TIP**

JESUS IS THE KEY

**STAFF**

JESUS IS THE KEY
JESUS IS THE KEY
FILLING MY CUP OF JOY TO THE BRIM
HELPING ME TRY TO BE MORE LIKE HIM
AND WELCOMING ME TO HIS ETERNITY
JESUS, JESUS, JESUS...IS THE KEY!

**GRACE**

BANK ACCOUNT IS FACING EMPTINESS
ALL MY FINANCES NEED REDEMPTI-NESS;
WALLOWING IN MY MISERY
I'M BROKE AND FRIENDLESS – YESSIREE

EVERY PROSPECT IS FULL OF GLITCHES
I NEED A WIN OR INSTANT RICHES

**TIP**

JESUS IS THE KEY!

**STAFF**

JESUS IS THE KEY
JESUS IS THE KEY
FILLING MY CUP OF JOY TO THE BRIM
HELPING ME TRY TO BE MORE LIKE HIM;
AND WELCOMING ME TO HIS ETERNITY;
JESUS, JESUS, JESUS...IS THE KEY!

**DORA**

OPEN THE DOOR, WHENEVER HE KNOCKS
PAY NO MIND TO LATCHES AND LOCKS, 'CAUSE...

**STAFF**

JESUS, JESUS, JESUS...IS THE KEY!

*At the last line, they all hold up their keys so that the cross is at the top. Tip exits right and then as the rest exit, he comes back on with a large sign saying: GIFTS BY GRACE, which he proceeds to hang up over the PARADISE INN sign on the black curtained center area. He exits.*

*Grace goes over to the side of the registration Desk and has a panel which reads: Gift Catalogue*

**PURLIE**

Now, let's go visit the gift shop before dinner.

**MEERA**

Can I get souvenirs for my friends?

**PURLIE**

Well, I'm not sure you'd call these gifts, "souvenirs" - they're a little more important than that. Let's let our gift shop Manager, Grace Charisma, explain.

**GRACE** *(sings)*

THE BIBLE IS FULL OF PROMISES
SEVEN THOUSAND LARGE AND SMALL
AND OUR PRIMARY AIM (IN JESUS NAME)
IS TO STAND AND CLAIM THEM ALL.

BUT THE BIGGEST AND BEST
THAT I'VE READ OR SEEN
IS THE PROMISE CONTAINED IN...
JOHN THREE SIXTEEN...

**MEERA**

..."that whosoever believeth in Him should not perish but have everlasting life."

**GRACE**

That's the one! And once anyone makes that "believeth" commitment, that's when the Gift Shop opens. You see... God wants the people in His kingdom to have all the right tools to be able to do the job He's called us to do.

**MEERA**

"Tools?" That sounds like a hardware store.

**GRACE**

Well, there's hardware... and software... but these are more like "holyware" God wants us to have the right equipment to do the job. Paul, in Ephesians, called this the "perfecting of the saints" (that' us!)... "for the work of the ministry." – and that means to spread the gospel.

**MEERA**

...so I can tell all my friends how important it is to get to heaven?

**GRACE**

Right! Now let's start with the "believeth" part. *(Recites)*

Roman 12, tells us all
How to begin, according to Paul;
How to determine your call, says Paul:

When we believe, God gives us a measure of faith
It's up to us to make that grow;
Then we are given the kind of gifts
That God has for us.... so...
We can reach out to others
(Friends, family, brothers,
And neighbors)...
So our labors will fulfill
This mission to be
In God's perfect will. *(Sings)*

IF YOU'RE LOOKING FOR THE PERFECT GIFT
YOU'VE COME TO THE PERFECT PLACE;
INSTALL YOUR SHARE... OF HOLYWARE
FROM AMONG THE GIFTS BY GRACE.

EACH GIFT WITH THIS LABEL
WILL HELP AND ENABLE YOU
AND GIVE YOU - FREE - THE ABILITY
TO PURSUE YOUR VERY OWN MINISTRY

YES, THIS IS THE PERFECT PLACE
TO SELECT WITH THRIFT
YOUR VERY OWN GIFT... BY GRACE!

And while you're Saint Paul-ing
You'll find your calling.

*As Grace names each of the six gifts, a staff member emerges from behind the center screen with a large display board depicting visual elements of that gift: Dora has PROPHESY which is a trumpet and scroll; Belle has TEACHING which has a slate blackboard and an apple; Anna has SERVING which is a mounted place setting; Purlie has ENCOURAGING which is a megaphone and pom-poms; Tip has LEADERSHIP which is a gavel. Grace gives the MERCY display to Meera (it's a Get Out of Jail Free card from Monopoly). The staff is then fanned out with their displays as Grace continues...*

Prophesy, teaching and serving;
Encouraging (giving a lift),
Being a leader, as well as a heeder;
Or maybe you have a mercy gift;
Maybe you have a mercy gift.

But whatever pursuit, or attribute
Here's a gift for any recruit –
A basket of fruit!

*Grace now produces a large basket, adorned with all kinds of fruit - apples, grapes, peaches, pears etc*

**MEERA**

A basket of fruit???

**GRACE** *(sings)*

LOVE, JOY AND PEACE
PATIENCE AND KINDNESS,
GOODNESS (TO FILL THE SOUL),
FAITHFULNESS, GENTLENESS -
FRUIT OF THE SPIRIT...

**PURLIE**

DON'T FORGET SELF-CONTROL;

**GRACE**

ESPECIALLY SELF-CONTROL!

**MEERA**

Wow! Do I need all that? That's a lot to remember!

**PURLIE**

Those are the free gifts from the Spirit of God. As you use them, you will find out which of those roles (serving, teaching, encouraging etc.) you are best suited for.

**MEERA**

...and why are those other things called "the ***fruit*** of the Spirit?"

**GRACE**

Oh, I can answer that!!

**PURLIE**

Watch out!

**GRACE**

God wants us to be full of such fruit. In Genesis, He said: "be fruit-ful."

**PURLIE**

See... I told you!

**GRACE**

...love, joy and peace are what makes you the ***apple*** of His eye...;
Patience and kindness are a wonderful ***pair***;
Goodness gives you ***or-range*** of possibilities;
...and if you don't have faithfulness and gentleness, you'll be ***melon***-choly.

**PURLIE**

Don't forget "self-control."

**GRACE**

Without that, you're ***plum*** out of luck!

**PURLIE**

It's time to move on, Meera...

**MEERA**

I wish I could have some of those fruit baskets sent to my friends.

**GRACE**

You can! We use ED EX...

**MEERA**

You mean: FED EX...

**GRACE**

No.... ED EX - that stands for Edification Extraordinary.

**PURLIE**

Come on... we'll be late for the Banquet

*As Purlie and Meera exit towards the left, Grace sings the last part of her song and then exits. As she finishes, Tip comes on ,as before, and place a large sign saying BANQUET HALL, first taking down the one that says: GIFTS BY GRACE.*

**GRACE** *(sings)*

YES, THIS IS THE PERFECT PLACE
TO SELECT WITH THRIFT
YOUR VERY OWN GIFT BY GRACE.

**TIP**

Dinner!.... dinner now being served in the Banquet Hall.

*As Tip puts up his sign and marches off, the Staff comes on to clear the stage and set up a dinner table. It is set for two, complete with checked tablecloth. As they finish this task, Meera and Purlie re-renter and are shown to seats at the table. Chef Anna Manna comes on and gives each a large MENU.*

**ANNA**

Now as I said earlier, we have two menus - one for Belshazzar's Feast (that's the non-kosher one); and one for King Solomon's Feast (that's the kosher one).

**PURLIE**

Let's try the one for King Solomon's Feast. I don't want to have to explain the "mene, mene, tekel, upharsin."

**ANNA** *(laughs)*

It's very tough anyway.

**MEERA**

It sounds awful...What is it?

**PURLIE**

It was the handwriting on the wall (if you remember your Book of Daniel).
Why don't I order for both of us? Now....for an appetizer....

**ANNA**

Felafel?

**MEERA**

No, I feel fine now. I have a new body - well.... a "loaner."

**PURLIE**

No, felafel is food. How are the barley cakes?

**ANNA**

Fine... they come with either the Faithful Mustard Seeds, or the Gethsemane olives.

**PURLIE**

The olives. Now for the soups....

**ANNA**

Well, we have either the Soup of the Seven Sorrows.. Or the Savory Esau Lentil Pottage.

**PURLIE**

The pottage... is it good tonight?

**ANNA**

Well, some people would give ***anything*** for it. How about entrees?

**MEERA**

Didn't I see a "Loaves and Fish Basket?"

**ANNA**

That's only for very large groups.

**PURLIE**

Let's see... there's the Fatted Calf Prodigal.... the Saint Peter's Fish... or the Altar Roasted Bullock a la Elijah.

**MEERA**

That sounds good.

**PURLIE**

Can we have it with the pomegranate sauce instead of the herbs of the field?

**ANNA**

Sure.

**PURLIE**

...and we'll have the vine leaves instead of the steamed wheat sheaves... and the haroseth rather than the millet pilaf.

**ANNA**

...and to drink?

**PURLIE**

We'll have the Promised Land Quencher...

**MEERA**

What's that?

**ANNA & PURLIE**

Milk and honey!!!

**PURLIE**

and don't forget some Sprouted Ezekiel Bread, ...with a little Sumerian Watercress.

*Anna closes her order pad, then turns and shouts off stage right...*

**ANNA**

Hey, Joe.... two number one's for Table four!!! *(Then to Purlie & Meera)*
Enjoy... and don't forget, we have some wonderful entertainment tonight.

**MEERA**

Wow

*On comes "Tip" to face the audience and make an MC-type announcement*

**TIP**

...and now, bretheren and sisteren, we bring you that new Salvation Rock Group – the Grateful Living!!

*Anna, Belle, Grace, Dora and Bea enter dressed appropriately as a singing group.*

**GROUP** *(sings)*

WE ARE THE GRATEFUL LIVING
MIGHTILY INTO
JOY AND THANKSGIVING;
IN A WORLD THAT SERVES UP
MAD AND HATEFUL;
WE BRING A PLATEFUL
OF GLAD AND GRATEFUL.
SELAH, SELAH, SAY LA, LA LA!

WE ARE SOME FISHERS CASTING
SEARCHING FOR SEEKERS
OF LIFE EVERLASTING
LET THE GOSPEL GOOD NEWS
COME RIGHT TO YA
AND THEN RENEW YA
HALLELUJAH!
SELAH, SELAH, SAY LA, LA, LA!

WE ARE THE GRATEFUL LIVING
TELLING OF GRACE FOR
ALL SINS FORGIVING
COME AND PACK YOUR SINS UP
BY THE CRATEFUL
COME JOIN THE LIVING
COME JOIN THE GRATEFUL
SELAH, SELAH, SAY LA, LA, LA!

SELAH, SELAH, SAY LA, LA, LA..... SAY LA!!

*The Group exits right. Purlie stands up, then Meera does the same - they move to the left*

**PURLIE**

Well, Meera, now you know all about the Rock of Salvation. It's time to show you what the shoals of judgement are all about.

**MEERA**

The whaaat?

**PURLIE**

Sure, Paradise Inn is a great place to go to... but if you want your friends to really understand how important it is to get here... and to be with you (when the time comes)... then you should make sure they know what the alternative is.

**MEERA**

The alternative?

**PURLIE**

Well, if you're not up here – you're gonna be down there. The best argument for making the choice to go to a heavenly place, is what happens to those who spend eternity at the competition.

**MEERA**

What's the competition?

**PURLIE**

Oh, it has lots of names – sheole, hades, the bottomless pit... but we call it: MOTEL 666.

**MEERA**

Where is it?

**PURLIE**

Just take that elevator... and press the WAY DOWN button. It's important that you see for yourself.

**MEERA**

Aren't you coming?

**PURLIE**

I can't. Just ask for my counterpart – Lucy Fur.... and hurry back.
Oh.. And Meera...? Hang onto your halo!!

*As this dialogue proceeds, the staff has come on to take away the dining table, settings etc. As they exit, "Tip" come on; takes down the BANQUET HALL sign and puts up a sign saying: MOTEL 666. Meera goes to the elevator as Purlie exits left. "Tip" then exits right, displaying a sign saying: WELCOME SINNERS! The Concierge station has now become a similar station, but with flames painted at the bottom and a sign on top showing LUCY FUR - Night Manager. Purlie, done up with a feather Boa and dark glasses re-enters as Lucy Fur. A musical vamp starts and she sings:*

**LUCY FUR**

I'M THE MANAGER HERE
AT MOTEL 6, 66
IT'S A REALLY HOT SPOT THAT WE'VE GOT
HERE ON THE RIVER STYXX;
UNREPENTANT SINNERS
ARE AMONG OUR PRIMARY PICKS
AS PERMANENT GUESTS
HERE AT MOTEL 6, 66

THE LIGHT IS DIM, AND GETTING DIMMER
HOPE IS SLIM, AS OUR GUESTS JUST SIMMER
TO ILLUSTRATE:
THAT THOSE "IN SIN," ETERNALLY
"IN-SIN- ERATE" (NOW AIN'T THAT GREAT!
AND IS IT HOT!
(PARADISE INN THIS IS NOT!)

I'M THE MANAGER HERE
AT MOTEL 6, 66
COME AND SEE THE RESULTS OF MY
DEVILISH BAG OF TRICKS
AS FREQUENTLY SEEN
IN THE LATEST FLICKS;
AND, OF COURSE, ROCK MUSIC LYR-ICS
(THEY'RE ALL MY SCHTICKS)
HERE AT MOTEL 6, 66 !!

Where we've got our share of celebrities
Those who majored in sin and sleaze,
Like Osama Bin – they all got in with ease.

They graduated here and now they've got
A lot of degrees
(Mostly centigrade)
And there's no shade as well
Here at my motel!

In our scriptural wing, there's Ahab, the King
And Jezebel, of course;
(The Phillistines were a really good source!)
There's Cain and Haman, and other "me pleasers;"
A couple of Pharaohs and lots of Caesars,
    And Jusas Iscariot -
    You won't find him.. At your glorified Marriott!

And here, from the underworld's trash heaps and sewers
We've drafted the dregs of evildoers
(It's a crop we've been creamin'
With the help of my top demon);
    The Hitlers, the Stalins, the Al Capones,
    The Borgias... and inventors of cellular phones...
    Just kidding...
    But they seem to be doing my bidding.

And our gloom surrounds all of the sounds
Of moans and groans;
So, our facilities may be a little bare bones;
    But you can stay in trim
    In our torturous gym
    Or maybe a swim, you can take
    In our nicely heated brim-
    Stone Lake;

It's hotter than h.... Hades
Measured in centigrade is
My perfectly swell... motel!

*As Lucy finishes her diatribe, Meera enters from the elevator - looks around, then says to Lucy..*

**MEERA**

Who are you? Where is this? Why is it so hot? – and what's that funny smell?

**LUCY**

I'M THE MANAGER HERE
AT MOTEL 6, 66
IT'S A REALLY HOT SPOT THAT WE'VE GOT
HERE ON THE RIVER STYXX;
UNREPENTANT SINNERS
ARE AMONG OUR PRIMARY PICKS
AS PERMANENT GUESTS
HERE AT MOTEL 6, 66

COME AND MIX
AT LUCY FUR'S BAILI-WICKS
HERE AT MOTEL 6, 66!

**MEERA**

Well, thanks (I think), Miss Fur.... but I really should be going.

**LUCY**

Wait! Don't you want to hear about our special promotions?

**MEERA**

I don't think so...

**LUCY**

We havea set of asbestos water wings for every new commitment... and once you're here... you can join our "Frequent Fryer" program.

**MEERA**

I'm allergic to second hand smoke.

**LUCY**

...and we have a Tobacco Hall of Shame.

*Meera has edged backwards towards the elevator, then turns to exit.. Lucy calls after her....*

**LUCY**

We'll leave the flame on fer ya!

*Meera exits through the elevator. Lucy exits left and changes back into Purlie as "Tip" comes on from the right; takes down the MOTEL 666 sign and puts up a new sign saying: MESSAGE CENTER. Meera comes out from the elevator, and see Purlie...*

**MEERA**

I got the message. Being part of God's plan sure seems like the way to go - before I go.

**PURLIE**

I think it's time for you to visit our Message Center. Belle!... Belle Tell, are you there??

*Belle, with headset, comes on and takes her place at the Registration Desk. She speaks into her headset.*

**BELLE**

Halo? Yes, Ma'am, you do have some messages. Here's one: John 14:2; Luke 10:20... and there's one more - Isaiah 35:10. That's it for now.
You're welcome... have a nice eternity....
Yes, Purlie?

**PURLIE**

I think Meera here wants to send some messages - to her friends. Those ones you just mentioned are good ones.

**MEERA**

...and I want to send one to my mother - I know she's anxious about me.

**BELLE**

Philippians 4:6 is the perfect message. And I have a good way of remembering it. You can sing along with me... if you remember the verse. *(Sings)*

BE ANXIOUS FOR NOTHING
BUT IN ALL THINGS WITH PRAYER;
AND WITH THANKSGIVING
MAKE YOUR WANTS KNOWN TO GOD;
AND HIS PEACE THAT PASSETH, ALL UNDERSTANDING
SHALL KEEP YOUR MIND AND YOUR HEART
SHALL KEEP YOUR MIND AND YOUR HEART

WHATEVER IS NOBLE
WHATEVER IS TRUE
IF IT BE LOVELY
AND IF IT BE PURE
IF IT BE JUST, OR PRAISEWORTHY AND FAITHFUL
LET YOUR MIND DWELL ON THESE
LET YOUR MIND DWELL ON THESE

REJOICE, REJOICE
AGAIN I SAY REJOICE

*While Belle has been singing, the rest of the staff comes on and listens. Then they repeat her song, with Meera joining in.*

**STAFF**

BE ANXIOUS FOR NOTHING
BUT IN ALL THINGS WITH PRAYER
AND WITH THANKSGIVING
MAKE YOUR WANTS KNOWN TO GOD
AND HIS PEACE THAT PASSETH, ALL UNDERSTANDING
SHALL KEEP YOUR MIND AND YOUR HEART
SHALL KEEP YOUR MIND AND YOUR HEART

REJOICE, REJOICE
AGAIN I SAY: REJOICE!

**BELLE**

But the most important message of all is the simplest. When you go back, Meera, and you want to share all this with your friends, remember ***that***. *(Points to her key)*

**PURLIE**

...and what Dora told you: "Jesus is the key!"

**BELLE**

...and if they ask, "why?" here's a little rhyming message that should help:

HE is our hope, when there seems to be none;
HE is our strength, when we most feel undone;
HE is our joy, when grief comes around;
HIS truth sets us free, when we tend to get bound;
HE is our healer, when we most need a cure;
HE is faithful and steadfast, when we need to be sure;
HE is our rock, when we're sinking in sand;
HE is our life, when death seems at hand;
And when you tell friends, it's important to say:
That to get ***here***, HE is the one true way.

**MEERA**

I can relate to all those things. Now I feel really equipped! - like Grace said... and I have a lot of work to do.

**PURLIE**

And you will have a very powerful testimony. But you still need one more thing.

**MEERA**

What's that?

**PURLIE**

Your Mother... and that hot chocolate! Let's go.

**MEERA**

I really hate to leave...

**PURLIE**

But the good news is... you'll be back someday.

*Purlie exits through the elevator as Tip takes down the Message Center sign - leaving the Paradise Inn sign in place. Meera exits opposite to get back to te wheelchair. We are now back to where they started in the first scene - the "sick room." Meera is in the wheelchair, waking up as the Nurse comes in followed by the Mother. Meera starts to speak rapidly... in a stream...*

**MEERA**

Mother!!!! I dreamt all about heaven... it's Paradise Inn... a wonderful place! There really is a Purlie Gates... and you have to chuck your baggage... there are lots of free gifts... and a fruit basket... and see "Jesus is the key!" Chef Anna Manna is in charge of wonderful banquets.. I sent messages by ED EX to all my friends... and I'm part of The Grateful Living... and ***nobody*** should go near Motel 666!!!

**MOTHER** *(to Nurse)*

Is she delirious?

*The Nurse feels Meera's forehead and checks her pulse*

**NURSE**

Her fever is gone – remarkable!

**MEERA**

I'm fine... there's no pain at all! *(She starts to stand up)*
You should be anxious for nothing, Mother.

**MOTHER**

That's funny... I was just reading that in Philippians!

**MEERA**

I prayed that, Mother... and God answered it. I'm healed, covered and delivered... and I know that when the time comes, I'll be heaven bound - and be with all my friends!

**MOTHER**

When you were born, Meera, I was very sick and I was afraid for you. That's why you are named "Meera" - short for "Meeracle." What's this? *(She picks up the halo which has fallen)*

**MEERA**

Oh, that's my ticket! ... and Mother? Now I have a real testimony!!.. and a lot of new friends!

*The Staff all comes through the elevator and lines up as a chorus for Meera's testimony song. Meera is now standing beside the wheelchair, the Mother and Nurse watching in amazement.*

**MEERA** *(sings)*

NOW I WAS SO FAR DOWN, I COULDN'T EVEN FIND "UP;"
CHECKED INTO SALVATION; AND THAT'S WHEN I SIGNED UP;
NOW I'M HEADED FOR THE RIGHT SIDE,
WHERE ALL THE SHEEP ARE LINED UP,
SO I'LL BE HEAVEN BOUND!

**STAFF**

I'M HEAVEN BOUND
ON THE GLORY EXPRESS
HEAVEN BOUND
CLOTHED IN RIGHTEOUSNESS
I'M TRAINED TO GO FORTH AND TO DO ALL I CAN
SO I'M BOUND TO BE PART OF
GOD'S HEAVENLY PLAN.

**MEERA**

NOW THERE IS HEAVEN OR NOT, IT'S UP TO ME TO PICK IT;
THE PAIN AND THE WOE NOW, I KNOW I CAN LICK IT;
I'M READY TO GET ROLLING
'CAUSE JESUS PAID MY TICKET
SO I'LL BE HEAVEN BOUND!

**STAFF**

I'M HEAVEN BOUND
ON THE GLORY EXPRESS
HEAVEN BOUND
CLOTHED IN RIGHTEOUSNESS;
I'M TRAINED TO GO FORTH, AND TO DO ALL I CAN
SO I'M BOUND TO BE PART OF
GOD'S HEAVENLY PLAN.

**MEERA**

I NOW HAVE SEEN THE LIGHT, THERE IS NO NIGHT, JUST DAY THERE
AND I'VE SEEN THE MANSION RESERVED FOR MY STAY THERE;
ALL ABOARD AND PRAISE THE LORD, 'CAUSE
THERE IS JUST ONE WAY THERE
YOU TOO'LL BE HEAVEN BOUND!

**STAFF**

I'M HEAVEN BOUND
ON THE GLORY EXPRESS
HEAVEN BOUND
CLOTHED IN RIGHTEOUSNESS;
I'M TRAINED TO GO FORTH, AND TO DO ALL I CAN
SO I'M BOUND TO BE PART OF
GOD'S HEAVENLY PLAN.

**MEERA**

WHERE ONCE I WAS LOST - NOW I AM FOUND
SO WHEN THE TIME COMES, I'LL BE...
HEAVEN BOUND! HEAVEN BOUND!

*The Staff now exits to the right side in a group, as "Tip" comes on with a CALL sign. He goes to stage left. As he mentions each "Call" and the character's name, that person comes forward to take a bow to the music of their particular song.*

**TIP**

And now... call for... The Nurse and Miss Bea Liever
Call for... Chef Anna Manna
Call for... Belle Tell
Call for... Dora Passki
Call for... Grace Charisma
Call for... Meera and her Mother
Call for... Purlie Gates and Lucy Fur

**PURLIE**

and Call for "Tip" the bellhop.

**ALL** *(sing)*

HEAVEN IS BEING WITH JESUS
HEAVEN IS KNOWING THAT HE
HAS PREPARED ME A PLACE
IN HIS FATHER'S HOUSE
WHERE HE'S LOVINGLY WAITING FOR ME.

THAT'S HEAVEN
THAT'S HEAVEN
AND THAT'S WHERE I WANT TO BE
FOR ALL ETERNITY.

THAT'S HEAVEN
THAT'S HEAVEN
AND THAT'S WHERE I WANT TO BE
FOR ALL ETERNITY!

**Curtain**

# 1st Corinthians 2:9

**Moderato**

Clark Tyler
*Arranged by Andrew Bell*

Em B7 C Em B7 B7
The eye has not seen the ear has not heard, and the heart can-not poss - i-bly know.
9 Em B7 C Em B7 C D
What won - der-ful things that God has pre-pared for all those who love Him and so.
17 Am Em D C D Bm7 G C G7 C
We can on-ly im-ag-ine and spec - u-late on what a-waits us thru hea-ven's pearl gate.

# Heaven

Clark Tyler
*Arranged by Andrew Bell*

23
Dm7 G C Csus4 Am7 Dm7 G
that's where I want to be; For all e - ter - ni -
1.2.3.
4. (End)
29
C Csus4 C C Csus4 C
ty.
rit.

# Paradise Inn

Clark Tyler
*Arranged by Andrew Bell*

19 C F C Dm/C Am7
Now most come by choice, no one by chance.
24 Dm7 G7 C Dm/C C F
One came by fi - e - ry char - i - ot. And once thru these doors
28 D7 D7
all Hea-ven is yours. Let's see them say that
32 G7 C
at the Mar - ri - ott. Come tar-ry at Par - a - dise

Coda
36
1.
2.
F
D7
When you check out on Earth check in - to a berth at
40
G
G7
C
G
Par - a - dise, Par - a - dise Inn.
43
C
G
C

# The Concierge

Clark Tyler
*Arranged by Andrew Bell*

G D7 G
G G#dim7 Am7 D7
E - ter-nal-ly at your ser-vice is the con- ci - erge. What
6 D7 Am7 G D G Em
hea-ven - ly guest des - erve is a com-pe - tent con - ci - erge. Who co - or - din - ates the
9 B7 D Em B7 C D7
joy that a - waits all of life's hea-ven bound grad - u - ates So
12 G Em Am9 D7 A7sus4 D7b9 G
1.
here I am Miss Pur- lie Gates, your con - ci - erge.

2.
16
G
B9
Em
C
E - erge. Your most re - spon - sy, not too fon - sy
20
Am7
D7
D7♭9
G
con - ci, con - ci - erge.
22

# The Baggage Anthem

Clark Tyler
*Arranged by Andrew Bell*

14
D G/D D A Gm C
it! The bag-age we have got would strech from Ne - va - da to Nan - tuck et. So
A
17
F Gm7 C7 Dm7 Gm7 C7
if your bag-age bag-age has come to be a drag, we are here to help you 'cause your bag-age is our
F
20
F Dm7 Gm7 C7
bag. We are here to help you 'cause your bag - age is our
22
F
bag.

# Jesus Is The Key

Clark Tyler
*Arranged by Andrew Bell*

20
E♭ B♭/F F7 B♭
hope 'cause I have the Key.
Spoken: Je-sus is the key.
B♭ Gm E♭ Cm7
Je-sus is the key.
26
B♭/F F E♭/F F B♭ Gm Dm Cm7 F Dm Cm F7
Je-sus is the key.
Fil-ling my cup of joy to the brim, help-ing me try to be
31
E♭ F Dm Gm9 C7 F B♭ Gm C7
more like Him, and wel-com-ing me to His e-ter-ni - ty.
Je sus, Je- sus,
36
F E♭/F F7 B♭ B♭
Je-sus is the key.
Verse:
There's old Sa - tan
Feel - ing bad, all
Bank ac - count is

41 Gm7 Cm F Dm
at my door a-gain, con-fi-dent he can up his score a - gain. Deal - ing his cards from
sick and fe - ver-ish mak-ing it hard to be be - liev - er - ish. Those aches and pains dis
fac-ing emp - ti-ness, all my fi nan - ces need re- demp-ti - ness, Wal - low - ing in my
45 Gm Cm F F7 E♭
un- der- neath. pro - bab - ly ly - ing thru his teeth. How can I beat that
cour - age me, I need some shots or sur - ge - ry. I'm at the end of
mis- er - y, I'm broke and friend - less, yes, sir - ee. E - ve-ry pro - spect
(Sung free and lyrically:)
49 Cm7 Dm7 F7 B♭ B♭/F F7 B♭
olden- tran- cer? If sin is the ques - tion, what's the an - swer? Je-sus is the key.
myen- dur - ance. I need a pre - scrip - tion and in - sur - ance. Je-sus is the key.
is full of glit - ches. I need a win or in - stant rich - es. Je-sus is the key.
54 B♭ Gm E♭ Cm7 B♭/F F E♭/F F B♭ Gm Dm Cm7
Je sus is the key. Je - sus is the key. Fil - ling my cup of

59
F Dm Cm F7 E♭ F Dm Gm9
joy to the brim, help - ing me try to be more like Him, and wel-com-ing me to
63
C7 F B♭ Gm C7 F E♭/F F7 B♭ End:
His e - ter ni - ty. Je sus, Je sus, Je sus is the key.
rit.
69
E♭ Cm Dm Gm7 Cm F7 Dm Gm
O-pen the door, then e - ver He knocks. Pay no mind to la - tches and locks 'cause
73
C9 F F B♭
Je- sus, Je - sus, Je- sus is the key.

# Bible - Promises

**In A Latin Style**

Clark Tyler
*Arranged by Andrew Bell*

# Gifts By Grace

Clark Tyler
*Arranged by Andrew Bell*

21
B7 F Dm7 G G9
place to se - lect with thrift your ve - ry own gifts by
24
C F Dm7 G C
grace.

# Fruits Of The Spirit

Clark Tyler
*Arranged by Andrew Bell*

C G7 C C Em F
Love, Joy, and Peace; Pa-tience and
mf
9 Am7 Dm7 G9 C Em G7 C
Kind - ness, Good-ness to fill the soul. Faith-ful-ness, Gen-tle-ness, Fruits of the
17 Am7 Dm G9 C Am7
Spir - it. Don't for - get Self Con - trol. E -
22 Dm G7 G13 1. C 2. C
spec - ial - ly Self Con - trol. trol.

# The Grateful Living

Clark Tyler
*Arranged by Andrew Bell*

C
C6 Am7 Dm7 G9
We are the grate - ful liv - ing
We are some fish - ers cas - ting,
We are the grate - ful liv - ing,
5 Dm7 G7 C6 Am7 Dm7 G7 Dm7 G13
3
might - i - ly in - to joy and thanks - giv - ing. In a world that
search - ing for seek - ers of life ev - er - last - ing. Let the Gos - pel
tell - ing of grace for all sins for - giv - ing. Come and pack your
9 C6 Am7 D7sus G9 C Am Dm9 G7
eats up mad and hate - ful, we bring a plate
good news come right to ya, and then re new
sins up by the crate - ful Come join the liv-

13 Dm7 G9 Dm7 G7 C Am7 Dm7 G9
3
- ful of glad - ed and grate - ful. Se -
ya. Ha - al - le - lu - jah!
- ing. Come join the grate - ful.
17 C6 Am7 Dm7 G7 C C6 Am7
lah, se - lah, Say la la la. (whistle melody)
20 Dm7 G7 C G7♭5 C6

# Motel 666

Clark Tyler
*Arranged by Andrew Bell*

18 Dm7 G7 C F B♭/F F B♭ F F
Mo-tel Six. Six-ty Six. The light is dim and get-ting
23 G7 B♭ F/A Gm C7/B♭ C7 F C/E B♭/D C F
dim mer, and hope is slim, as our guests just simmer To ill - us - trate that
28 B♭ F C B♭ C B♭ F C/E B♭/D C C
those in sin e-ter-nal-ly in - sin-er - ate. Now ain't that great?
33 F Dm C7 F
"And it is hot! Par - a-dise Inn this is Not!" I'm the man-a-ger here at

38 Dm Gm C F B♭/F F G7
Mo tel Six Six-ty Six. Come and see the re - sults of my
42 C F B♭/F F F Dm Gm C F B♭ F
de-vil-ish bag of tricks, As fre-quent-ly seen in the lat-est flicks. And of course
47 B♭ C7 F C/E Dm C C7 C13 F Dm
rock mu-sic ly-rics, they're all my schticks here at Mo-tel Six
52 Gm C F F C C13 F
Six-ty Six. I'm the man-a-ger here at

57 Dm Gm C F B♭/F F G7
Mo-tel Six Six-ty Six. It's a real-ly hot spot that we've
61 C Dm/C C F B♭/F F Dm C/D Dm G7
got, here on the ri-ver Styx. Un-re-pen - tant sin-ners are a-mong our pri-mar-y picks
65 C Dm/C C C7 F Dm Gm C
as per-ma-nent guests here at Mo-tel Six, Six ty - Six.

69 Dm Gm A7 Dm B♭ C7
Come and mix at Lu-cy Fur's bai- li - wicks, here at
73 Dm Gm C7 F B♭/F F
Mo-tel Six, Six ty - Six.

# Be Anxious For Nothing (Phil 4:6)

Clark Tyler
*Arranged by Andrew Bell*

# Heaven Bound

Clark Tyler
*Arranged by Andrew Bell*

**In A Ragtime Style**

C F Dm Gm C9 A7 A
Now I was so far down I could-n't ev - en find up. Checked in - to sal - va- tion and
Now there is heaven or not it's up to me to pick it; each pain and each woe now, I
I now have see the light there is no night just day there, and I've seen the man- sion re-
5
G7 C F F♯dim7 Gm C9
that's when I signed up. I'm head - ed for the right side where all the sheep are lined up. So
know I can lick it. I'm rea - dy to get rol- ling 'cause Je - sus paid my tick - et then
served for my stay there. All a - board and praise the Lord 'cause there is just one way there. You
8
Gm C7♭13 F F B♭/F F7
I'll be Hea- ven bound. I'm Hea - ven bound on the Glo - ry ex-
can be Heav- en bound.
3
8va

12 A7 Dm/A A7 Dm B♭/D Dm G7 F/C C Dm/C
press. Hea - ven bound, clothed in Right-eous-ness
(8)
17 C C7 F Gm/F F C7 B♭/C C7
I'm bound to go forth, and to do all I can. So I'm bound to be
22 B♭ F C7 1.2. F B♭/F 3. F B♭/F Gm7
part of God's Hea-ven-ly plan. plan. Where once I was
rit.
rit.

26
C7
B♭
F
Am
Dm
lost I am found. So when the time comes I'll be
29
C7
F
C7
F
Hea - ven bound. Hea - ven bound.
rit.

## Chapter 9 - SO, WHAT'S ENTERTAINING ABOUT THE DEVIL?

Teaching young children about the possibility of hell is a very tricky business. Although the threat is very real, scare tactics do not seem appropriate. Eternal punishment, damnation, hellfire, the bottomless pit etc. are all there in the Bible – depicted, described with clear instructions on how to avoid. Whether it is appropriate to get into all this within the context of Sunday school, is something that should be carefully thought through. As I pondered this, I realized that a better point of attack on the problem may be the character of Satan.

The reason for this fits perfectly with my approach to teaching children in this age group (6 to 12). Christian doctrine concerning damnation, judgement and eternal "conditions" is a little tough to handle; however the problem of temptation and the continuing threat of Satan's activities (sin) is something of the here and now that kids could easily understand. If I was going to train my youngsters and equip them to be effective witnesses, they needed to understand the problem of sin and where it comes from. Tying this to the character of Satan was the obvious way to accomplish this.

Satan not only appears in person in the Bible (in the Garden of Eden, in the Book of Job and in the New Testament in the Temptation and in Revelation), but we are given a multitude of clues as to his character, his methods of operation, his tools, his tactics, his influence, his results, his helpers, his effect on people and his complete biography. That is quite a lot. Satan is referenced by name as the tempter of David (I Chron 21:1), the accuser of the high priest (Zechariah 3:1 &2); and both Isaiah and Ezekiel speak of his being cast down from heaven.

What emerged in my thoughts was not the classic depiction of the personification of evil... the loathsome, hideous, magician of the Faust story as shown by Mephistopheles, but something quite different. What I saw was a multi-faceted , slick manipulator in a number of differing guises that children could easily recognize. That word, "recognize," was one of the three "R's" that I decided to concentrate on – recognize, resist and respond. Those were the things that God's word tells us to do when confronted by evil and temptation.

Clearly, you can't resist and respond if you don't recognize, so that's where I started. OK, so what are those character traits that would make it easy for kids to recognize Satan when confronted? Here's my working list:

| | | |
|---|---|---|
| crafty | powerful | attractive |
| dangerous | deceitful | seductive |
| mocking | accusatory | subtle |
| murderous | lying | contemptuous |
| rebellious | thieving | tempting |

In addition, Satan is occasionally successful, but not victorious; he knows God's word (and twists it to his use); he commands legions of demons to do his bidding; but he can't make us act against our will. Now that is a longer and more detailed resume than most people have... and the Bible tells us his whole story from beginning to everlasting end.

James 4:7 represents, in this regard, one of the great "how to's" among foundational truths. It says, simply: "resist the devil, and he will flee from you." The word "resist" is active, instructional and not subject to multi-interpretation. With proper illustration, children can easily grapple with this. That is why in the play, "Exercising Faith," our pint-sized, faith-filled wrestler, Miss Mustard Seed, graphically takes a large family Bible, literally stands on it, and body slams the Power of Darkness. The children all understood that to win out in battles such as this, it wasn't always necessary to do intensive battle as the angel Michael did (Daniel: 10; 12-15) for 21 days. "Resist" therefore could mean recognizing to the point of conscious avoidance.

Similarly, in an earlier play, the secret agent, James Bondage (you know who), reveals the tools of his trade. His favorite "tool" is - discouragement. Doctrinely speaking, discouragement is not a sin, but it sure can provide an opening for the devil to do his thing. This became another dimension to the concept of "resist." When "Paradise Inn" came along, the lovely little girl who played the lead character, Pearlie Gates (the concierge of the "Inn"), was also cast as the devilish Lucy Fur, night manager of Motel 666. In the latter role, she was both attractive and diabolical, bragging about her successes, mocking the amenities of heaven, and suggesting that allegiance to her "program" would be fun. Even kids under the age of 6 got the point.

Portraying the problem of evil as something delusional or even ridiculous gave the children something they could understand, relate to and take appropriate action against. In the Christmas story, the horrific instinct of King Herod to eliminate the threat of a rival King (Jesus) was treated by introducing the character of Herod's Astronomer Royal. This silly spinmeister looks at the star in the East as a possible vindication of his own warped astrological claptrap. Thus, the Astronomer Royal's musical interpretation of the "Bright New Star," became an introduction to the real meaning as sung by the shepherds and the Wise Men.

In "Come to the Garden," the tempter/Serpent was a young man who said he was a salesman of "apple futures." In the teaching lead-up to this play, I explained that in Genesis, the serpent was only condemned by God to crawl around on his belly ***after*** the fall of Adam. Thus, presumably, the serpent got around in some other fashion ***before*** his successful act of temptation. Yes, that was an obscure point, but the kids loved it and it made all kinds of sense to them.

So presenting the dangers of sin, the prospect of eternal damnation and the wiles of Satan, was certainly necessary, but didn't have to be horrifying to be understood. And the best part was the number of adult heads nodding agreement to these presentations.

## Chapter 10 - A CHECKLIST OF THE OBVIOUS

At the risk of stating the obvious in the form of a checklist, this chapter is designed to state the obvious in the form of a checklist - a checklist to help any Sunday School teacher to successfully produce one or more of these musical plays.

**Don't make it a requirement for your cast to memorize anything.** In the end, they will anyway, so it won't matter. If it helps them to read off a page of script or a 3 X 5 card, that's fine as long as they do it with feeling. The important thing is for them to sound credible.

**The melody is not as important as the words.** Don't limit yourself to "trained" singers. Non singers can be good actors and the importance of the lesson (or message) transcends technical musical perfection.

**Experts in mnemonics can probably tell you why, but reciting verse is easier for children than reading lines of script.** Just make sure they don't "sing song" it. They should also pause after a rhyme, because rhymes will be anticipated and sometimes will bring a laugh.

**Make sure everyone speaks s-l-o-w-l-y.** The reason that this is critical is that as children become more comfortable with their part or their lines, they tend to speed up the delivery. When performing before an elderly audience, or in a large auditorium, this is disastrous. The director should have a hand signal for "slow down."

**Emphasize that every word (even little ones) has three parts - a beginning, a middle and an end.** This stricture will ensure that enunciation and slow speaking dominates. Clearly, certain words of scripture ("redemption," "obedience," as well as proper names) are hard for children to articulate. They can, but it takes practice. My favorite example of this is young, talented Kristen who struggled with "mene, mene tekel upharsin." When she finally got it, she was thrilled that it got a big laugh during the performance of "Paradise Inn."

**Two "musts" before every performance - prayer and a bathroom break.** The need for prayer and taking authority over missed lines or gaps, or recalcitrant sound equipment, is obvious. The second "must" is that any type of anxiety causes a need for a bathroom visit. When one has to go, they all will.

**"Cheat" towards the audience.** This has nothing to do with an ethical lapse – it is simple jargon for letting the audience see the face of the performer. If an audience only sees the back of a performer's head, they will not hear the words.

**Keep hands occupied.** I learned the hard way that if a child does not have something to occupy his/her hands, then matters of personal hygiene will undoubtedly be taken care of. Hand gestures to help illustrate words in songs, hands on a prop or a script card...solves the problem.

**Insist on proper dress for performances.** To emphasize the point that your children/performers are in ministry, make sure that all girls are wearing dresses; all boys in nice shirts and dress pants. No tank tops, blue jeans, baggy pants, or even sneakers. Even if there are costumes, make sure that underneath there is proper attire. Nursing home residents grew up in an age of "proper attire," and really like to see children in it. It also signals to the children how important their appearance is. If they look good, they will sound good.

**Avoid gaps during performances.** Make sure that if there is a slip-up, or a missed line, or a delayed entrance, that the kids know how to overcome, so there are no long pauses. If there are, it will kill the momentum and throw off the whole cast. Their tendency is to go back and repeat their lines until they get it right, but this is sloppy and really not necessary. The director should have a signal for "moving on," or even cuing them on how to proceed. Delayed entrances can be overcome if the piano player adds some background music from a just-sung song. Directors and stage assistants need to be prepared for such eventualities.

**Don't let anyone "step on a line."** The children will not always know what might get a laugh or win applause. Teach them to pause at such moments or to take a cue from the director about when to proceed. It may be necessary for one of the assistants to start applause at the end of a song. Just make sure that this is consistent as feelings will get hurt if one child wins applause and another doesn't. Audiences also like to be told when to applaud.

**Choreograph the curtain calls.** Endings are always hard. A performance can be improved by programming exactly when the children should bow, or leave the stage at the conclusion. At nursing homes, this can merely be done by introducing the children by name to the residents. Then when they go to hold hands or pray with each, there is some helpful familiarity.

**Stage logistics are critical.** Split your cast in two and have half enter from one side and half from the other, if possible. This keeps chatter and fooling around to a minimum, but will take some practice to have it all flow. Have an adult assistant be a traffic manager at each side. If there is a puppet stage, make sure and adult assistant with a script is there to cue and guide. If hand held mikes are used, make sure the handling and flow are well-rehearsed. Tape marking (with names) where each child should stand is critical. Who cares if it shows. When stage movements flow well, the production looks very solid.

**Back-ups (understudies) are a good idea.** Sore throats, flu and other happenstances, do take their toll. Make sure you have trained replacements for key roles. You will find that most kids know all the solo roles anyway.

**All eyes are to be glued on the director**. Smaller children have a tendency to have eyes wander. If, during choruses, they have been trained to watch the director at all times, a big problem will be avoided. The director can even "mouthe" the lines or the lyrics. Kids follow this, and only **they** can see it. The piano player should also carefully watch the director (position the piano, so this is possible) for those "slip-up" moments and remedial action.

**Individual practice tapes are a must.** Forget quality of the singing, and concentrate on giving each child (soloists and chorus members) a tape of their song(s), with two things: first, a voice and piano rendering of the song; and second, a music only version they can sing against at home. It is very easy to tell who has and who has not used these between rehearsals!

**Teach proper puppeteering.** Several children, who may not want to perform, will want to work the puppets (if you have them). This is not an easy assignment. They have to be taught to hold them high enough to be seen over the masking curtains; to move the mouths carefully in synch with the words; to make sure the lower part of the puppet's mouth moves (otherwise the puppet head will flip back); and to take their cues from the embedded puppet director. If two puppets are "on" at the same time, one should watch the other while it is speaking. If puppeteers are seated on stools, adjust the height of these so that the puppets can be uniformly seen, when "on."

**Props are extremely important.** First, they can add an element of humor. Second, they enhance the "visuality" of all the words in the script and the lyrics. Third, they prevent performers' hands from doing things you would prefer them not to do. The usual rule is that someone 50 feet away should be able to see the prop, read the lettering or understand what it depicts. Three-inch high lettering is standard for this. Make sure props are numbered and arranged in the order of use, so the stage assistants can hand them out properly and retrieve them in good order. Props are also an excellent way of disguising lyrics or script lines for use by the performer.

**Have a minimum of six run-throughs.** Even though these plays are written for simplified blocking and stage movement, children in this age group need to be totally familiar with how all the pieces fit together. In addition to the practice tapes, any individual rehearsals, or specialized segmented work, it is important to have a minimum of six full length rehearsals. Obviously more is better, but six will eliminate gaps, miscues and a variety of performance problems. Don't worry about a disastrous dress rehearsal; the performance will be fine. Kids love audience reaction and will rise to the occasion!

**Take time for pre-rehearsing teaching.** While the children will be anxious to start rehearsing, you should be sure and schedule sufficient teaching time for the lesson plans. Remember you are "equipping the saints for the work of ministry." Believe me, that once your students understand the message and the lesson, their performance will be considerably enhanced. Use games and role playing to teach the lessons. Avoid Christian and doctrinal "jargon." Make sure your students know where (and how) to find something in the Bible. Each should bring a Bible to class so you can demonstrate this. Remember that the active definition of someone "hearing" something is: can they repeat it, retain it and act upon it? If a scene, or a song or a message continues to be a stumbling block, leave it out and move on. These plays are written "accordion style" so that this is possible.

**Involve as many adults as you can.** Because these presentations are ministry, get as many church members as possible involved in the production and outreach. Making props, sewing costumes, copying scripts, handling stage logistics, make-up, backdrops, sound, piano & guitar help, publicity, snacks, teaching assistance - are all critical needs and will spread the "ownership" of the production.

**Programs, posters and invitations.** Every child likes to see their name in print - have a program. Friends, neighbors, extended family and others will respond to a personal invitation. It's okay to print an invitation, but scribble a personal note on it urging them to come and witness something quite different. Nursing homes love to have simple posters to put in elevators, meeting or dining rooms. We have been fortunate in having supermarkets, convenience stores, libraries and other places which don't usually display church-oriented material, put up a poster. Give it a try.

**Make constant checklists.** When you do a presentation, such as these, there will be a million details to follow up on. Make constant checklists of these and put a "disciple of forward progress" in charge of each item. That way, nothing falls between the cracks.

**When in doubt, call the author**. The author is semi-retired, and doesn't mind being called, asked questions or even asked to come and help, advise, and/or participate. There is no charge, other than reasonable out-of-pocket expenses (and maybe a home-cooked meal or two) for this service. I look at it as part of the Great Commission!